The Literary Community

Selected Essays: 1967–2007

Ted Solotaroff

D1523060

Also by Ted Solotaroff

The Red-Hot Vacuum

A Few Good Voices in My Head

Truth Comes in Blows: A Memoir

First Loves: A Memoir

An Age of Enormity by Isaac Rosenfeld (editor)

Writers and Issues: An Anthology of the Sixties (editor)

Best American Short Stories, 1978 (editor)

Many Windows: Stories from *New American Review* and
      American Review (editor)

The Schocken Book of Contemporary Jewish Fiction
      (edited with Nessa Rapoport)

Alfred Kazin's America (editor)

The Literary Community

Selected Essays: 1967–2007

Ted Solotaroff

Introduction by Russell Banks

The Sheep Meadow Press
Riverdale-on-Hudson, New York

All inquiries and permission requests should be addressed to:

The Sheep Meadow Press
P.O. Box 1345
Riverdale-on-Hudson, NY 10471

Designed and typeset by The Sheep Meadow Press.
Distributed by The University Press of New England.

Printed on acid-free paper in the United States. This book meets the guidelines for permanence and durability of the Committee on Production
Guidelines for Book Longevity of the Council on Library Resources.

Library of Congress Cataloging-in-Publication Data

Solotaroff, Ted, 1928-
    The literary community : selected essays, 1967-2007 / Ted Solotaroff.
        p. cm.
    ISBN 1-931357-59-5
    1.   American literature--History and criticism. 2.   United States--
Civilization. I. Title.

PS121.S65 2007
810.9
                                                    2007038865

Contents

Part Four

Part Five

Introduction

By Russell Banks

I read perhaps half these essays when they were first published in journals like *The Nation*, *Granta*, *American Poetry Review* and so on. Reading them again, in some cases more than a decade later, and in the company of essays that I somehow missed back then, is like greeting an old friend and picking up our last late-night conversation right where we stopped, as if neither of us had left the table. Further, it's as if in the intervening years the conversation has been marinating in both our minds, and as a result we find ourselves with freshened intelligence and depth able to expand upon the ideas, arguments, and opinions that we shared the last time we spoke. More than any other critic working today, Ted Solotaroff *shares* his thoughts. His essays are like personal, two-way conversations, as if he were listening to us as much as addressing us, listening to us as individuals, weighing our ideas, no matter how ill-considered or ill-informed, taking our feeble counter-arguments seriously, respecting our opinions even as he supplants them. He makes it easy to take his point, to accept his argument, to make our own opinions agree with his.

He was like that as an editor. I speak from long personal experience, going back to 1967, when I was first beginning to submit work for publication. I was still at college when, to my astonishment, he accepted one of my short stories for *American Review*, then the most distinguished and widely distributed literary journal in the country, and later published more of my work in its equally distinguished successor, *New American Review*. My gratitude as a reader for the mere existence of those journals was only exceeded by my gratitude for his willingness to include me as one of the contributors. In the early 1980s he became my book editor at Harper & Row, later Harper-Collins, until he pushed back from the editorial desk and retired from publishing and turned to writing his luminous memoirs and many of these essays.

Sitting at a table and going over one's fiction manuscript with Ted Solotaroff during those years was an experience very like reading these essays today. He was an old-fashioned *literary* editor, a type that almost doesn't exist today, certainly not in the employ of the media conglomerates. His constant concern was for the book, the author's book, not the publisher's. It was a privilege, a kind of blessing, to have him as the first reader of one's manuscript, even if it was an early draft —perhaps *especially* if it was an early draft and still in woeful need of extensive revision—because he brought to it the same quality of mind, the same intelligence, honesty and rigor, the same breadth and depth of reference and allusion, the same personal modesty, that he brings to the subjects of these essays. Working with Ted Solotaroff— and you always felt that you were indeed working *with* him—made a young author feel that he or she was a vital part of a community of writers living and dead, writers who mattered, Ted Solotaroff's literary community, the people and books he embraces and analyzes in these essays. He made you feel, because of his loving attention and high standards, that your poor manuscript was potentially the equal of John Fowles's or Raymond Carver's or Saul Bellow's, among the writers he engages here.

As an example I will tell one story. In 1984 I completed and turned in what I thought was the finished manuscript of my novel, *Continental Drift*. A few weeks later we met at his office on East 53rd Street to discuss it. It was my sixth or seventh novel, and I was pretty certain that it was better than any of its predecessors. Maybe it needed a tweak here and there, a few minor cuts, a quick comb-through, but nothing major. Ted sighed and looked at the ceiling for a long moment, then pushed the manuscript across the desk to me. "You've told the story, told it well," he said. "And I can certainly publish it as it is. And will, if you want. But you haven't finished the book. There's something missing at the end. There's something you've backed away from, as if you're afraid of the implications of the story you've told." There was an empty, unwritten space he'd imagined out there beyond the novel I'd turned in, and until I filled it I would not have written the best novel I was then capable of writing.

I had no idea what he meant, and he couldn't (or wouldn't) tell me any more than that. He told me to go home and not look at the manuscript for a week or, if possible, a month. And not to worry, because he would happily publish the novel if it came back unchanged. I did worry. Ted Solotaroff was the best reader of fiction I knew. And if he said there was something missing at the end of my novel that was not an ending, then I had better find a way to write it. Then a month later I woke up one morning and knew with startling clarity that my novel was missing an antiquated device called an *envoi*. It's a charge directed by the author to the book itself, designed to give the book a proper send-off by making explicit its intentions. My *envoi* was perhaps a little long, but it ended as it should: "Go, my book, and destroy the world as it is." In an age of irony, who says such a thing? Well, Ted knew that there was no irony anywhere in *Continental Drift*, and that was perhaps its main virtue. If it was intentional on my part (and it was), then I needed the courage of my convictions to come right out and say it. So I did, and as a result wrote a better book than would otherwise have been possible for me.

In his famous essay, "A Few Good Voices in My Head" (included here, happily), he speaks of having learned early on to rely on "practical criticism," which means "not only trusting your first impression but also using your imagination to take the measure of a work rather than merely interpret it." It's what obliged him as an editor and allows him as a critic to search for the book the author intended or hoped to write, rather than the book the editor and critic wanted to read. His analytical powers are great and are amply deployed in these essays (see especially "The Young Camus", "Woman's Fate: The Stories of Alice Munro", and "One of Us: The Poetry of Hayden Carruth"), but it's the power of his imagination that separates him from other critics. That, and the sweet lucidity and precision of his prose, and especially its transparency. He compliments Stanley Kauffmann's memoir, *Albums of a Life*, by saying, "He casts his light rather than standing in it; his prose is a polished window rather than a mirror." One could say the same of Ted Solotaroff.

There is, of course, a vividly realized personality here. Though they are primarily literary in scope and subject matter, these are personal essays, after all, written in the great American tradition of Emerson, Mencken, Kazin, Baldwin, and Sontag (*that* literary community). Throughout, one senses behind the sentences the presence of a wryly skeptical man who nonetheless manages to keep himself always open-hearted and -minded, always ready to adjust his first impressions as new information comes in. He's nobody's fool, that's for damned sure, and never was; yet even so, he's willing to make himself vulnerable, to reveal his early errors of judgement, his youthful indiscretions and vanities, and his guilty pleasures. The narrator of these essays is very good company. His casual-seeming asides can be shrewdly double-barreled, as when he describes Shimon Peres as "ironic and a bit wistful as well as tough, a kind of Jewish Mario Cuomo who inspired more respect than confidence." And he can be incredibly kind, especially to writers whose books he feels have been under-valued or otherwise neglected.

In the final section of the book, there are five essays in which he makes explicit what he means by "the literary community". I wish I had read them when I was young, back before Ted Solotaroff took my early stories for *New American Review*. I wish every young writer in America could read those five essays. They could serve as an extended seminar on every writer's apprenticeship, for, taken together, they contain more useful information about the writing life in America today and its big-picture meaning than can ever be extracted from a two-year MFA creative writing program.

I'm grateful that this book exists and intend to keep passing it on to both new and old members of the literary community—writers, of course, but book-lovers of all types. This is a book that affirms our connection to one another through literature, and explains how and why, in this media-driven, image-obsessed, post-literate world, that connection is ever more necessary. As he says on reading Isaac Rosenfeld's criticism, "I knew in my Jewish bones, well before Matthew Arnold confirmed it, that literature was first and last a criticism of life, and now I had found a voice that embodied this viewpoint in a warm, masculine, somehow familiar way. It was less like discovering a writer than like finding a terrific older brother." The next voice you hear will be Ted Solotaroff's. It will be like finding a terrific older brother.

Preface

The essays and reviews in the following pages span most of my career as a literary editor, critic, and occasional teacher of writing. The majority were written in the past fifteen years or so and haven't been been collected before. The others, taken from two earlier collections, long out-of-print, are ones that I still feel are useful.

In selecting and going over all of them again, I've done a fair amount of editing to clarify or strengthen what I was trying to say at the time. With a few of them I've wanted to say something else or more and have indicated that by adding 2007 to the year of its original publication. I've also taken the opportunity to retitle a number of them.

Virtually all of the pieces on individual writers are essentially positive ones. As with people, I find that I have more to say about writers that I admire than about those I don't. This does not preclude registering judgments that spring from a lessening of interest or esteem, for the point of reviewing an author is to deliver the experience of reading him or her, and to be less than candid is to weaken the conviction that has otherwise come to praise. One's convictions—judgments that wish to convince, beginning with oneself—are really all that the reviewer-critic has to go on, both to guide him and to break fresh ground. Nonetheless, the positive review or essay comes from a different place in the psyche than the negative one: the first being powered by affection, the second by aggression; the first seeks to welcome and explore, the second to keep out and tear down. In my younger years, I wrote a fair amount of negative criticism, generally to deflate a prestige that I thought was unwarranted or to point up a literary/cultural tendency that I thought was pernicious—often both at the same time, the one providing the context for the other. And, of course, I did it to make my mark, status-hunger and aggression being as closely synchronous as the right hand and the left. In my later years the one has declined with the other.

When I started out as a reviewer critic I was much influenced by Edmund Wilson. His main principle, at least as I took it, was "justness of characterization," which he had gotten, I believe, from Sainte-Beuve. In making that my objective, I also adopted his main method of characterization which was to draw (in both senses) close to the author and the work by paraphrasing it in a way that conveyed one's judgment of its power, depth, artistry. One time, at a literary conference, I was reproved by a famous critic who said that when she read this kind of review, particularly if it was well done, she felt no need to read the work itself. She much preferred the mode she practiced which was to take up a general idea that the work either invoked or provoked and develop that, using the text as examples and stalking points. Were I as brilliant with or as impassioned by general ideas as she was, I would have tried my hand at it but then I would have been writing for a different audience than the one I wanted to reach.

During the course of my career as a literary journalist as well as an editor, I developed the conviction that literature is too important a human resource to be left in the hands of the literati. To come to this conviction and to continue holding it, I've had to undo most of the intense elitism that came with identifying early on with the modernist tradition that was so much in the air when I decided to become literary. Most but not all. Though I've written, edited, and taught in the spirit of being inclusive rather than exclusive, I still believe in high standards, if not the seven-foot one of the great modernists. I learned to adjust these standards to the common reader, who I assume to be a serious one, at *Commentary*, my first writing venue and editorial position, and took them with me into my subsequent career in mainstream publishing where it quickly became apparent that if you didn't fight tooth and nail for your high standards, you would soon have no standards other than that of immediate or potential marketability.

This collection also brings together the essays and talks I've given about the career and practice of serious writing from the point of view of an editor, practitioner, and teacher in MFA programs. For personal as well as professional reasons I've had a particular affinity for the gifted younger writer and have tried to pass on what I wish had been told to me when I was standing in his or her shaky shoes.

T.S.
April, 2007

The Literary Community

PART ONE

The Telling Story:
Walter Benjamin and Mona Simpson

Walter Benjamin, in his magisterial essay "The Storyteller," argued that the art of storytelling was dying out, that it was being superseded by the modern media of information and by the story's younger and more topical relative, the novel. There are reasons to believe that, writing in 1935, Benjamin was gloomily prophetic, but there are other reasons to believe his prognosis was unduly narrow.

In an interview (*American Review* 15, 1972), the novelist John Barth speculated that it may be the novel, as we know it, that is passing out of literary history, but this "doesn't mean the end of narrative literature, certainly. It certainly doesn't mean the end of storytelling." Arguing against the article of the modernist literary faith which holds that plot—the constitutive element of storytelling—is a retrograde device, Barth wrote that there are "ways to be quite contemporary and yet go at the art in a fashion that would allow you to tell complicated stories simply for the aesthetic pleasure of complexity, of complication and unravelment, suspense, and the rest." One can add that beyond the writer's pleasure, there still lies the reader's, however sophisticated he may be, in the well-told story—a pleasure that may have become distracted, displaced, and undernourished, but one that is programmed into his nature as surely as gazing meditatively into a log fire (and not unrelated to it), a pleasure that can be so quickly and powerfully revived by a true storyteller like García Márquez. And no less basic in the human creature is the pleasure of telling stories. Indeed, the need to do so, as any bartender will tell you.

Benjamin's use of the term "story" corresponds more closely to what we would call a "tale": i.e., it has its roots in the oral tradition, its favorite domicile was the hearth or the workroom, its archetypal artists were the peasant, the seafarer, the artisan; for "it combined the lore of faraway places, such as a much-traveled man brings home, with the lore of the past, as it best reveals itself to natives of a place." Thus its favorite venue was not the here and now but the more philosophical there and then. For its principal distinguishing feature, in Benjamin's view, was its heuristic value. It dramatized a moral, practical instruction, or illustrated a proverb or maxim. In other words, the tale was spun into a useful fabric, one that provided counsel for its audience, "counsel" being understood, as Benjamin puts it, less as "an answer to a question than a proposal concerning the continuation [and significance] of a story which is just unfolding." And because such stories were typically drawn from the ways of the world, from shared or readily communicable experience, their counsel becomes "the epic side of truth," namely wisdom, which, like storytelling itself, Benjamin believes is dying out.

As I understand Benjamin, then, the story is less an evolving art form than an ongoing if fading cultural resource: a vehicle for communicating and passing on the wisdom of the race by producing "astonishment and thoughtfulness." Though open to individual embellishment, its nature is to be repeatable; hence the narrative line is clear and coherent: it introduces a situation, complicates it, and then resolves it. Like, say, Gogol's "The Overcoat" it does not depend upon psychological explanation for its psychology is characteristically simple, evident; but it withholds explanation, part of its art, to allow the listener or reader to grasp its import by means of her own imagination and insight. Further, it is the lack of dependency on psychological nuance that contributes to, in Benjamin's lovely phrase, the "chaste compactness" of the story and enables it to be remembered and retold.

This "chaste compactness" is achieved by the craft with which a storyteller like Hawthorne hews to the main lines of a person's character, tracing them through situations that test and illuminate them, thereby casting a glow on the manners, mores, and attitudes of the tribe, animated by a man's life process flowing through them. Benjamin frequently relates the story to "natural history," the disparate, variable, mutable ingredients and events of the world which nonetheless draw ineluctably if fortuitously on to a predetermined end, which is death.

The storyteller is conversant most of all with fate and mortality. His art—layer upon layer of transparent incidents moving both indeterminately (suspense) and inexorably toward a fixed ending—is derived from his feeling for natural history. Indeed the older the storyteller, whether historically or personally, the more likely he is to identify his vision of life with nature and the "great inscrutable course of the world," and hence the more conversant he will be in communion with the transitory and mortal. But whether he is as early as Herodotus or as late as Nikolai Leskov, the nineteenth-century Russian writer whom Benjamin uses as his principal touchstone and source of examples, the signature of the true storyteller is found in the movement of his tale toward completeness, the sense it leaves of an earned definitiveness of experience, however open its meaning to speculation and mystery. In a remarkable passage, Benjamin associates death and storytelling:

> It is characteristic that not only a man's knowledge or wisdom but above all his real life—and this is the stuff that stories are made of—first assumes transmissible form at the moment of his death. Just as a sequence of images is set in motion inside a man as his life comes to an end—unfolding the views of himself under which he has encountered himself without being aware of it—suddenly in his expressions and looks the unforgettable emerges and imparts to everything that concerned him that authority which even the poorest wretch in dying possesses for the living around him. This authority is at the very source of the story.

Part of Benjamin's explanation for the decline of storytelling is that death and its revelations have been pushed from the realm of domestic, lived fact to the periphery of our awareness by the ways in which we isolate ourselves from the dying and the dead. The point is typical of Benjamin's approach to the problem of the story. He does not concern himself with the arguments, familiar by 1935, that the conventions of plot are falsified by the random, provisional, indeterminate aspects of reality, that the freestanding, solid, explicable characters, more or less bereft of an unconscious, are belied by psychology as well as by our own inner life, that fiction with a moral in tow or designed to illustrate a maxim is immediately suspect of simplifying experience and subverting art. Since virtually all didactic fiction in recent times is a form of propaganda for authoritarian systems, the genre is doubly dubious.

To be sure, Benjamin would say he is talking about "counsel," not thought control. And he would attribute the decline of counsel and wisdom to the fallen value of experience itself, whether of the person or the community or the race, its supersession by the bewilderment of man in the face of his incessantly changing society and a world that has gotten out of hand and has passed beyond the human scale of understanding and judgment. Hence the story is dying because of the incommunicability and incommensurability of being-in-the-world. He points out that the men returning from the First World War were silent rather than full of stories, and the novels that were later produced were "anything but experience that goes from mouth to mouth." What they communicated instead was mostly the enormity of modern warfare, the overwhelment of the person. As he puts it,

> A generation that had gone to school on a horse-drawn street car now stood under the open sky in a countryside in which nothing remained unchanged but the clouds, and beneath these clouds, in a field of force of destructive torrents and explosions, was the tiny, fragile, human body.

What are we to say fifty years further along in the acceleration of history, which hardly requires war to reduce persons to random social particles? The mass society does that very readily, while its culture further undermines the communicability of experience by its various modes of pseudo communication, the more pseudo the better, as the TV ratings testify. Benjamin, who died in 1940, did not live to see his military image expand across the social spectrum and move to an even more drastic incommunicability of destruction (Auschwitz, Hiroshima, Dresden) but he was already well aware of the media of information as a conquering adversary of the story. The product of the up-and-doing middle class with its preference for the factual and the explicable, the daily flood of information, works directly against the function and value of the traditional story. In drawing upon the ways of the world, Benjamin's storyteller is indifferent to the verifiability of his account and offers no explanations for life in the there and then. Like man himself, the imaginative interest on which story does depend has diminished to the meager, wisdomless "news story."

One can see how the primacy of information over story has penetrated and altered our reading habits by comparing the child's to the adult's way of taking in a story. Still relatively innocent of the penchant for news, the child's request to "tell me a story" is qualitatively different from his parents' "Let's see what's in *The New Yorker* or *Ms.* this week." Like Benjamin's weavers at their looms, in which the rhythm of the work induces a receptivity to narrative—Benjamin calls it "self-forgetfulness"—the child, relaxed in his bed, creates a special state of attentiveness in which the story provides a passage from the day's activities through contact with otherness, preferably with a touch of the strange. The imagination takes over and leads the self toward contentment and rest. The process is perhaps similar to the much more abbreviated, out-of-the-blue imaginings in an adult that presage that he is about to drop off.

But though adults also typically use bedside reading to put the day behind them and prepare for sleep, they do not open themselves to story in the way the child does. If an adult is reading a magazine and comes to a story, his mindset does not alter and prepare to receive the rich and strange, but rather slightly adjusts itself to assimilate more indirect kind of information, presented in a more personal but often no more imaginative form than the articles: the way we live now, etc.

Most magazines most of the time reinforce this tendency by providing stories that do not come from afar, whether in time or place, but are rather news from the private sector, usually in keeping with the magazine's characteristic interests and tone, and the class imagery of its editors and readers. A few popular magazines, such as *Esquire* and *The New Yorker*, which are responsive to literature, will sometimes publish stories that have little or nothing to do with the rest of the content, but the fictions of Barthelme, Borges, or Bashevis Singer no doubt seem esoteric to most of the readers and have the air of distant relatives or odd guests of the family.

The media are not the only lethal impediments and adversaries to Benjamin's notion of the story. There is also the novel. It departs from the story at its very outset, its formative years being not in the oral tradition but in the printed word. The effect of this medium is, typically, to distance the writer from his audience: Instead of a man among men, who "takes what he tells from experience—his own or that reported by others. . . and in turn makes it the experience of those who are listening to the tale," the novelist keeps his narrative to himself and has to be his own audience until he is finished. Anyone who has successfully told a story to a circle of people and then, encouraged by her performance and their responsiveness, has tried to write it is aware of how the spontaneity and intimacy of the oral turns into the self-consciousness and detachment of the written. It is partly this difference that Benjamin has in mind when he goes on to write about the novelist in what seems to be a rather arbitrary and extreme way:

> The novelist has isolated himself. The birthplace of the novel is the solitary individual, who is no longer able to express himself by giving examples of his most important concerns, is himself uncounseled, and can not counsel others. To write a novel means to carry the incommensurable to extremes in the representation of human life. In the midst of life's fullness, and through the representation of this fullness, the novel gives evidence of the profound perplexity of the living.

Defoe? Fielding? Or, even more notably, Dickens?—the writer whose novels took their place at the hearthside of countless Victorian households, who was so much the counselor of his society, whose fullness of presented life was so securely organized and intuitively understood that it provided his readers with intelligence rather than bewilderment: Benjamin's storyteller with endless staying power.

But if one thinks about it, the further Dickens traveled in his career, the more his figure begins to take on the lineaments of Benjamin's novelist. In the later novels like *Little Dorrit*, *Great Expectations*, and *Our Mutual Friend* the fullness of life burdens rather than elates, as it did the younger Dickens, while his faith in its center—the enterprising middle class—collapses and turns into despair and contempt. His later protagonists and spokesmen, such as Arthur Clennam, Pip, Bradley Headstone, far from being counseled, are respectively stifled, bewildered, consumed by hate. Instead of the élan of curiosity, wit, and broad imagination, the relish in oddity, the confidence in the natural, the decent, the just, whose figures by and large win out, the later novels are driven by darker energies, a welling up of the destabilizing, destructive, and perverse forces of society and character which lead toward the study of the demonic that was beginning to take form in the unfinished *Mystery of Edwin Drood*. Instead of the sense of intimacy between Dickens and his characters, in the later novels he seems to stand alone, brooding over individual conditions and social forces that denature his people, isolate them, imprison them. Once his faith in progress, nurtured by the course of his own life as well as by the age, declined and turned mordant, he increasingly found life to be, in Benjamin's term, "incommensurable," and his main recourse if he was to go on writing was precisely in developing an increasingly complex and centrally placed psychology. It is also interesting that as this development was carrying him beyond and against the expectations of his audience, Dickens developed a need that became obsessive to appear before them in public readings, as though sensing that while he was losing his hold on them through his published words, he might still regain it through his actual voice, reinvoking the mutual spell of intimacy through recourse to the spoken.

And yet, and yet…Dickens continued to write stories to the end, short ones as well as the elaborately plotted late novels, which remained his only way to organize and to some extent comprehend life's fullness and perplexity.

For Benjamin the "short story"—a term he uses only once—is less a development of the traditional story than another example of the various abbreviations of the forms and processes of the past by the modern means of productivity. Rather than carrying on the craft of the tale, as it did Poe's and Mauppasant's, the short story is, to his mind, an abbreviated novel. In any case, he writes about the story as though Chekhov, Mann, Kafka did not exist, though he also wrote perhaps the best single essay on Kafka and was, I suspect, haunted by him. He even begins his essay with a story about Potemkin, who was undergoing one of his paralyzing depressions and paralyzing the state as well. A petty clerk, Shuvalkin, deciding to attack the problem directly, entered Potemkin's room with a sheaf of state documents, and emerged triumphantly with them signed; only to discover they had been signed "Shuvalkin…Shuvalkin…Shuvalkin." The story, Benjamin writes, "is like a herald racing two hundred years ahead of Kafka's work. The enigma which beclouds it is Kafka's enigma." He uses several other stories to illustrate the range of the doomed transactions of Kafka's cosmically burdened characters with the world and its authorities, but he deals with Kafka as not so much a storyteller as the creator of a theater in which, like the classical Chinese, happenings are reduced to gestures, though in Kafka's case generally incongruous, enigmatic, confused, or futile ones.

But certainly Kafka was a storyteller of the there and then, and there is probably no deeper illustration of Benjamin's favorite kind of story, in which the elements of myth and fairy tale interpenetrate the natural, than "Metamorphosis." To be sure, Kafka is without counsel and there is no more perfect witness than his protagonists to the profound perplexity of the living in the midst of life's fullness, no author who has carried the incommensurable to a further extreme. And yet Kafka was full of stories, and even parables, myths, and fables.

I agree with Benjamin about the human usefulness he finds to be the story's defining ingredient, but I believe that it can be conveyed by other means than the counsels of the there and then. The contemporary short story is typically concerned with the here and now, particularly in cultures like ours, in which the new, the perplexing, the ominous, the misleading constitute our central universal. It is no accident that the storytellers of the there and then are today largely found in Latin America, where the past still flows through and shapes the present, often tragically so. I believe that the usefulness of the contemporary American story lies precisely in its fight in behalf of the human scale of experience and its communication against the forces that seek to diminish and trivialize it. I find that most stories that interest me accept the incommensurability of experience and struggle against it to make sense of the otherwise senseless, to locate the possibilities of coherence (in both senses of the term) in the otherwise incoherent flux of a society whose members are dazed by its mutability and by the babbling of its media about this "event," that "trend," which flatters our knowingness while impoverishing our understanding.

2.

In the middle of life's fullness and perplexity, I come upon the first story in last year's Pushcart Prize anthology, "Lawns," by a young writer named Mona Simpson. It begins:

> I steal. I've stolen books and money and even letters. Letters are great. I can't tell you the feeling, walking down the street with twenty dollars in my purse, stolen earrings in my pocket. I don't get caught. That's the amazing thing. You're out on the sidewalk, other people all around, shopping, walking, and you've got it. You're out of the store, you've done this thing you're not supposed to do, but no one stops you. At first it's a rush. Like you're even for everything you didn't get before. But then you're alone, no one even notices you. Nothing changes.

Unlike Benjamin's archetypal story and like the standard contemporary one, this story has a narrator whose character is complex, full of psychological nuances. She is both brazen and reflective, devious and forthright, without compunctions but troubled as though she were bereft of them, both empowered and emptied by her secret vice. It's not easy to make up one's mind about her, mainly because her compulsive stealing comes across less as a pathology than as, say, an orphan's behavior, though we learn early on that she is not an orphan, that her father drove her to school and left weeping. She is a freshman at Berkeley, a top student, who works Saturday mornings in the mailroom of her dormitory, where she commits most of her thefts. She steals money, packages of clothes and cookies, and letters, but only letters addressed to three of her former high school classmates, who had belonged to the elite group:

> And now I know. Everything I thought those three years, worst years of my life, turns out to be true. The ones here get letters.... And like from families, their letters talk about problems. They're each other's main lives. You always knew, looking at them in high school, they weren't just kids who had fun. They cared. They cared about things.

This widening view of a poignant kleptomaniac takes into account her otherwise "normal" behavior. She falls in love and begins to sleep with a fellow student, a handsome boy who cuts the campus lawns. Glenn was once subject to trances but is now healthy; both of these aspects draw her to him. "I'm bad in bed," she blurts out at one point but thrives on his reassurance and her own gratitude. Her performance in school also fortifies her. When she is questioned about the missing packages and mail, she easily wards off the threat: "Four-point-oh average and I'm going to let them kick me out of school? They're sitting there telling us it's a felony. A Federal crime. No way, I'm gonna go to medical school."

The complex aura of the narrator's account of herself proves to be a foreshadowing of the proposal the story now makes, in Benjamin's terms, "concerning its continuation," from which its "counsel" is derived. The narrator's father, who appeared briefly and enigmatically in her thoughts, now turns up for a surprise weekend visit. The proposal is daring, less from the fact that they sleep together than from the matter-of-factness that they will do so:

> So he's here for the weekend. He's just sitting in my dorm room and I have to figure out what to do with him. He's not going to do anything. He'd just sit here. And Lauren's coming back soon so I've got to get him out. It's Friday afternoon and the weekend's shot. OK, so I'll go with him. I'll go with him and get it over with.

During her account of their behavior, both in his hotel room and in the five years since he initiated it, the reader experiences the "astonishment and thoughtfulness" that Benjamin designates to be the final cause of the storyteller's art, that which clears and deepens the space in our minds the story will henceforth occupy. What is most remarkable about the relationship is her tone of unremarkableness. The narrator speaks of the present state of affairs much as she did of her thefts:

> So next day, Saturday…we go downtown and I got him to buy me this suit. Three hundred dollars from Saks. Oh, and I got shoes. So I stayed later with him because of the clothes, and I was a little happy because I thought at least now I'd have something good to wear with Glenn. My dad and I got brownie sundaes at Sweet Dreams and I got home by five. He was crying when he dropped me off.

The sexual fire and brimstone we associate with incest is notably absent. She speaks of her father's attentions as she would those of any unwelcome older man, a high school teacher or a family doctor, say, who had seduced her and whom she continues to indulge. The conventional scenario of domination has been displaced by the perversely conventional one of exploitation. She hates her father less because he is her father than because he is so sheepish and jealous: "Jesus, how can you not hate someone who is always begging from you."

In a passage quoted earlier, Benjamin speaks of the emergence of "the unforgettable" in the face of the dying man as conferring an "authority [that] is at the very source of the story." The force of this statement is particularly pertinent to "Lawns":

> He waited till I was twelve to really do it. I don't know if you can call it rape. I was a good sport. The creepy thing is I know how it felt for him. I could see it on his face when he did it. He thought he was getting away with something.

It is just here that the story calmly places its finger on the heart of the matter and becomes unforgettable. As the passage goes on, describing the rape, or whatever, in its understated way, the father's expression presides over it with the authority of sin, which proves to be what the counsel of the story is about. Its wages quickly prove to be his moral undoing as a father and a man and her guilt-free ability to take whatever she wants:

> My dad thought he was getting away with something but he didn't. He was the one that fell in love, not me. And after that day, when we were back in the car, I was the one giving orders. From then on I got what I wanted.

This, of course, she has learned to do from him, in his principal act as a role model, which has the authority of the expression on his face of "getting away with something," at the most impressionable moment, to put it mildly, of her life.

The proposal of an unmanned, lovesick father and an adaptively perverse daughter enables what has come before in the story to cohere with what follows. She is frightened now by her father's importunity because she now has something important to lose, namely her newfound stability and hope, her place with Glenn at life's feast. She calls her mother, a self-absorbed lawyer she has heretofore despised, and asks her for help. Here the story enters the realm of the topical but resists settling there, guarding itself against the topical's superficial counsel of information and knowingness:

> She found this group. She says, just in San Jose, there's hundreds of families like ours, yeah, great, that's what I said. But there's groups. She's going to a group of thick-o mothers like her, those wives who didn't catch on. She wanted me to go into a group of girls, yeah, molested girls, that's what they call them, but I said no, I have friends here already, she can do what she wants.

She tells Glenn, who quickly drops her. Desolate again, she turns to her roommate, Lauren, who at one point takes her for a ride. They stop in front of an elementary school in a mixed neighborhood and watch the children playing at recess. Lauren then speaks to her, in a way that redeems the topical by placing it in the human scale:

> Eight years old. Look at them. They're eight years old. One of their fathers is sleeping with one of those girls. Look at her. Do you blame her? Can you blame her? Because if you can forgive her, you can forgive yourself.

The "thoughtfulness" of the reader is fostered in two ways by the story. The first, as I've been suggesting, is by Mona Simpson's making her own proposal about an incestuous relationship and keeping it free of the current fashions of reductiveness that surround it as a social problem, a hot media topic, and a feminist cause. In the clear space she has come to in her mind, the narrator thinks about her past and tries to take into account her father's view of the good times they've had together. She finds that her memories are no worse than equivocal. Then she goes on:

> But that's over. I don't know if I'm sorry it happened. I mean I am, but it happened, that's all. It's just one of those things that happened to me in my life. But I would never go back, never.

Her acceptance may seem shallow or perverse to the knowing and the militant. But it is no more so than her determination is and indeed grounds it. She wants to be what the story proposes her to be—an individual rather than a generic victim, someone who has a life rather than a case history or a legal brief or a gender grievance. The story is painful precisely because the narrator presents herself less as the victim than as the daughter of her father, whose attachment has kept her vulnerable even as her contempt has enabled her to exploit the situation. At one point earlier in the story, still a bit squeamish about being in bed with Glenn, she reflects:

> It's so easy to hurt people. They just lie there and let you have them. I could reach out and choke Glenn to death, he'd be so shocked, he wouldn't stop me. You can just take what you want.

The exaggeration of people's vulnerability here is itself telling—an outcropping of the psychopathology of her everyday life. But it is also a perception of the human condition that the dominated share with the dominating, and, in this instance, that one side of her mind shares with the other. Part of the psychological authority of the story comes from its easy intercourse between the normal and abnormal, the natural and unnatural: It tacitly counsels us that this is also true of its subject, which is why incest is such a deeply implanted taboo and sin. It is normal for a daughter to do her father's bidding, to want to please him and be admired by him, just as it is for a father both to exercise authority and to fondle and dote on his daughter. Moreover, it is in the context of the natural that the unnatural asserts itself most clearly and forcefully in our minds, because it becomes both sharply focused and commensurable in the human scale. For example, the most unforgettable moment in Terrence DesPres's *The Survivor* is not in his full account of the terror and privation of the death camps but in his brief passage on what it must have been like to wake up each morning at Auschwitz. The forming of this kind of insight, this sudden flare of light in the dark which naturalizes the unnatural and restores it to the human scale, is what we look to in the literary imagination as a resource of thoughtfulness.

The second way that "Lawns" conduces the reader to reflect is by its movement toward healing, which in the story also takes on a kind of natural aura. Sometime after he rejects her, the narrator meets Glenn on campus:

> I felt the same as I always used to, that I love him and all that, but he might just be one of the things you can't have. Like I should have been for my father, and look at him now. Oh, I think he's better, they're all better, but I'm gone, he'll never have me again.

Her words here and elsewhere convey a sense of time's changes and attenuations, of her progress being an aspect of what Benjamin calls "the great inscrutable course of the world." There is no one "reason" offered by the story as to why her wound is healing over. The good she initially received from Glenn, her confessions, the counsel of her roommate Lauren, her mother's belated support, and so forth have all contributed, but the number and variety and mixed effects of these agents indicate that they have no common denominator except the way one good thing can lead to another, just as one bad thing in her life has led to others. The connections are left to our thoughtfulness to establish. Again, this is not to imply that the story is complacent about incest, that it is proposing that time heals all wounds, so what's all the fuss about, the hotlines and support groups and alarming statistics? Such a reading induces thoughtlessness by stripping the narrator of her individuality, the story of its psychological nuances and grasp of natural history, and by countering its proposal with a position. That is, it turns a telling story about human nature into an antifeminist document, which flatters our knowingness while impoverishing our understanding.

Toward the very end of the story, the narrator tells us that she has begun to steal mail again—"not packages and people I know" and only one letter every Saturday ("I'm really being stern"), because she feels desolate and in need of excitement. Then, on the last Saturday of the story, she receives a letter addressed to herself, the first she's gotten. There is no return name and address on the envelope;

it comes from Benjamin's great inscrutable course of the world. But since she knows it is not from Glenn, who has another girlfriend now, she throws it away and finishes her work for the day:

> And then I thought, I don't have to keep looking at the garbage can, I'm allowed to take it back, that's my letter. And I fished it out... and I held it a few minutes, wondering who it was from. Then I put it in my mailbox so I can go like everybody else and get mail.

And so ends Mona Simpson's "Lawns," a story that takes on the fullness and perplexity of contemporary life and provides the kind of counsel that Benjamin speaks of as the "the epic side of truth"— namely wisdom.

(1978, 1987)

A Dream of Ray Carver

For days after I learned that Raymond Carver had died an image of his face would appear in my mind. The face was not that of the stricken man I had seen for the last time two months before, but of Ray in his prime—boyishly spruce and expectant, his face slightly averted, listening in that cocked way of his. It was strange to think of him as dead and to see him so alive, like studying the sealed photograph of a particularly striking face attached to a tombstone, as I had done in the Novodevichy cemetery in Moscow after visiting Chekhov's grave.

It was also strange to be so haunted by his presence since I hadn't known him that well. We were together probably ten or twelve times, always in professional or social situations. The closest we had come to a personal conversation were the few occasions in recent years when he and Tess Gallagher, my wife Virginia and I had gotten together during their visits to New York, or once when we had met up in London and gone to the British Museum together.

Ray recalled that sweet time in London in a letter he wrote to Virginia toward the end of his life. He said that the four of us were "lucky people, all things considered." Virginia and I took this to mean that he had sensed that we, like Tess and himself, had lucked out in finding each other in middle age. We also took his words as another outcropping of the courage and gratitude with which he had come to terms with dying in one of his last poems, the extraordinary one called "Gravy."

No other word will do. For that's what it was. Gravy.
Gravy these past ten years.

Alive, sober, working, loving and
being loved by a good woman. Eleven years
ago he was told he had six months to live
at the rate he was going. And he was going
nowhere but down. So he changed his ways
somehow. He quit drinking! And the rest?
After that it was *all* gravy, every minute
of it, up to and including when he was told about,
well, some things that were breaking down and
building up inside his head. "Don't weep for me,"
he said to his friends. "I'm a lucky man.
I've had ten years longer than I or anyone
expected. Pure gravy. And don't forget it."

So, at first I thought that my bright image of him was honoring his wish to he remembered for what he had been given rather than for what had been taken away. With that explanation, I figured that the image would fade. But it didn't: it continued to recur, its vividness still filling the hole that his death had punched out in my sense of rightness. His face wasn't lodged there in the soft way of grief but in a firm one, as though its vitality was a kind of message—something being given to me or possibly being asked of me.

The third day or so the image changed: his face was no longer in its listening mode but had turned to me, his eyes looking to make contact. He was less the literary figure and more the person, whom I felt I had known less well. I sensed that I was being visited and perhaps instructed by the gift of his friendship, that he had meant more to me than I had recognized or acted on when I'd decided not to fly across the country to attend his funeral. His eyes had his open, welcoming, sincere (there's no other word for it) look that brought out one's own sincerity, what was left of it. They also had his gentleness: unlike most of the writers I've known from working-class backgrounds, there had been little, besides his passion for fishing, that was macho about him. His smile was that of a boy who was close to his mother, and he carried himself and attended to people in a careful way that made him seem more like a minister than a writer, particularly a famous one. As for his reputation, he wore it with a kind of naïve pride, like the beautiful tweed jacket he had bought during his reading tour in England, and this too was endearing, particularly when one remembered from his fiction and his autobiographical essays how far he had come and what he had overcome on the way.

I began to believe that this imaging of Ray was coming from the soul, telling me that I had been privileged to know a rare person, a *mensch*, as we Jews say, a real sweetheart, as Ray would have said—a brave man with a highly developed feminine side, the type of man I most cherished and wanted to be. This brought to mind Chekhov, another of my models of conduct, and Tolstoy's famous remark to Gorky about Chekhov: "What a beautiful, magnificent man: modest and quiet, like a girl. He even walks like a girl."

Ray had picked up Tolstoy's words and used them in his final published story, "Errand." An account of Chekhov's last days, it has a documentary character that makes it unlike any of Ray's other stories that I'm aware of; yet it becomes a Carver story all the same by the laconic yet brooding way it deals with the dark, oncoming facts of the event and its aftermath ("...the injection didn't help—nothing, of course, could have helped") and from the expressive power with which he endows a commonplace object—in this case an errant champagne cork—to concentrate both the chill and poignancy of the death. There is also, of course, another chilling and poignant story that is telling itself between the lines, a story based on implicit similarities, beginning with the detail that Chekhov had "peasant's blood in his veins."

A few weeks later Tess asked me to speak at the memorial for Ray in New York. This meant the writer as well as the man, so I stayed up one night reading his stories. The fact was that I hadn't read many of them until then. Except for "Errand," I had respected his fiction rather than cottoned to it. His typically small-town isolates were of marginal interest to me; they didn't seem to see or feel or learn much beyond their insecurities, the bleakness of their prospects, the force of their streaks of envy, jealousy, cruelty, shame, dishonesty, or some other twisted energy that flared up like a chronic fever in a meager, congested life: the unemployed salesman who pressures his wife to lose weight so that he can watch men ogling her: the drinker and adulterer who drives himself to begin to put his family's life in order by secretly getting rid of their messy dog; the baker who torments the couple whose child has been run over about paying for the birthday cake they had ordered. I admired the integrity of Carver's work—his firm grasp of damaged lives for which there was little help or hope and his bluff style that conceded nothing to literary entertainment or embellishment. But his vision was too limiting, to my taste: the world seen from the barstool, the forsaken marriage bed, the car rubbernecking the traffic accident.

That was my superficial response. What I remembered best was his astonishing essay "Fires," in which he said flat out that the main influence on his fiction had been his long subjection to the needs and caprices of his children. He and his wife had been teenage parents, uneducated and unskilled, working at one "crap job" after another, subsisting, stretched thin, losing hope and heart until

> "everything my wife and I held sacred, or considered worthy of respect, every spiritual value, crumbled away. Something terrible had happened to us... It was erosion and we couldn't stop it. Somehow, when we weren't looking, the children had got into the driver's seat. As crazy as it sounds now, they held the reins, and the whip."

That kind of rockbottom honesty was electrifying: it generated the power and light of his stories. But it didn't make me a fan of the stories. It mostly made me wonder how the sweetness of the man had survived the bitter erosions and defeats the writer kept recounting and imagining.

That night and on into the early morning I read through most of *Where I'm Calling From*, his new and selected stories. I found myself giving up my dismissive respect or, rather, having it pushed aside by assent. At first it took a literary form, a fascination with the exactness of the writing—common language that "hit all the notes" as Carver once put it, and with the subtle variations of the emotional burden that I'd read too glibly as an obsessive gray doom that fogged in his people's world. What I had taken to be a grim reductiveness was, when seen over the long haul, a finely calibrated ruefulness: a more tender and interesting and philosophical kind of understanding. As one of his characters in the grip of an unwarranted but intractable jealousy, comes to see: "Yes, there was a great evil pushing at the world. . . and it only needed a little slipway, a little opening."

Those wrecked marriages and stalled affairs and misfiring bar seductions and sprung friendships: each testified in its own distinctive way to the erosion at the heart of things that he spoke about in "Fires." I also began to see that his understanding of it had widened over the years and become more nuanced: the blue-collar ruts of the earlier stories branched out, as it were, into the mazes of better-educated people, the undercurrent of menace or perversity was giving way to more uncanny and strange threats, like the blind friend of the narrator's wife in "Cathedral" or the good-bye letter from the wife in "Blackbird Pie" that is not in her handwriting or style. But he still refused to brighten or soften the testimony of his narrators about their secret meannesses, screw-ups, losses, and the prose remained homely and unsparing, as though a naked lightbulb were burning in their minds. The ruefulness was built into the "unique and exact way of looking at things" he recommended, just as it was built into the lives he trained it upon…just as it was built into my own. The pity was in the telling itself and it began to get to me, to chasten my way of reading him. The last story I read was a late one called "Menudo" about a man who can't sleep, who is on the verge of breaking up two marriages and is thinking about his previous one:

When Molly and I were growing up together, she was a part of me and, sure, I was a part of her, too. We loved each other. It was our destiny. I believed in it then myself. But now I don't know what to believe in. I'm not complaining, simply stating a fact. I'm down to nothing. And I have to go on like this. No destiny. Just the next thing meaning whatever you think it does. Compulsion and error, just like everybody else.

I read those words again and then again. They could have been my own words through much of my adult life. Like Carver, I had married too young, had held the same kind of high hopes and values along with the same low jobs, had also tried to raise two children with more despair and panic than care and money, had witnessed the same terrible slow entailment and foreclosure of that striving first love. Though my ordeal hadn't gone on as long and as hopelessly as his, and though I had been spared the grimmer consequences he had known as an alcoholic, it had left some of the same scars and kinks of error and compulsion that he wrote about. For most of my adult life that passage in "Menudo" could have served as the "unspoken meditation of my heart" (a phrase from the Yom Kippur liturgy), which I usually managed to evade or gloss over.

I finally went to bed, fell asleep, and had a dream. I was driving my new Honda Accord, the first quality car I've owned. One of the warning lights came on, the one that tells you to head for the nearest repair shop. It was a dark, cold, snowy night with no traffic, no pedestrians. A Ray Carver night in the sticks, except that I was in New York. I drove past a couple of garages, the kind that are inside buildings. I found a place to park in the street and went back to the first garage. A surprisingly friendly mechanic there told me to bring the car in, he'd work on it. Much relieved I went outside and walked to where my car was. It was gone. I couldn't believe that even in New York a car could he stolen that fast and I walked up the street looking for it, thinking I'd gotten its location wrong. But though there were other cars that looked like mine, none of them was, and when I got to the end of the block I knew that it was gone for good. I began to panic, to go crazy in my lifelong way. When I'd calmed down a hit I remembered that I'd parked the car near a second garage and thought that perhaps they had taken the car in. But no, they hadn't seen or heard of it.

I woke up then and lay in a daze of revelation. The dream seemed like a Ray Carver story about losing him. It was also about the panic and craziness of suddenly losing one's assurances, of once again being down to nothing. It was about the permanent ruefulness that the passage in "Menudo" had led me to recognize in myself.

Some of what is written here, including the dream, comes from what I said at the memorial. Since then the image of Ray's vitality and the dream have taken on a further meaning.

A month or two before his death I had abandoned a long piece of writing that dealt with a surrogate version of those desperate years. I'd adopted a jaunty style to make it less depressing, livened it up with a romantic relationship from a later period, provided a strong therapist to lead my character out of the wilderness, and modified or left out most of my actual mistakes and pain and, most of all, harmfulness. For several years it had been fun to write, off and on, but just as it was, heading into the crisis I had suddenly lost interest and conviction. Its liveliness now seemed willed, a smiling whine, its issues psychologically precious, its narrator ungrounded in an actual life and hence increasingly arbitrary, and the way ahead tedious. I thought I'd been writing a novel that went deep into the process of psychotherapy but now saw that I had been seduced by a facile first-person voice, had managed to ignore most of what I had learned about fiction from editing, teaching, and criticizing it, and was writing still another narcissistic first novel, possibly quite like the one I would have written thirty years ago if I'd had the freedom.

All of which was disappointing but not heartbreaking. I told myself that I had only postponed an apprenticeship, that like most novelists I've worked with I'd written an unpublishable first novel, had gotten a lot of vanity out of my system, had learned about certain mistakes by making them. Perhaps I'd rewrite it in the third person and let more of the world come into it. In any case, my experience with the process would be useful, one way and another. Asked to speak at a writing program last summer, I quickly recycled the main lessons into a lecture entitled "The Pits of Fiction."

But my "mature" response to the failure has proved to be facile too. Hidden and defended by egotism, the real cause began to reveal itself as I was revising this essay. For I'm as sure as one can be about such matters that Ray's image in my mind and the dream, whatever else they're about, have to do with that abandoned manuscript, that the opportunity was taken away because I finally got bored with kidding myself. To write with any sustained energy and interest about those years of losing my way, of anguished trial and error, I would have had to go back into how I came to be down to nothing and tell about the force of error and compulsion in my life. For that's the bedrock of what I've been given to know and I am still learning about thirty years later, since all too often the knowledge slides into obliviousness. To establish that bedrock I would have had to tell about the bitter, crazy side of premature marriage and child-rearing: those Medusa truths that even shielded by time and forgetting can still make my heart as heavy as stone

In his *Paris Review* interview Carver speaks of turning one's life's stories into fiction. "You have to be immensely daring, very skilled and imaginative and willing to tell everything on yourself....What do you know better than your own secrets?" He's not saying that telling them guarantees anything, for fiction is more likely to fail from lack of skill and imagination than from evasiveness. What he is saying is that if you want the energy and authority that comes from telling your secrets, they had better be the real ones: the ones that make you go through their pain again. Otherwise the writing will be coming not from the secrets but from the defenses against them and the fiction will not be the bread of experience earned in the sweat of your brow but rather the cake of fantasies that you can have and eat too.

I think I see now why the image of Ray in my mind had so much vigor—the vigor that comes from honesty—and why my dream was a secret told in a Carveresque way. As I read him now and write about him he has come to seem less like a dead friend than a vital ally. I imagine that when Chekhov died many Russian writers felt the same way: that his fiction was itself a friendship. What one wants most in a friend is both candor and empathy, rarely found together. Chekhov's vision was less relentless than Carver's and he had more social range, but they started from and came back to the same ruefulness: a radical honesty and empathy about ordinary lives and how they go wrong.

Gorky wrote that in Chekhov's presence "everyone felt an involuntary desire to be simpler, more truthful, more oneself." This was also Ray Carver's gift as a person, as I've said earlier, and one that is literally conveyed by his stories and poems as it was by Chekhov's stories and plays. It explains, I think, much better than does the fashionable talk about "minimalism" and "rural chic" why Carver has been the most influential writer of his generation. He had the kind of gift that circulates: the common touch raised to the next power, the power of art, that can he conveyed intact to his readers and brings out, as my dream did, the giftedness in them, the possibility of getting down to the charged and freighted basis of our lives. To God's honest truth, as he would have said, and as he did.

(1989)

Radical Realism: John Fowles

It is strange that a novelist as superbly imaginative as John Fowles should be content to write within the canons of conventional text-book realism. Of the four stories in *The Ebony Tower*, three have simple, linear structures—situation, complication, resolution—the incidents rationally linked through the probable interactions of credible characters, the action and theme neatly illustrating each other. The fourth story is somewhat more open-ended and covert: a picnic in the country that ends in a disappearance and, by implication, a suicide. One has to draw the connections for oneself and see the sudden gathering storm at the end as an epiphany. But this is a technique that Joyce was practicing in "Dubliners" at the turn of the century and that is still being practiced routinely in the pages of *The New Yorker* and elsewhere.

Yet each of these stories is anything but obvious or thin. However conventionally they begin and proceed, there comes a point when their issues dramatically engage and take on complexity and power—as though one had picked up a familiar object, casually examined it, and suddenly found it shaking in one's hands. By the same token, Fowles's seemingly typecast characters—a lascivious old artist meets his decorous young critic, a timid literary scholar is ripped off by an aggressive hippie—have a way of slipping out of their mold, surprising us first as individuals and then as the strange faces that our most intense encounters tend to confer.

The popular writer turns life into clichés, the artist of realism turns clichés back into life. But why start with clichés in the first place and why tie yourself down to the restrictions and reductions of a plot?

Why all this outmoded literary law and order? It's as though a brilliant playwright came upon the scene, a master of illusion, who insists upon practicing the three unities.

One may believe Fowles enjoys being so clever and also the rewards it has brought him as a writer of highly intelligent fiction that manages to be very popular. But judging from *The Aristos*, his "intellectual self-portrait," he has more ambitious goals in view: in his quiet, detached way, just as much as Mailer does in his clamorous, self-regarding one, Fowles wants to create a revolution in the consciousness of his time. Still, if this is so, surely he must suspect that his fiction is going about it in the wrong way. Tidy narrative structures, well-rounded characters, consistent points of view, lucid prose, accurate descriptions of times and places—aren't these the techniques, at our late stage of modernism, that confirm the most retrograde bourgeois tastes, that are valuable only so that they can then be superseded or, better yet, undermined, if not destroyed, by the writer's innovations? Learn the rules so that you know what you're doing when you break them—so the young writer is told. Learn the craft so that you can then practice the art: craft being what all writers are supposed to be able to do, art being what only the individual writer can do because true art is the creation of new *forms* of consciousness, which only the individualist can achieve. Right?

Wrong. Partly wrong in theory and increasingly wrong in practice. New consciousness does not necessarily require new forms in literature any more than it does in any other field of writing. When Shakespeare wrote the "Dark Lady" sonnets, he was doing something original in love poetry, and hence for love itself, though he left the sonnet form undisturbed. And while it is true that new literary forms can provoke new consciousness, it tends more often to work the other way around. In any case, modernism, which has tended to identify originality and individuality with formal innovation, has left the writers who still subscribe to it increasingly high and dry: i.e., rarefied and empty. Or as Fowles himself puts it in *The Aristos*: "There is the desperate search for the unique style, and only too often this search is conducted at the expense of content. This accounts for the enormous proliferation in styles and techniques and for that only too characteristic coupling of exoticism of presentation and banality of theme." If you don't think he's right, pick up an anthology of current "experimental" fiction or poetry and see how much genuine new consciousness you find and how much of the same surreal solipsism, forlorn or abrasive or sardonic. Talk about conventionality.

In one of Fowles's new stories, "The Enigma," John Marcus Fielding, a wealthy Conservative M.P., a model of respectability and responsibility, mysteriously disappears. An astute young detective is assigned to the case, who after weeks of checking and interviewing comes up empty-handed. Finally, he goes to see the girlfriend of Fielding's son, another of those grave, bright, smashing young women whom Fowles likes to write about, who are, as in Henry James, the sunlight and moral agents of his world. "Sergeant Mike Jennings," he says to the girl, who is somewhat puzzled by this spruce public-school graduate on her door step. "The fuzz."

They hit it off very quickly and she tells Jennings several somewhat compromising things she has kept from the other investigators: that Fielding, though he could barely manage to indicate it, had seemed to admire her independence of spirit and that, the evening before he disappeared, she had mentioned she would be going to the British Museum the next day, the last place Fielding was traced to. After some charming fencing with Jennings (few writers bring the sexes together as happily and subtly as Fowles does), Isobel reconstructs Fielding's disappearance by putting him in a story in which the author, who believes in giving his characters and hence himself the perils of freedom (there is a fascinating discussion of this question in Chapter 13 of *The French Lieutenant's Woman*), finds himself with a character who has decided to vanish without a trace.

What has eluded Jennings through his scientific police work comes in buckets to the literary Isobel as she draws out the implications of her own two meager clues and produces so shrewd a scenario that it eventually convinces the smitten but all the more skeptical Jennings. For several related reasons, Fielding has chosen to play the "God game" by absconding (the theme that wells up so powerfully at the end of *The Magus*). But the underlying point of the story is that there is a wisdom that passes scientific understanding embedded in the narrative process itself, one that can weave intuition, imagination and the generative logic of storytelling into deep but lucid inquiries into human conduct and destiny.

Hence for fiction to abandon narrative is rather like having science abandon the scientific method because some phenomena are too elusive or enigmatic or distortable to be fully understood by its methods. Fowles's practice of providing or suggesting alternative endings to his previous two major novels is not just cleverness but an acknowledgment that narrative art, like science, like reality itself, terminates in paradox and mystery: the double ending being a kind of fictional equivalent of Bohr's principle of complementarity.

An awareness of the toll that the decline of narrative has taken appears to be rapidly growing these days: Reynolds Price spoke of it in his review of Graham Greene's latest novel in the *Times Book Review*, so has John Barth in *New American Review* 15; it is also evident in the growing influence of such writers as Fowles, Borges, Nabokov, and Garcia Márquez, who are revitalizers of the art of narrative, surprise witnesses at the otherwise mostly bootlessly academic inquest of the novel.

Fowles's contribution has been twofold. In *The Magus*, he creates what might be called an existential narrative, using realism itself to mock and alter its assumptions. The novel is made up of a huge mesh of incidents, most of which are as convincing as they turn out to be duplicitous. A sensible and evasive young Englishman takes a job teaching on a Greek island, becomes a habitué of a rich man's estate, and soon finds his credulity being serially flattered and betrayed. His relationship with a demonic millionaire and his entourage becomes a treacherous terrain of psychological traps and moral land mines which eventually pervade the rest of his life, until daily reality appears to crumble and human existence resembles the behavior of subatomic particles: probability contending with chaos, the knowable with the unknowable. This plot (in both senses) in which Nicholas

Urff finds himself (in both senses) is an extraordinary if exasperating creation that employs all the nuances of verisimilitude, not to confirm our worldliness but to undermine it, so that the world's randomness, contingency, and hazard can be revealed in their full truth and power as the price we pay for the functional rationalism of everyday life.

This is Fowles's master theme and objective: to restate the terms of mental freedom. In *The French Lieutenant's Woman*, Fowles uses the conventions of nineteenth-century romantic fiction not only to write a brilliant study of Victorian manners, morals, and morale but also to do something no less interesting and more difficult—to portray the seeds of the future blowing into "the age of steam and cant," sowing what we call modern consciousness in three young people—a stifled governess, a bored gentleman and amateur scientist, and his ignorant but fashion-minded servant—each pursuing her or his own image of independence to ends they would never have dreamed of.

None of the four long stories in *The Ebony Tower* has the originality of those two novels or even the tour-de-force quality of Fowles's *The Collector*, a shocking parable of contemporary class warfare confined to two characters in two rooms. Fowles tells us that these new stories were written as variations on some of the themes of his novels, and they do tend to have a kind of relaxed, less layered feeling about them. But if you haven't been reading Fowles, you'll find them magical enough and a good way to begin the ascent; if you have been reading him, you'll have the pleasure of making connections.

The richest and most expressive one is the title story, about two days that shake the life of a successful young "color painter" and critic. David Williams's abstract canvases are as attractive, rational and low-keyed as his character, his marriage, his existence. The gifted son of two architects, he has had his way paved into the art world and he has sensibly made the most of it. Writing an essay on Henry Breasley, an Expressionist painter whose work has gone through many changes while his life in France has remained consistently scandalous, Williams travels to Brittany to interview him.

In his late seventies, Breasley is still going strong, indeed painting the major pictures of his career—a series of "dreams" in a forest setting—and living with two English girls, whom Williams finds sunbathing in the nude when he arrives. He is surprised to find that Breasley still has the dress, manners, and affable inarticulateness of the English upper-class he fled so long ago; but once he is in his cups, the angry old lion in him stirs and begins to claw at Williams and his tradition of "obstructs." "Triumph of the bloody eunuch…Spunk. Any spunk. Even Hitler's spunk or nothing…Not fundamentals…Fundaments… All that goes with them. That's reality. Not your piddling little theorems and pansy colors….Mess of scientific pottage. Sold the whole bloody shoot down the river…." Or as "the Mouse," the more sophisticated and fetching of the two girls, puts it for him: "Art is a form of speech. Speech must be based on human needs, not abstract theories of grammar. Or anything but the spoken word. The real word."

By the end of the next day, Breasley's words and his new work, the pagan atmosphere of the household, the adjacent forest and the coolly alluring Mouse, have cast their spell and Williams has succumbed. He has come, he feels, to the end of his careful way; Breasley's way is just a step across and the Mouse (Breasley's nickname has nothing to do with her temperament: it stands for Muse with the female O added) is holding out her hand. But at the crisis point, Williams's habits of dutifulness reassert themselves, he hesitates, and is lost. Driving back to Paris, he realizes that he has been defeated all along his front, or rather, that a longstanding ramifying defeat has finally been exposed:

> One killed all risk, one refused all challenge, and so one became an artificial man. The old man's secret [was] not letting anything stand between self and expression; which wasn't a question of outward artistic aims, merely styles, and techniques, and themes. But how you did it; how wholly, how bravely you faced up to the constant recasting of yourself.

Hence vanity, prejudice, and amorality are as essential to a Breasley as paint and canvas. And terrified of them, the tolerant, diffident, considerate, self-evasive Williams has not the wherewithal to change. His experience "remorselessly demonstrated what he was born, still was, and always would be: a decent man and eternal also-ran."

In seeing through himself, Williams also sees into the prison where his painting has led him. Breasley was right there too. "Turning away from nature and reality had atrociously distorted the relationship between painter and audience: now one painted for intellects and theories. Not for people; and worst of all, not for oneself." The result has become an art of outer space—daring, quickly banal, frozen—in which only the artist and the critic in their special space suits exist and have value.

The closing pages of *The Ebony Tower* are, of course, an assertion of Fowles's own guiding values, and they go a long way to explain and justify his practice of writing about live men, women and issues in searching narratives. In restating the tradition of realism, he finds his mode of opposition and his medium for recasting himself. At one point, Williams asks the question that haunts most contemporary artists, composers, and writers alike—are they living in the sterile aftermath of modernism, in one of the dead spots of cultural history:

> Art had always gone in waves. Who knew if the late 20th century might not be one of its most cavernous troughs? He knew the old man's answer: it was. Or it was unless you fought bloody tooth and nail against some of its most cherished values and victories.

Amen.

(1974)

Woman's Fate:
The Stories of Alice Munro

Alice Munro has begun to loom as the mother-figure of contemporary fiction—fecund, wise, dauntingly capable. Her purview is the private history of women's lives in the small towns of the Ottawa Valley, where she has lived most of hers, with occasional sweeps to Toronto and Vancouver. Her provincial straightforwardness, steadiness and clarity are set against an urbane sophistication, like that of the great stylists of 1920s realism, a Katherine Anne Porter brought up to date.

For American readers she might as well be writing from the Ohio Valley, so similar are the cultures now, so applicable is her penetrating insight, so much in the American grain are her pragmatic experiments in handling time, point of view and new textures of verisimilitude. We are in the middle of an age of renovated realism in fiction, in which much of the new work has been done in the short story, and Munro seems to me as much an architect of the female wing as Raymond Carver has been of the male.

Like most contemporary realists, both are domestic writers of the emergent lower and middle classes, whose main adventure, struggle and defeat is marriage, along with its previews, second chances and aftermaths. Both Munro and Carver have the authority of seeming to write directly from personal experience without the blind spots and obtrusiveness of the ego one finds in Cheever or Mary McCarthy. Even those stories whose pain or problem seems most personal and complex take place in a clarified air of objectivity. Moreover, unlike their immediate predecessors the metafictionists of the 1970s, their innovations in storytelling place a democratic trust in the insight, empathy and moral imagination of the common reader, wherever he or she may still be. They create unexpected individuals rather than walking tropes, the difficulties of life rather than of art.

It is just here that Carver and Munro part company, for he is a minimalist, mostly, and she a maximalist. He uses the magnifying glass of the story form to focus a small, telling situation and to concentrate the ray of his vision to make it flame. Munro uses her glass to explore, bit by magnified bit, the narrative configuration of a life (as when we ask, What's his or her story?) and to take in as much as possible of the ground as well as the figure. Rather than a sudden flare of revelation, Munro provides a mounting glow of implication. Put your hand into one of her full, limpid, flowing stories and you feel the current of a destiny.

One of Munro's strengths as well as a source of her appeal is that she is so firmly rooted in an older feminist sensibility and sexuality: Willa Cather meets Edna O'Brien. Women are the bearers of her values, but she writes about their experience, contemporary as well as past, mostly in terms of their relation to men. Husbands and lovers provide the shaping events of their lives, the chief circumstances of their power and failure, and are the moon of their moods. Their jobs are nominal; their careers are secondary; they have few female friends, and even their children tend to exist on the periphery of their lives, certainly of its story.

In "Vandals," one of the stories in her new collection, Bea Doud, a typical Munro figure, has left an earnest, agreeable high school principal for a taxidermist who is "rude, and testy and slightly savage." Was that the reason? she asks a correspondent:

> She would hate to think so, because wasn't that the way in all the dreary romances—some brute gets the woman tingling and then it's goodbye to Mr. Fine-and-Decent?... But what she did think— and she knew that this was very regressive and bad form—what she did think was that some women, women like herself, might be always on the lookout for an insanity that could contain them. For

what was living with a man if it wasn't living inside his insanity? A man could have a very ordinary insanity, such as his devotion to a ball team. But that might not be enough, not big enough—and an insanity that was not big enough simply made a woman mean and discontented. Peter Parr, for instance, displayed kindness and hopefulness to a fairly fanatical degree. But in the end, for me… that was not a suitable insanity.

What her new man, a taxidermist, gives her is not only his fiercely guarded preserve of stuffed and active wild life but, more to her point, a life surrounded by his "implacability." A vain as well as ironic daughter of the first family in Carstairs, addicted to the star turns of serial love affairs, Bea finds that Ladner's harsh indifference is indeed the climate she needs, and she thrives as half of one of those "interesting" older couples in baggy pants and flannel shirts one sees in country towns. But then he suddenly dies and she soon loses her hold again, her skid greased by another aspect of his implacability she hadn't allowed herself to be aware of. Munro brings this out in another narrative line that she threads through loops in Bea's, about a young girl, Liza, from the shanty next door whom Ladner cruelly seduced and who returns after his death, a born-again Christian, to trash their property.

It's remarkable how many times and ways Munro can place a woman in a man's shadow or have it cross her life at its dividing line without seeming to limit or repeat herself. She taps a rich vein in the broken marriages and seized sexual opportunities of the Sixties era (one survivor looks back at it "as though she had once gone in for skydiving"), but the male madness they are escaping from or into comes in various forms and depths and from many different places and times.

Thus the stories in *Open Secrets* develop Munro's master theme from various locales and from dramatically unexpected angles. In "A Wilderness Station," which mostly takes place in the early 1850s, the male insanity is all too literal. Annie McKillop, a young woman from the workhouse in Toronto, is brought to Carstairs, which is just beginning to be cleared from the forest, by her new husband and his brother, orphans like herself: Simon barely out of his teens, George barely into them. Their story is told in a series of letters, led off by a taciturn memoir of George's published some fifty years later about their iron-willed struggle to survive in the wilderness, which ends with Simon's death in a logging accident and George and Annie going their separate ways. From several letters that follow—an exchange between the settlement minister and the law officer in Walley, the new county seat, and then by Annie herself—the truth slowly emerges, like bandages and then scar tissue being stripped away from a deep wound, that Simon was murdered by George, who was provoked by his sadism, which Simon had also practiced on Annie's body. Her main letter describes her discovery of the ax wound, the struggle to get Simon into a shroud, his hasty funeral service and burial in a blizzard, and the long night's vigil in which she saves George from a catatonic withdrawal, only to have him henceforth look at her in the same murderous way his brother did, which drives her slowly mad so that she confesses to the murder. This is just extraordinary writing, a fictitious document that deserves to live forever in the annals of the frontier ethos and the brutality and terror it inflicted on women.

Despite its biblical references and overtones, "A Wilderness Station" is not an indictment of patriarchal oppression. Munro's imagination is constitutionally dialectical: In this case she is as engaged by Annie's coping process as she is by the victimizing one. Annie's confession is both her mind's effort to quiet a maddening dissonance of fear and guilt brought on by both the brothers and a naïvely resourceful attempt by a resourceless woman to survive the sub-Arctic winter in the new county jail. It is also an opportunity for Munro to provide the religious and medical viewpoints—which attribute Annie's behavior to a dereliction of wifely duties or playing with the devil or reading too many romances—as part of the institutionalized male insanity that women had to endure; but this, in turn, is played off against the sympathetic skepticism of the Clerk of the Peace, who enables her to recover and find a place in his home.

Munro then jumps the story ahead fifty years, a characteristic strategy of hers to reenergize her imagination and her reader's, by projecting a final coordinate of Annie's destiny and letting the reader draw the line of implication to it. Also, Munro often shifts the time frame and point of view to cover social ground—in this case the transformation of Carstairs from Hobbes's state of nature to prosperous farms and genteel households in little more than a generation. The writer of this final letter is the daughter of Annie's benefactor who recalls a trip in her new Stanley Steamer, which ends with her taking Annie to meet her former nemesis, George. But since he is by that point senile, the meeting is mostly an ironic non-event and the jocular tone of the letter consorts oddly with what has come before, like hooking a parlor car onto a cattle train. When Munro falters, it is usually in the daring end game she has set for herself. This is true, I think, of "Vandals" too, in that Bea's vamping her way into Ladner's life and Liza's payback create a weak parallel of the title, particularly since Ladner's seduction of his nymphet remains emotionally cryptic in the telling, a mistake that Munro doesn't often make when it comes to the sticking point.

There are two great stories in *Open Secrets* that deal with the male shadow on women's lives. One is a beautiful three-part variation on the theme of being carried away, in its double meaning of love and death. Its main figure is Bea Doud's mother, Louisa, who has come to work in the town library after a brief career as a commercial traveler. There she picks up the torch that a soldier writing from the front in World War I has been carrying for her. Jack Agnew is a self-educated worker—"The last book I took out was very good—H.G. Wells, *Mankind in the Making*. . . I am a person tending to have his own ideas always." Louisa has been the woman of his dreams, which he can finally reveal to her, since he is unlikely to return alive given the carnage around him. What he doesn't tell her is that he is already engaged to a girl of his class.

A few months later a rueful Louisa tells her story to a kindly and sensible former comrade of the road, Jim Frarey, who regards Jack's behavior as all too understandable. She is gentled by him and then warmed by his whiskey, she slips out of her embarrassment. "Do you think me inexperienced?" she asks. "So they passed into a state of gingerly evaluation—which he knew well and could only hope she did—full of small pleasant surprises, half-sardonic signals, a welling-up of impudent hopes, and a fateful sort of kindness."

Another writer would be content to cash in her finely played hand at this point and take in the pot of ironic changes she has counterpointed. But Munro is only getting started. As another maximalist storyteller, Thomas Mann, put it, "Only the exhaustive is truly interesting." A good deal more eventful and much less talkative and explicit than Mann in his stories, she has much the same kind of imagination, which finds the shape and meaning of a life or a culture in the ongoing play of its oppositions.

This interweaving of contraries is everywhere present in Munro's work, from her phrasing to her view of a society. It is particularly marked in her treatment of sex and its politics—her real interest. In her story "Oranges and Apples" (to be found in *Friend of My Youth*), one of the few Munro tells from a man's point of view, Murray comes home from his department store to discover his wife, heretofore an aloof but reliable mate, slowly writhing on the lawn in her bathing suit and their friend and lodger watching her from his room.

> In the presence of her child in the middle of the day, in her own back yard, she lay on the grass inviting him. Promising—no, she was already providing—the most exquisite cooperation. It was obscene and enthralling and unbearable.

The last three embattled adjectives express the wedge experience that splits Murray's life henceforth into a before and an after and also reveals the core of the marriage that marks both. A self-assured working-class girl, Barbara has used the marriage mainly to give herself a literary education; but in the Realpolitik of the relationship she has always controlled her eager-beaver husband as she "balances contact with absences," which the scene on the lawn so graphically carries to the next power.

As Munro knows and knows, it is their women who make husbands into men, that it is sex that makes the strangest bedfellows, that if the woman is on her back, the man is on his knees, or vice versa, as Isaac Rosenfeld once put it. The title story in this new collection uses a missing girl to create circles of perverse behavior, in one of which the wife of a prominent attorney comes to recognize the sadomasochistic twist of her marriage in the dominating way a farm wife holds her husband's hand.

The remarkable combination of fullness and focus that Munro achieves comes from her subtle creation of patterns that enable seemingly disparate elements of her story to talk to each other. In "Carried Away," Jim Frarey's explanation that Jack Agnew didn't expect to come home in one piece ironically stations itself at the side of a factory accident a few years later in which Jack literally loses his head. Similarly, the hardheaded working-class view of marriage that implicitly locked Jack into his betrothal becomes explicit when the factory owner, Arthur Doud, visits his widow only an hour or so after the accident and finds her laundering curtains for the wake and worrying about getting Jack's books back to the library. Her surprising behavior not only rings true but casts a retrospective light in the reader's imagination on what the marriage had been like and on the force of Jack's dreams of another life in his correspondence with Louisa. Or again, after Arthur Doud returns the books, Jack's death sparks his relationship with Louisa, and his sudden proposal to her is a reprise in a sober minor key of her dalliance with Jim Frarey.

Munro has still one more hand to play in "Carried Away," and it is a virtuoso one. Thirty-five years later, a recent widow and manager of the Doud factory, Louisa travels to London, Ontario, for consultation about a heart condition. On the way to the bus home, she notices that a labor organizer named Jack Agnew is to speak at a rally. As she waits at the temporary depot he suddenly joins her, a late middle-aged man with a sporty look who has risen in the world just as she has and who tells her, in his old way, that "love never dies." Offended, she thinks, "Love dies all the time, or at any rate it becomes distracted,

over laid—it might as well be dead." When he leaves she notices he
has the backside of Jim Frarey. Then a group of black-clothed Men-
nonites from the area come to sit near her. It is a scene of exquisite
equivocalness in which the two meanings of "carried away" come
together. Even to say it is a dream of a dying woman conceptualizes
it beyond, and short of, its own telling, its deeper realism. Just as the
heart signs no documents, the soul leaves no clear set of tracks, and
the story ends in its own spiritual space, sealed by a final flashback
to the sound of sleigh bells disappearing into the countryside, which
Louisa heard when she first came to live in Carstairs.

If "Carried Away" is written, as Mark Twain would say, with "the
calm confidence of a Christian with four aces," Munro's other masterpiece in the collection, "The Albanian Virgin," is written with the
guts of a burglar. The first-rate story writers all have something of
the safe cracker in them, since they have to get in and get out, having sprung the combination to a novel's worth of rich material. But
here Munro has outdone herself. Again, she runs two parallel narrative lines that eventually meet. The first concerns a Canadian tourist
who is accidentally shot and carried off by a primitive mountain tribe
in the Balkans in which male insanity reigns supreme. Lottar, as she
comes to be named, learns to live within it as a "virgin," a solitary, androgynous herder of the sheep, and is eventually rescued by a Franciscan priest slightly less savage than his parishioners. It may, or may not,
be only a story made up by an esoteric old bohemian named Charlotte who goes around Vancouver with her fierce-looking, maniacal
Balkan husband, Gjurdhi, selling old travel books from a wagon. One
of their stops is the bookshop of a much younger narrator who enters
the story with her own tale to tell of flight from male domination by
a refined husband and a crude lover, and who has taken up a subsis-
tence life style and a solitary search for her identity. She is the lamb
to Charlotte's lioness ("Imagine this old fraud still being on the go,"
she remarks, picking up a book by Anaïs Nin), and that Munro can
keep their experience, plus that of Lottar, convincing and reverberating in tandem is sort of like Houdini cracking a safe into which he
has locked himself.

Toward the end, Munro gives the story a more explicit signature than usual. Charlotte and Gjurdhi have vanished, the building in which they had lived in their blithe squalor has already been gentrified. Feeling a dismay "more menacing than any of the little eddies of regret that had caught me in the past year," the narrator heads back to her bookstore:

> I felt as if I could as easily walk another way, just any way at all. My connection was in danger—that was all. Sometimes our connection is frayed, it is in danger, it seems almost lost. Views and streets deny knowledge of us, the air grows thin. Wouldn't we rather have a destiny to submit to, then, something that claims us, anything, instead of such flimsy choices, arbitrary days?

A similar passage appears in "Oh What Avails," one of the best stories in Munro's last collection, *Friend of My Youth*; but then again the threat of the vacuous, random, queasy universal lies at the back of many of her works, as it does of our lives, crouched and ready to spring, whenever we lose or seriously risk our "connection." The narrator, though, soon regains hers, for back at the bookstore—like the Franciscan waiting for Lottar or Ladner for Bea or Jack for Louisa—her unlikely lover has arrived, bearing her fate.

(1994)

Melville, Poe, and Doctorow

In what used to be the canon of American fiction, there is a sharp break between Hawthorne, Poe and Melville and the post-Civil War figures such as James, Twain, Howells and Crane. The dark meditative tales and romances (what Hawthorne called "blasted allegories") of the first group suddenly give way to realistic stories and novels, and an intensely literary language drops a level to embrace the fresh current of the spoken idiom. One of the several fascinating features of E. L. Doctorow's *The Waterworks,* which takes place in 1871, is that it settles in the mind like a kind of missing link in American fiction's evolution. Hints and glints of Poe are embedded in its twinned interests in mystery and science, its detective-story format, its necrological overlay, its protagonist—a brilliant, noir, disinherited literary journalist—its man-about-New York ambiance, even a mansion named Ravenwood.

The other writer who haunts the book's pages is Melville. Not the Melville who wrote the novels so much as the one who had ceased to do so, who would have been walking these harsh teeming streets on his way to his job as a customs inspector, his moral imagination gripped between the evils of rampant industrialism and even more rampant political corruption. Melville's provenance in *The Waterworks* is less a matter of literary traces than of a great shadow cast on Doctorow's moral imagination, urging him to see darkly and negatively all the way to the end of sanity and morality, and to make a distinctively American allegory of it, updated from the era of the New England oversoul and whaling industry.

At the same time, *The Waterworks* is controlled by a direct, reportorial realism that looks back to the urban, industrial-age fiction of Crane, Upton Sinclair and Dreiser. The New York that it holds in its bifocal lens is both a factual and prophetic place, the young power-struck metropolis of the Gilded Age and at the same time a "panoramic negative print, inverted in its lights and shadows" of the city for sale that had a centennial of sorts in the Ed Koch era. Doctorow's New York, with its horse-drawn traffic jams, its humming industrialized waterfronts, its real estate boom north of 42nd Street, is also a city of homeless veterans, ruined children, a cynical younger generation, a massively extortionate politics, a screaming press, a humming stock exchange, a plague of fires.

> It was a pungent air we breathed—we rose in the morning and threw open the shutters, inhaled our draft of the sulfurous stuff, and our blood was roused to churning ambition. Almost a million people called New York home, everyone securing his needs in a state of cheerful degeneracy. Nowhere else in the world was there such an acceleration of energies. A mansion would appear in a field. The next day it stood on a city street with a horse and carriage riding by.

Doctorow is a remarkably resourceful writer. He casts his imagination into an era of American history and makes it his own turf, an accurately rendered, resonating "repository of myth," as he says in one of his essays. Viewed together, his novels form a highly composed vision of American history, its phenomena turned into firm images pointed in our direction. Most of them set in and around New York, each book is a kind of relay network between its time and ours, keeping our awareness in touch with the American collective unconscious. For example, his narrator reports that as the sluice gates of the city reservoir, then at 42nd Street, are opened, "the water thunders in. . . as if it were not a reservoir at all, but a baptismal font for the gigantic absolution we require as a people."

Except for Gore Vidal, I don't know of another novelist who is doing this job, an enormously important one in an age when the sense of the past shortens and falls in value from year to year, so that the new becomes merely what is trendy at the moment.

Doctorow's sense of the past is more textured than Vidal's and less tendentious. He has a 20/20 social imagination that sees his subject steadily in its presentness to itself, and whole in its permanent implications. He also has an unusual versatility of voice that adapts from book to book, tuned to the representational demands and distinctive feeling of the material: the homely, earnest prose with an edge of twang in *Welcome to Hard Times*; the counterpoint of the personal and the objective, of rage and detachment in the political indictment of *The Book of Daniel*; the mix of the demotic and the elegant in the class novel of the Depression, *Loon Lake*; the sinuous lyricism of a prewar Bronx childhood in *World's Fair*; the clipped cadences of America marching into a new century of affluence and violence in *Ragtime*; and so forth. As a stylist, Doctorow has developed into the literary counterpart of the young Barry Bonds—he hits for both distance and percentage, runs the bases like a street thief and ranges all over his political position in left field.

As Melville would say, *The Waterworks* is "an inside narrative." It is inhabited by the mind, imagination and soul of its narrator, the former city editor of the *New York Telegram*, writing some decades after the sensational events he witnessed but was unable to report at the time. The Tweed Ring is at the height of its power, its tentacles everywhere. A middle-aged bachelor, McIlvaine lives for his work: "My newsman's cilia were up and waving. The soul of the city was always my subject, and it was a roiling soul. . . . As a people we practiced excess. Excess in everything—pleasure, gaudy display, endless toil, and death."

It takes an imaginative man to tend a roiling soul, and McIlvaine has been waiting since the passage of the dead Lincoln along a dumb-struck Broadway for the spawn of the assassination, "some soulless social resolve," to declare itself. He is thinking riots, another to add to the draft ones, as well as the gang riots, the police riots, the internecine Irish riots, the recent general riot he has witnessed. But what comes from Lincoln's grave, as he puts it, proves to be suitably spectral and macabre.

The young freelance book reviewer Martin Pemberton turns up one morning in his sardonic Union greatcoat and attitude (the War was fought by two confederacies; New York has no intellectuals, only newspapermen and clergy) to declare that his father, supposed to be some months dead, is still alive. At Columbia, Martin had discovered that his vaunted father, Augustus, had made much of his money in furnishing the Union troops with "shoddy" as well as in slave trading, so McIlvaine takes the young man's remark as another of his metaphors for their "city of thieves, raucous in its dissembling." Yet it soon turns out that Martin has seen his father not once but twice, both times riding in a white municipal stagecoach with a group of moribund old men in black coats and top hats. (Black and pale white are the primary colors of the literature the novel is bouncing off.) Shortly thereafter Martin disappears. His "cilia" waving like mad, the astute McIlvaine winds his way through the high and low life of the city in search of his guilt-ridden young rebel, who was last seen by his fiancée saying, "Either I am mad and should be committed, or the generations of Pembertons are doomed."

The shade of Poe shortly thereafter visits the novel in a more brilliant way. McIlvaine has turned to Edmund Donne; the one honest police captain in New York, who quietly leans upon Martin's friend Harry Wheelwright to tell what he knows, which is mainly of a nighttime trip to Woodlawn Cemetery to open Augustus Pemberton's grave. The darkness, the white mist, the prying open of the coffin, the effort to take heart, the shriveled figure within that is not Augustus but a small boy with a red bow and patent leather shoes. Well, Wheelwright's story does take one back to how scary Poe used to be. Watching Martin look down into the grave, Wheelwright "heard a moan . . . an awful basso sound . . . not in his voice at all but brought up from the lungs of a shaggy ancestry . . . a million years old." Doctorow's touch is quicker, more suggestive than the Master's, enabling the reader to frighten himself.

Poe's M. Maupin was the first of the gentlemen sleuths, his mind so detached and powerful that he needed only "ratiocination" and a bit of casual observation to solve the crime. Poe placed him in Paris because that's where gentlemen of genius amused themselves outwitting the bourgeoisie—in this case the diligent but short sighted police. Doctorow's lanky, methodical, austere Donne is the professional law-enforcement officer of the democratic future. Instead of clues recollected in leisure, he depends upon knowing the city as though it were a village, on informers, on composite portraits of suspects (he is the first in the field here), on his gift for making witnesses conform to his expectation of them, and on his nose for paper trails. All of these are effectively deployed in the course of the hunt, most notably Donne's use of documents. Combing through the account books of the Tweed Ring that had been given to McIlvaine by the dissatisfied City Sheriff, Donne notices an anomaly—a charter for a new orphanage for which no money has changed hands. Its physician is Wrede Sartorius, in whose Adirondacks sanitarium Pemberton père was reported to have died; its director is Eustace Simmons, Pemberton's erstwhile slave trader. The Home for Little Wanderers ties in with an informer's report of a child-buying ring—another anomaly, since the city provides so many street children for the taking. All of which suggests an explanation for the boy that Martin and his friend found in the coffin.

From this point on, the novel is increasingly dominated by the figure of Dr. Sartorius. Though McIlvaine and Donne are pursuing him, he moves into the story like an advancing general, preceded by awed rumors, reports and skirmishes. A preternaturally gifted surgeon who arrived from Germany in time for the Civil War, he turned his field hospital into a laboratory for revolutionary techniques that could treat head wounds and restore joints, amputate a leg in nine seconds, an arm in six—no small mercy at the time. But mercy was not his motive; knowledge was. He was a pioneer as well in post-operative treatment, his theory and practice anticipating the work of Pasteur and Robert Koch. All in all, McIlvaine concludes in his circumspect way, Colonel Sartorius's army career was "brilliant and masterful and brave. It's important to understand this. . . . We are speaking of the noble lineaments of the grotesque."

When Donne arranges a police raid on the Home for Little Wan-

derers that Sartorius founded, it turns out to be a model of enlightened institutional child care. On the other hand, some of the children are missing and most are prematurely aged. Also, in a basement
cell is the missing Martin Pemberton, near death and in a catatonic
state.

   Martin's relationship with Sartorius has been an intense one that
follows the arc of a long spell. What drew him into it was the genius
of the man, one of those who make "the world seem to exist for
the sake of their engagement with it." After being abducted, Martin
has spent months in the doctor's one-man research institute devoted
mainly to extending the doctor's encyclopedic knowledge and incidentally to prolonging the lives of his father and the five other
benefactors Martin had glimpsed in the horse car. Though he is
soon aware of the connection between the orphanage and the huge,
domed garden he beholds (in which the zombielike moguls waltz
with deaf and dumb attendant concubines amid an array of erotic
statuary while they await the injections and infusions that maintain
them), Martin nonetheless is soon disarmed by Sartorius's presence
and mission. His impressiveness consists not only in the learning and
prowess that have brought him and his clients to the frontier of life's
struggle with death but also in his awesome detachment from his
own ego. In his Zen-like objectivity and curiosity, he is the ultimate
embodiment of science for science's sake. He records his findings in
meticulous Latin but is beyond the need to publish them, though he
likes having Martin around to talk to and allows him free run of every
place but the treatment rooms. Eventually this attitude of amorality
proves to be too much for the disciple; though willing to sit for an
early version of an EEG, he balks at contributing bone marrow to
the enterprise, and goes into a tailspin of conscience that ends in the
cellar of the orphanage and his own zombielike state.

   The novel's main focus of interest and claim to permanence is the
character of Sartorius. His slim, resolute figure bestrides the modern
era, one foot in his time, one foot in ours, Faust without Mephistopheles, or rather, a Faust whose Mephistopheles has become the

power structure of the state, in this case the State of New York. For his enormously expensive program has been funded by the Tweed Ring, which built the orphanage and expanded the city's waterworks at Croton to create Sartorius's laboratory and human conservatory. This is the city's "soulless social resolve" that emerged from Lincoln's grave. When Tammany Hall is finally breached by a *New York Times* exposé of the magnitude of the take, and Tweed flees, he is last seen by a Cuban fisherman who reports that he was babbling about being the god of the city where "they have learned the secret of eternal life."

All of which may seem a bit too dated and mythy for the sophisticated, hard headed reader of today to note the prophecy. Instead of eternal life we have Elisabeth Kübler-Ross and Sherwin Nuland, hospices and living wills and the increasingly portentous figure of Dr. Kevorkian: what a psychologist I know calls "Death Lib." But with a small adjustment of the lens, we can look all the way up the road to the nexus of science, money and politics that hove into view just the other day in the report that linked the debilities and pain found among veterans of the Gulf War to mass inoculations of esoteric and insufficiently tested antidotes for germ and gas warfare.

Which is not to say Doctorow is writing a cautionary tale for our times. As McIlvaine stoutly puts it, "We did not conduct ourselves as if we were preparatory to your time. . . . New York after the war was more creative, more deadly, more of a genius society than it is now." Also, his interests are metaphysical as well as political. The far side of his consciousness has a visionary edge, so that the horror of Sartorius's show is not only in its objective disruption of the natural relationship of the generations, which is but the next step from the common practice of child labor at the time, but also in the rent it makes in moral consciousness itself, revealing the darkness and chaos of a universe that negates the understanding and faith of the human bond. In an extraordinary passage toward the end, McIlvaine, whose own soul has been permanently roiled by the events he has witnessed and suffered, dreams of Sartorius observing with terrifying intentness a child's boat struggling in a heavy sea that soon takes it under. The dream goes on to recapitulate and dramatize other images of the radical noetic experience that he has been given by "my darkbearded captain," who, like Ishmael's, has struck through the paste board mask of appearances. But though Melville went farther than any writer of his time in his negation of the regnant ideology of spiritual optimism, he was still standing ankle-deep in the sea of faith. "O Nature and O soul of man! how far beyond all utterance are your linked analogies. Not the smallest atom stirs or lives on matter, but has its cunning duplicate in mind." Sartorius has come out of the sea and taken the next step. When we last see him, standing as calmly as ever against a background of maniacs in the asylum to which he has been dispatched, he dismisses McIlvaine's and the novel's final, awed question about his moral views with a brief lecture on biology that turns the page to the modern mind.

> The truth is so deep inside, so interior, it operates—if that can be said to be the verb—in total blindness, in the total disregard of a recognizable world that would give us comfort, or in which we might find beauty or the hand of God—a point where life arcs in its first sentient glimmerings. . . senseless and unalive, and quite. . . mindless. . . as it is in black space.

As in cosmology, so in ethics. Just before McIlvaine's interview with Sartorius, there is one with Dr. Sumner Hamilton, whose board of examiners has voted to commit their colleague rather than have him tried and hanged, alternatives to which Sartorius himself is indifferent. He "answered only the questions he felt deserved an answer. We ended up trying to formulate questions he respected." One of the pointed ones is whether Sartorius's defense of his deployment of scientific method suggests that his experiments would someday benefit schoolchildren as they did soldiers; to which he replies with a smile, "You're not suggesting, Doctor, that I am to be distinguished from you or your colleagues. . . or indeed anyone else in the city. . . in observing the laws of selective adaptation. . . that ensure survival for the fittest of the species."

According to Hamilton, who has read Sartorius's notebooks, no child died directly from or was even impaired by his procedures; they suffered only a certain devitalization of the will to live. But such temporizing is beside the point of the pioneer's position. The closer the knowledge of how contingent, mutable, "membranous" the physical organism is, the more, as Sartorius testifies, it "cleanses the natural scientist of ennobling sentiments, pieties which teach us nothing." As for his patients and donors, they are hardly more pathetic than people in society, "all of them severely governed by tribal custom, and a structure of fantasies which they call civilization" but is only a blind allegiance to electromagnetic impulses "that constitute the basis of our actual living."

The medical tribunal ends up feeling more implicated than judgmental, forced to admit that their genius, with his blood transfusions and hormone infusions and marrow transplants, has been developing a medical technology that is perfectly consistent with his previous achievements. So, too, is the enlightened orphanage and the highly civilized conservatory. Of course he went too far, Dr. Hamilton concludes—beyond sanity and morality, to be sure, but, after all, how firm are their boundaries? His crime was a matter of excess.

Which brings us back to McIlvaine's early formulation of New York as a city of excess, and to the modern fusion of intellect and power. The narrative and thematic weave of *The Waterworks* is a powerful assertion of artistic strategy and tact. In dwelling on what it is saying, I have scanted what it is doing, notably growing a novel of deep, transitive ideas on the trellis of nineteenth-century genre fiction, complete with melodrama, domestic sentiment, a villain crushed by his own strongbox, and even an ending of two happy marriages. It is also, as I've suggested, Doctorow's own meditation on the great tradition of American fiction, and his claim to his place in it as both a recipient and a contributor.

(1994)

Tetz/Sinyavsky:
A Secret Agent of the Imagination

During the six years before his arrest in 1965, Andrei Sinyavsky must have led a strange double life. In the literary circles of Moscow, he was known as a leading research scholar at the Gorky Institute for World Literature. He also wrote regularly for *Novy Mir*, a journal that was cautiously attempting to liberalize Soviet letters. Of the essays and reviews that Sinyavsky produced in this period, and to this end, those that have been collected and translated in *For Freedom of Imagination* reveal him to be not only a keen literary critic but also a politic one, who coolly argued for individuality and complexity as being in the best interests of the literature produced by and for a Communist culture.

Meanwhile, he was writing, and publishing in the West, under the pseudonym "Abram Tertz." His electrifying book *On Socialist Realism*, as well as his stories and two novels, were so intensely individual and complex, so firmly ironical about Soviet positivism, and so intrigued by the "dark and magical night of Stalin's dictatorship" and its aftermath, that it is still difficult to relate the sober, circumspect, relatively orthodox scholar to the free, mordant, and occult spirit who wrote under the disreputable name of Abram Tertz, which is taken from a song about black markets, ribaldry, Jewishness, and other anti-Soviet activities that recur in his fiction.

This dangerous double life as a secret agent of the imagination became the ground of his fiction, furnishing both material and tone. His two novels, like his stories, are about divided men who are ruled by suppression and surveillance, both external and internal, as well as

53

by sudden bursts of psychic energy. They inhabit a narrow fringe of being that is swept by forces of authority, parapsychology, and paranoia. The first Abram Tertz novel, *The Trial Begins*, opens with its putative author being visited by two plainclothesmen, who scoop up the characters and punctuation marks from a page of his writing and then announce: "You are being trusted." A huge fist, visible through the wall of the writer's room, appears in the sky; other walls open so that he can observe the lives led behind them. One man is singled out, and a voice behind the fist tells the narrator that this bureaucrat is "my beloved and faithful servant. Follow him, dog his footsteps, defend him with your life. Exalt him!" The last the writer cannot bring himself to do. The man in question, Prosecutor Globov, is indefatigably fatuous and longs for a sensational public trial of a Jewish doctor to "clear the air." Globov and his fellow officials present a cheerful, friendly face to the world; their politics are "all inside them, hidden in that secret place where other mortals kept their vices." The writer attempts to suppress his account of Globov's circle, but his rough drafts are retrieved by a device installed in the sewer pipe, and he is convicted of slandering his "positive heroes" by not "portraying them in all the fullness of their many-sided working lives."

As elsewhere, life follows art in the Soviet Union. When Sinyavsky was revealed to be the infamous Abram Tertz and was put on trial with the poet Yuli Daniel, who had also published pseudonymously abroad, the proceedings were conducted under the spell, as it were, of the paranoid legalism, distortion, and defamation satirized in *The Trial Begins*. Sinyavsky has X-ray vision of the pretenses and crudities that stuff the shirts of the Soviet authorities, and though enigmatic and jocular, he cannot help but draw blood. His wit is as eccentric and deadly as Gogol's, and seems as much in possession of him as he is of it. Again like Gogol, he loves to play with the supernatural, to see double. "Art is jealous," Sinyavsky writes. "Moving away from inexpressive 'givens,' it—by force of its burning imagination—paints a second universe in which occurrences unfold at a heightened tempo and in a bared form."

So it is in his brilliant second novel, *The Makepeace Experiment*, in which a bicycle mechanic turns mesmerist and leads his back-woods community through a reenactment of the history of Bolshe-vism, complete with a population that comes to believe anything he tells them and that he isolates from the rest of the world by drawing a psychic curtain around the community. The tale is told by an old librarian, who is under the spell of a spirit from the nineteenth cen-tury, one Proferansov, a friend of the great eighteenth-century French chemist Lavoisier and of Tolstoy. The novel becomes a beautifully fused mixture of old and new Russian illusions and phantoms, while, prey to the mischances and perversities of power, life draws slowly on to the only freedom that is safe and complete.

The theme of possession by a demonic force that drives men to express themselves, to act out their fantasies (with the result that they usually end up in Siberia or dead), runs through Sinyavsky's *Fantastic Stories*. A young workman goes to the circus and, inspired by the ac-robats and a sleight-of-hand artist, "the Manipulator," decides to en-liven his dull life by performing similar feats. After picking a pocket, he is off on a series of manic adventures: The world cooperates and even for a time seems to become a circus in which he is the star per-former. But eventually Konstantin commits a burglary and shoots "the Manipulator," for which he is sentenced to Siberia. One fine morning, though, as he marches with the work gang, his inspiration returns, and Konstantin goes leaping and hurtling toward freedom until a guard's bullet sends him into a climactic and terminal somer-sault.

In one form or another, the "extraneous and magnanimous super-natural power" that brings Konstantin to the fulfillment of his destiny visits each of Sinyavsky's heroes. "The Icicle" concerns a man who briefly acquires the gift of clairvoyance, and, with it, visions of the transmigration of his soul and of other souls. Sinyavsky seizes upon this motif with a particular intensity: the previous incarnations that the character helplessly witnesses provide an insight into the nature of the self.

Men are so made that they never find their appearance quite convincing. When we look in a mirror, we never cease to be amazed.
"Is that ghostly reflection really mine?" we ask. "It can't be."...I
imagine that there is someone inside us who violently objects at
every attempt to persuade him that the person he sees in front of
him is none other than himself...and so we begin to bluster, and
make faces as though to express our skepticism about the appari-
tion defiantly stuck there in front of us.

Shortly thereafter, the narrator, having watched several of his past fu-
nerals, is horrified by a vision of "himself" being hanged in a later in-
carnation; it is as if the face of his future torment were staring at him
across the desert of time. In the story "You and I"—a chilling study
in the dynamics of schizophrenia—there is a similar queasy fluidity
and separation of the ego in a parapsychological context, this time
carried to pathological lengths by a character who spies on himself.

All of which suggests not only the habitual direction of Sinyavsky's
imagination but also the extreme tensions under which he labored
in his double life as a writer. Such tensions proved to be very fruitful, since they placed him in immediate touch with the inner, secret
life of a society ruled by a literally mesmerizing terror and faith.
Sinyavsky's ventures into the occult are seldom more than an irony
away from a critique of the monstrous idealism of Stalinist thought
control. At the same time, Sinyavsky rightly speaks of himself as an
"idealist," and his inspiration, like his peril, lies in his responsiveness
to demonic and psychic forces, as well as political ones. In his story
"The Graphomaniacs," which Sinyavsky at his trial suggested might
contain "certain autobiographical features," one of the legion of Soviet scribblers announces that the only purpose and hope of writing
is "self-suppression":

That's why we labor in the sweat of our brow and cover wagon
loads of paper with writing in the hope of stepping aside, overcom-
ing ourselves, and granting access to thoughts from the air. They
arise spontaneously, independently of ourselves...You composed

one thing yourself, so that it's worthless, while another thing is not yours and you don't dare, don't have the right to do anything with it….And you retreat…in terror at your own nonparticipation at what has taken place.

The sense of being ruled "from the air" is restated near the end of "The Graphomaniacs," when the main character, returning to his family from a writing spree, suddenly feels that his motions are being controlled by "someone's fingers as a pencil is guided over the paper." Like the dark street, the sleeping houses, his whole long unsuccessful life suddenly seems to be part of a relentless literary composition. He raises his fist toward the sky and shouts, "Hey you there—the grapho-maniac. Stop work!...You're unreadable."

For a writer to maintain himself in this incredibly paradoxical, threatened, and divided mode of existence without going dumb or mad, he must have sources of unity deep in his nature. In Sinyavsky's most recent writing published in the West, "Thought Unaware," he reveals himself to be a secret Christian. The nakedly personal medi-tations assembled under this title seem, at first glance, a far cry from anything else he has published either as Tertz or as Sinyavsky—so di-rect and austere are they, so single-mindedly committed to the Chris-tian account of the world and of the moral world within. Sinyavsky's reflections on God, faith, death, sin, prayer, nature, create some of his most luminous and moving writing. And the more one ponders these reflections, the more intimately they seem connected to the affirma-tive moments in his fiction, as well as being the sustaining ground of his irony and satire. Just as "the graphomaniac" is a negative, comic, covert image of the God to Whom Sinyavsky ardently subjects him-self and all his values, so the imagery of his other fiction—as well as the framework of his enigmatic essay *On Socialist Realism*—emerges as a sardonic transmutation of the Christian worldview, correspond-ing to the corruptions and perversions by which its mysticism still manifests itself in politics, art, the occult, sex, etc. Thus "Thought Unaware" not only provides the unifying matrix of Sinyavsky's art but indicates the abiding sanctuary of "selflessness," which, I suspect, has enabled this writer to endure his situation.

It is worth noting that the word "Christian" does not appear in any of the writing collected in *For Freedom of Imagination*, not even in the long essay on Pasternak's poetry. Here, as elsewhere in the collection, Sinyavsky's point of view is entirely secular and "progressive," and he justifies Pasternak, another secret Christian, as a Soviet poet who fulfilled his primary Marxist obligation to reflect, in a positive way, the history of his age. As an orthodox critic and liberal, in his public guise, Sinyavsky had to be deliberately obtuse in dealing with Pasternak, the Russian writer with whom he is probably in greatest sympathy, if he hoped to rehabilitate the latter's reputation and to champion his methods and values as the basis for the renewal of Soviet poetry. Such, in general, are the narrow ideological boundaries within which Sinyavsky could safely and productively operate as a Soviet critic.

Even so, he manages to impart a great deal of literary education, functioning as both a liberal spokesman and a teacher of the tribe, a role traditional for Russian writers, whom even the Bolsheviks honored as "the technicians of souls" before they began to destroy them. Standing where he does, thirty years after the modernist tradition was almost totally wrecked and abandoned, Sinyavsky is like a sophisticated architect who has inherited a spacious but decayed mansion, full of dry rot and violations of the building code. Much of his criticism is a kind of basic renovation, laying new foundations, clearing out the debris, replacing warped doors and windows, bringing in power. To impose the rudimentary principles of freshness, concreteness, and individuality, he constantly calls on the assistance of Mayakovsky, who appears to have become the Soviet Homer, and uses his precepts and verse to reproach the official poets for their vague, abstract, repetitious, hackneyed, inaccurate, derivative, depersonalized, feeble, and supremely smug verse. What they most notably lack is what Mayakovsky called "tendency," which Sinyavsky defines as "a living, formative, creative principle in verse, a movement which breaks down dogmas and clichés and does not permit compromises and wishes to live in a new way, an individual way."

Polite but devastating, he addresses the literary hacks: asking, for example, Yevtushenko to live up to his claim that he has abandoned his superficiality, Sinyavsky writes with an immediate feeling for the imaginative power of poets like Akhmatova and Frost. His strongest essay deals with the poet and diarist Olga Berggolts, whose ability to seize her experience, to identify—and make the reader identify—her individualist responses with the inner life of her country and people, represents for Sinyavsky the right direction for a truly Soviet art: "the unity of the personal and the general which forms our way of life."

The closest Sinyavsky comes to pointing his criticism toward the nature of his own creative work is in an essay on science fiction. Wishing to free this genre from the encroachments of socialist realism that have made it ludicrous—its timid fantasies often lagging a decade behind the realities of Soviet science—Sinyavsky offers an eloquent redefinition of science fiction as a form for rational hypotheses that envision an "ever more difficult, beautiful, and therefore fantastic goal." Just as the spiritual images of Olga Berggolts are able to reveal the "true existence" that lies behind and illuminates the dull inexpressiveness of everyday life, so Sinyavsky argues for a fiction that uses the imagination of the future to reveal what he terms in *On Socialist Realism* "the grand and implausible sense of our era."

It is just here—in the realm of the visionary—that Sinyavsky and Tertz touch and join. Here, and in an epigram of Gorky's that, as both Tertz and Sinyavsky, he frequently quotes—and that, for the time being, as he serves his seven-year sentence in a forced-labor camp, can stand as the motto of this great writer and man—"the madness of the brave is the wisdom of life."

(1971)

George Konrád's Burden

Some years ago, when I was traveling in the Soviet Union, I was taken to the studio of a Georgian artist. Much of his work had a strong erotic or religious feeling, sometimes both together. We became friendly and I asked him whether all of these sensuous curves and devout figures and symbols might not get him in trouble. He replied that he was a Georgian artist, that he painted the culture of his people: his female forms expressed their regard for the generative principle, his saints were the bearers of their history of oppression and resistance. At one point he showed me a painting of a kneeling male figure shackled to a post by a collar and chain: it was titled "Self-Portrait." What about that? I asked. Couldn't it be taken as a protest against the restrictions of the artist in Soviet society? "People can think what they want," he snapped. "The chain and collar is my art. I cannot escape from it, but it is what holds me to my place in the world. It is an obsession but it also tells me who I am, why I live. I painted it just after I recovered from a dangerous illness." When I returned to Moscow I related the incident to a writer who knew the artist. "I couldn't tell whether he was serious or ingenuous or evasive or cynical." "All of them," the writer replied. "Like most of us."

I sometimes think of that story when I read the work of the East European dissident writers: Sinyavsky, Aksyonov, Konrád, Kís, Kundera, Hrabal, et al. There is an apparent common touch about them—a direct relation to the creaturely life of their people. On the other hand, they are subtle, devious, unexpectedly brutal, macabre—a kind of theatrical trafficking in the forbidden feelings as well as subjects, an easy recourse to the inhuman. There is also the obsessiveness that

60

haunts their pages, a stylistic equivalent of the fatedness that presses down on their characters, both confining them and weighting them, giving them a dimension beyond themselves, the sense of having a destiny, however wretched or absurd it may be.

All of which, along with the political risks, goes into the perception of an inner necessity that we admire in these writers and for lack of which so much Western writing seems to be about the bearable lightness of being. Each of George Konrád's three novels is essentially the monologue of a Hungarian intellectual who can't stop talking because he feels so constrained by his experience, so burdened by the oppressivenesss of life behind the Iron Curtain, and so needled by his conscience that he must keep trying to deliver himself or at least exhaust himself into silence. One of his speakers is a case-hardened social worker; the second is a community planner in a treacherous bureaucracy; the speaker in *The Loser*, Konrád's new novel, is a scarred and callous dissenter. Each of them is shackled to a situation that is unyielding and highly equivocal but from which he draws his saturnine vigor and lucidity, his "solitary invective," as one of them puts it. Though they are distinct individuals with their own voices, they are brothers under the skin, a family of deep-sea divers, existentially speaking, weighted by their fateful positions, encased in inner concerns that enable them to resist the external pressures of the state that would otherwise disable them. Because they continue to choose the role that entraps them, the tone of their voices runs the full register of irony—baleful, mordant, sardonic, sarcastic, chagrined, wry, the tone of a fallen humanism.

Konrád's first novel, *The Case Worker*, is the most artistic—a short work of formidable black pathos. It is a tour through the lower depths of Budapest, conducted by a welfare worker who is resigned to "the faulty nature of things," who merely "steers the suffering this way and that," but who soon begins to succumb to the guilt of his dreams, the curiosity of his reveries: Gorky meets Kafka. One of his cases is a five-year-old idiot whose father has never recovered from being unjustly denounced and imprisoned as a Nazi collaborator.

Old Bandula begs in the cafés, cannot hold a job even as an orderly in a morgue, but insists on keeping the boy, against the protests of his neighbors. Lying on the bare springs of his bed, while the naked child, tied into his crib, plays with scraps of food and his wastes, the former minor official tells the caseworker, T.:

> Remember all those principles, rules, and punishments? If I may say so, you're still a slave to all that. You rarely think of yourself—only, let's say, when you have a toothache. None of that applies to me. I'm no more human than my son. Let's have a cigarette. I'm a freak. Of course, that, too, is a human word.

T. is fascinated by this brink of being, this last-ditch sense of responsibility the broken man and his permanently dazed wife insist on defending against the authorities. Then one day they abruptly abandon it, pass into the "terrible inviolable freedom" of suicide, and T. finds himself sitting on Bandula's bedsprings and watching the child, as hairy, healthy, and reeking as a bear cub, gnawing on his vanished mother's brassiere. Another life, not much more lurid and phantom-like than the one T. is leading, begins to stalk his mind: he can give up his job and family and settle in here, keeping the child from the horrors of the children's asylum, taking in piecework for a living.

The experience of replacing Bandula is no less compelling for being a reverie—indeed, so intense and graphic is it that many readers may mistake it for the fact. Moreover, by the end of his long day of imagining his new life T. finds that the wound of his own despair has somehow closed. He places the child for the time being and goes back to his other cases. "Let all those come who want to; one of us will talk, the other will listen; at least we shall be together."

Like Dostoevsky, Konrád is both a psychological terrorist and a compassionate witness; and in exercising these talents with the Bandulas and the other inhabitants of their woeful slum, along with the teenage suicides, battered wives, crippled workers, and other examples of nature's and society's derelictions that T. broods about, Konrád is carrying on the great theme of nineteenth-century Russian fiction—

the forging of the human bond between the privileged consciousness of the writer and the mute despair of his people.

He has also carried it forward to stand over against the actual mentality of state socialism. Though *The Case Worker* does not deal with politics as such, Konrád is intent on pouring back into Hungarian consciousness the personal, the disruptive, the irremediable elements in life that Communist culture tries to leach out by its relentlessly collectivist, nationalistic, and positivist ethos. In a historical analysis, *The Intellectuals on the Road to Class Power*, that Konrád wrote with Ivan Szelényi, the authors describe the "marginal" writers who have taken the risk of distancing themselves from the official state culture because "in speaking of the human condition they could not derive from socialism optimistic solutions for the problems of illness, loss, death or even disappointment in love." *The Case Worker* is this wry comment armed and barbed and delivered with shattering force.

The City Builder lacks this clarity, concentration, and fierce intentionality. In the main, Konrád is an intellectual who writes novels rather than the other way around. The point of view of each of his novels is a closely held first-person one, and given Konrád's penchant for commentary and self-scrutiny, we are almost always listening to the teller rather than to the tale: Consciousness is all. This is one reason why the reverie in *The Case Worker* is such an appropriate and effective device. But in *The City Builder* there is little to alter and complicate the speaker's awareness, to take him where he hasn't been. Konrád runs an intermittent narrative thread through the speaker's successive states of mind, opaque with metaphor and paradox, within which he struggles to explain and justify, lament and revile his situation as a guilty ex-husband and father and as a technocrat in a regime that has betrayed him and his ideals. The book aims to evoke and personalize the class consciousness of the intellectuals who participated in and still serve the revolution, but it does so in such a generalizing, introspective, and cryptic way that one suspects Konrád may have written it in spite of himself, haunted by the sense of the Hungarian thought police looking over his shoulder.

What saves *The City Builder* from the kind of rhetoric with which

French radicals preen and torment themselves ("Assuming reality—even if only in name—is humiliating. Opening the window of my cramped and constant world to let in time, I try to figure out who is scratching and whining in this dark room . . ." and so on), what gives the book Konrád's stamp, is the intense nagging that is going on behind the screen of his language between the speaker's sardonic resignation and his restless conscience: a couple that can't get along and can't stay away from each other; a perverse dialectic that generates the remarkable energy of his sensibility even when it falls into a manner. In the clear stretches of the speaking, that is, when the force of events—the war, the Holocaust, the 1948 revolution—provide expressive scenes to go with the sound track, the planner's monologue suggests the genuine testament it might have been.

The Loser is Konrád's effort to write that testament. It is nothing if not specific and outspoken: the direct experience and evolving attitudes of a veteran Hungarian radical. Bearing the same identifying initial, T., as the speaker in *The Case Worker*, he too has been through it and through it. Even more so: his horrors being political ones—battlefields, torture chambers, prison cells, and Central Committee meetings. Committed to the concrete, which in this case weighs a ton, Konrád makes himself shoulder the burden of T.'s involvement in Hungarian history: from his entry early in World War II as a student antifascist to his exit in the mid-1970s as a prominent dissident who ends up in a mental hospital, where he finally can free himself of politics and can stop lying.

The grandson of a prominent Jewish merchant, scholar, and seer, and the son of an emancipated, even somewhat decadent land developer, T. loves the former but imitates the latter, his early life being highlighted by his precocious seductions. Even as an antifascist courier he remains something of a *flâneur*, though less so than his younger brother Dani, who becomes his accomplice and betrayer, a man whom the politics of terror will deprave rather than merely corrupt. T.'s heady apprenticeship abruptly ends when he is caught, badly beaten, and forced to watch his girlfriend hang by her arms while he continues to withhold information. During the war he serves in a brutalized forced-labor battalion, lives with a partisan peasant woman, fights with a group disguised as Hungarian soldiers, is captured by the Russians, contracts spotted fever, is packed into a prison train with five thousand other victims, most of whom die en route. The Red Army indoctrinates him and sends him back to Hungary as a propagandist; with his field radio and megaphone he creates droves of defectors, who are then shipped off to Siberia. By the time the war ends, he has become a member of the antifascist elite—most of them erstwhile poets, scholars, and editors who will soon come into power and, after a few euphoric and benighted years, will, one by one, fall haplessly from it into secret prisons and graves.

Some of T.'s descriptions of the carnage, pillage, rape, and genocide of the Balkan front have a laconic Goyaesque expressiveness which gives them a place in the annals of the viciousness and pathos of war. Also he has a clear-eyed view of the way men act—in both senses of the word. He presents the early Communist regime as a provincial version of the Stalinist theater of cruelty—the sadistic and treacherous officials wiping out the sensitive and principled ones, though with a good deal of counter behavior on both sides. His later experience with the 1956 uprising and in the subsequently emerging twilight world of the dissident community—in both of which he plays a reluctantly prominent role and pays the price—is treated as a theater of the absurd, in which every one tried to keep a brave or at least a straight face, beginning with himself:

> The truth is, you knew when to make compromises that, though necessary for survival, did not destroy your legend. You knew when to step aside and smile enigmatically, and when to scatter your private aphorisms through the urban folklore.

Yet the overall effect of T.'s adventures in the inhuman and his reflections on "the historical-philosophical farce" he has acted in tend to work against each other, to be dulling, finally, rather than illuminating and chilling. Again, it's mostly a matter of the primacy of the speaker's voice and consciousness. The Konrádian mingling of cynicism and scruple soon takes on its own theatrical air, a striking of poses. The guerrilla and freedom fighter with his machine gun, the propagandist armed with his Bolshevik brutality, the self-serving dissident, live on too easy terms with the man who has been there and suffered, who has seen too much of pain and death, brutality and treachery. Many of T.'s adventures strike a superficial note, as though they had happened to someone else, and on the deepest matters he tends to be evasive: As his girlfriend hangs before his eyes and says to him, "It's real bad," he tells us:

> At that moment something in me died. There was now a murderer in place of my former self, who was willing to sacrifice his love and would do the same to his own son, just so that he shouldn't have to say anything....I knew I was an accomplice related to those who had tied me up. All that was working in me was my insanely obstinate resolve to stay the way I was....Sacrifice exists for itself, as does hatred, and everything exists for death....I lifted my head and looked at Sophie's tortured lips, which were beyond forming words. I no longer wanted to save her spent body.

So much for Sophie, who will soon be cut down so she can die, as we learn in an afterthought, at Auschwitz. She will not trouble T.'s conscience again, which is not surprising since she is hardly present in his thoughts here. T. is not becoming an accomplice of torture before our eyes. He is becoming a facile existentialist, formulating a studied response to a moral crisis he has stripped of its anguish.

So it will go through most of his moments of crisis. Whether he bravely refuses to betray his colleague and friend during the purges, or refuses to falsify his past under torture, or agrees to deliver the opposition government's foolhardy order to the Soviet minister in 1956, thereby ensuring himself another prison sentence at the very least— T.'s consciousness of what he is doing and why has much the same lack of affect that characterizes his acts of compliance with brutality. Here he is speaking of his state of mind as a Communist official:

> Oppression is simply an educational tool; let the people learn that they can wish only for what we wish for. First they'll be beaten into submission; then, through us, they will regain their self-respect.... What else could I become but a Communist? The war was over, but the fighting went on between old and new, good and evil. The bourgeois hoards, the Communist fights. He considers more and more of the hoarders his enemies; he provokes them, hurts them, and this makes him proud of himself. This part is fairly easy; what's more difficult is to fall in love with the party.

No doubt such thoughts were thought. The point is that T. merely takes them in the stride of his sardonic equanimity. "Today I cannot argue with the man I was then: I look at him as though he were my son, though I am not moved by him." To be sure. But we are also to believe that the T. who begins speaking in this book from a mental hospital in a whirl of frightened and guilty images is a man worthy of our sympathy; just as he is at the end, when, in his final encounter with the inhuman, he assists his demonic brother in hanging himself but refuses to join him in death. From first to last, though, the immense destructiveness that T. has witnessed and immersed himself in has done little more than reinforce his essential aloofness—the ground tone of his voice, the bottom line of his experience.

Such aloofness may well overtake a Hungarian intellectual who chose the road, even only part of the way, to class power. As T. tells himself at one point: "Here's your chance to spill the beans about your class, to blurt out its unconscious secrets, write its collective memoirs." But what this comes down to are such "beans" as:

> It was quite a lark; a historical sleight-of-hand: with your pals you laid the foundation of intellectual class power, which was pretty nasty at first but which will in time become more pleasant and it will never be supplanted by another kind of power.

Whatever such aloofness may gain for the book as a document it loses as art. Aloofness is never a basis for art, because the way to the depths is closed to it; it lacks the will to struggle, being secretly preoccupied with the wounds of the ego. Hence T.'s conflict between awareness and conscience is often weak and equivocal and, unlike his counterpart's in *The Case Worker*, unable to be resolved: one reason why Konrád has to bring in the tangential issue of the brother's murder of his girlfriend and his suicide to end *The Loser*. Except that the ending does remind us of what T. actually is: He is less a loser, since he has never had much, morally speaking, to lose; he is mostly an accomplice, which would have made a better title for the novel.

And yet there are many moments when he is more, when he does not make light of the crushing weight of his experience, when the writing sheds its fitful, ambivalent ironies and becomes closely knit by strong feeling. These moments often have to do with T.'s pious grandfather and with his moral legacy, which now and then enters T.'s mind to strengthen or enlighten him. "Like drunkards we live in a fog of self-love," he remembers his grandfather saying, "and, confusing good and evil, we grope our way in the darkness and laugh when our neighbor falls"—words that prophesy the political nightmares to come. At one point, T. comes upon a pile of fresh corpses in a forest, victims of a Nazi death squad:

> The naked bodies are sexless; I can see they shielded the backs of their heads like infants as they were toppled over by a round of machine-gun fire….A bearded man's head rests on a young girl's whitened thighs; the cold groins are as indistinct as a frozen indentation in a dirt road. Now you know how perishable is he who is so very like the earth, how little he differs from the clay he was fashioned from—he who was created by God in His image.

And T. goes on to speak of the good and evil in this creature, of the one who "slipped a piece of bread to those hiding in the henhouse," and of the one who "pulled an old man in a hat from a woodshed." Another voice seems to be speaking to us at such moments of deep creaturely feeling rather than the garrulous T., alternating between his world- and self-weariness and a certain glibness. It is a voice buried deep in his nature, a source of energy and direction for the struggle his author might have made to provide a more engaged and deeper account than this one of the nightmare of history that continues to obsess him. There is enough material in *The Loser* for five novels. I hope that the next time, Konrád chooses, as he did in *The Case Worker*, to redeploy the extraordinary strength of his consciousness and the passion of his concern to bear the full weight of one of them.

To be sure, there is a certain glibness or patness of my own in making this recommendation, an American who was spared the wars in his time and otherwise has so light a burden of history to bear and to unbare, and who has been free to speak in any voice he chose. What makes the literature from the other Europe so fascinating to us is partly the otherness of its literary conditions. The peril and predicaments that give weight and significance to the Georgian artist or the Hungarian novelist are, after all, what have weighed on and shaped his ways of expressing himself. One's literary imagination and moral imagination don't always track.

(1983, 2007)

Saul Bellow:
The Lines of Resistance

One afternoon a few years ago I was returning to New York from a lecture I had given. The subject was recent Jewish American writing: Bellow, Malamud, Roth: aspiration, suffering, spiritual self-discovery, and so forth. My audience had risen to the theme, as suburban Jewish ladies will, and, rocked along by the Long Island Railroad, I was still bemused and touched by the mood of idealism I had induced. The soft facts of life are not to be discounted, I thought; otherwise why has man developed sentiments? It's only a matter of refining them, of educating and thereby strengthening the impulses to be good and true. The other solitary passengers in the car, I imagined, carried the same "counsels of the heart" that I had been talking about and that were stirring in my own. Then, moved to place more of the world within my transforming awareness, I looked out the train window.

There were the outskirts of Queens. It was about four on a winter afternoon, the sky about thirty feet up, the flats looking like a testing ground for biological warfare, the horizon smoking away. Then the train passed a small town: impacted files of bungalows and long slabs of brick two-families, a huddle of gas stations around an intersection, an all-purpose shopping center, then the wasteland again. What had been swamp twenty-five years ago was now a community, but every-thing conveyed a sense of the grimness of things, as though only the tenacity of the inhabitants kept such places from sinking back into the landfill of ashes and garbage. All of it seemed terribly remote to my vision and obdurate in its own: its aspirations were expressed by the TV antennas, its values were "property" and "Blue Book." Queens was the social contract writ large, and, placed against it, any better scheme of life seemed evanescent. Go tell it to the owners of those brick two-families, shouldered together like a team making a goal-line stand, protecting those few feet of lawn in the back. "The counsels of the heart"? My own heart sank. And who was I to say they were wrong—the millions of them? So they would never read Saul Bellow.

All of which came back to me as I was reading *Mosby's Memoirs*, a new collection of Bellow's stories. Hot for uplift, I had apparently missed the basis. Not that Bellow isn't a humanist but that he is also a realist: his fiction begins about the point where my little shock of recognition left off: the resistance, density, intractability of our lives. This is why his imagination is so strong. It has to be: it grapples and lifts the full weight of a man's existence. This, in turn, is why his characters are so real: Joseph, Leventhal, Wilhelm, Henderson, Herzog, whose principle might be, "I am burdened, therefore I am." In "A Father-to-Be" a young research chemist rides the subway to dine with his Jewish princess of a girlfriend and finds himself studying with disgust a smug middle-aged man in a stylish overcoat and blue suede shoes: the very prototype, Rogin realizes with horror, of what their prospective son would be like in forty years:

> What a vision of existence it gave him, Man's personal aims were nothing, illusion. The life force occupied each of us in turn in its progress toward its own fulfillment, trampling on our individual humanity, using us for its own ends like mere dinosaurs or bees, exploiting love heartlessly, making us engage in the social process, labor, struggle for money, and submit to the law of pressure, the universal law of layers, superimposition.

The beginning is Schopenhauer, the ending is pure Bellow. The law of pressure, layers, superimposition: that is how he builds up figure and ground, so that Rogin's ride on the IRT on a Sunday night becomes as effortful and portentous as a bad dream.

As most of these stories indicate, Bellow has an extraordinary ability to enter directly into the mixed conditions of a particular life or experience and conduct the reader toward a general truth embedded in it. Three of the six stories—and they are the three that matter most; they may well be masterpieces—mine the ore of common life: a mismatched old woman in the Utah desert trying to hold onto her house and independence; a white intellectual trying to deliver relief checks in the Black Belt; a physicist meditating on the rise and strife of his immigrant Jewish family. Against the dullness, stupidity, hopelessness of Hattie's struggle in the Utah desert, against the terrific vacuousness and gloom of the Chicago ghetto during the Depression, against the stridency and acquisitiveness of the Braun family—a steady and searching pressure of consciousness is exerted, encompassing and at the same time animating, preserving phenomena both in their literalness and multivalence. In "Looking for Mr. Green," George Grebe slowly makes his way through a tenement in the Black Belt:

> He began to climb to the third floor. Pieces of plaster ground under his feet; strips of brass tape from which the carpeting had been torn away marked old boundaries at the sides. In the passage, the cold reached him worse than in the street; it touched him to the quick. The hall toilets ran like springs . . . . Then he struck a match in the gloom and searched for names and numbers among the writings and scribbles on the walls. He saw WHOODY-DOO-DY GO TO JESUS, and zigzags, caricatures, sexual scrawls, and curses. So the scaled rooms of pyramids were also decorated, and the caves of human dawn. The information on the card was, TUL-LIVER GREEN-APT. 3D. There were no names, however, and no numbers.

Along with the strength of observation, an imaginative idea is working through this material like yeast in dough, and eventually it will make the story rise, as the passage itself does, to indicate something of the inner truth of our human relationships and to restate it in action. The decay of the tenement, the regression to the primitive cave-like conditions of shelter, the atavistic markings, the gloom, the anonymity stand at one extreme; the ex-classicist Grebe and his address-cards and Relief checks at the other. The social nexus between them has collapsed, revealing in a particularly naked form what Grebe's erudite boss refers to as "the fallen world of appearances." This is the terrain that Grebe must cross, full of fantasy and tension, for the "faltering of organization [has] set free a huge energy, an escaped, unattached, unregulated power from the giant raw place." At the beginning of the story, Grebe feels he might as well be looking for Mr. Green in the jungle, but—as he comes to realize, and this makes him press on in his search—the adversity of appearances is an aspect of the general fate in a city like Chicago, where neighborhoods such as this one rise and fall into ruin every fifty years. Amid so much flux, what then abides?

> Objects once so new, so concrete, that it could [not] have occurred to anyone they stood for other things, had crumbled. Therefore, reflected Grebe, the secret of them was out. It was that they stood for themselves by agreement, and were natural and not unnatural by agreement, and when the things themselves collapsed the agreement became visible.

As one of his other clients helps him see, this "agreement" is a function of human trust—and need: "the need that keeps so many vast thousands in position." The reality system is no different, finally, from the money system. When Grebe finally finds Mr. Green's address, he is met by a naked, drunken, obscene, angry woman who refuses to identify herself. But having learned what he has learned, Grebe gives her the check: she stands for Mr. Green and Grebe has to trust too.

This metaphysics of the human bond, as Grebe scornfully reminds himself, is pretty remote to the immediate conditions in this blighted jungle. In the face of such misery, he can only mark the honest direction of his imagination—the question of whether "there is something that is dismal and permanently ugly" in the human covenant—and press on to deliver his very real check. As Norman Podhoretz points out in a concise and trenchant reading of the novels up to *Herzog* (in *Doings and Undoings*), Bellow's social and political bias has been pretty much the neo-conservative one, with which Podhoretz associates his pessimism, his refusal to arraign the institutions that produce his characters' malaise, his damming up and deflection of rage, and his tendency to end his dark novels on an upbeat note. The detection of this bias is accurate but to ask Bellow to drop it and to adopt a more radical one is to ask him to turn his art, and the ideas and emotions that support it, upside down. What Bellow knows before he knows anything else—knows in his bones—is the settled weight and ambiguity of existence, both inner and outer. It is precisely from this feeling for the accumulation of circumstance, contingency, error, conflict, paradox, anomaly, *as an individual experiences it*, that he derives his amazing descriptive power— a power, incidentally, that makes *Seize the Day* the best presentation of Manhattan middle-class angst that I know of. To open his art to meliorative politics would be to rob it of its specific gravity and to place Bellow outside his own sense of the perdurable and the changing from which he draws his clues to the "axial lines" of a life and its place in the scheme of things. He is at heart an essentialist: man and his nature are absolutes and what is most true is what most preserves a man in his emotions and duration and kind. To the "law of layers, superimposition," Bellow has no solution: but the mastering emotion he prescribes and through which he conducts his protagonists is not love, as Podhoretz says, but remorse: the active kind, that lifts some of the burden of mismanagement off the spirit and allows it to breathe.

Take Hattie Simmons Wagoner, a "city woman," still proud of her Philadelphia connections, her china, linen, engraved stationery, who has been eking out an existence for twenty years at Sego Desert Lake, with the local Indians and Mexicans, the dudes from the nearby ranch, the six white residents. Mistress of a long-departed cowboy, companion and servant to another old divorcee, whose house she has inherited, Hattie is a "character": a "cheerful, plugging, absent," and hard-drinking old woman of seventy-two, who keeps her canned goods on her library shelves and more than anything else wants "to be thought of as a rough, experienced woman of the West." One day, driving drunk and fast as usual, she stalls her car on a railroad crossing, and while it is being towed off, her arm is broken. She tries to go on against the odds, which include a record of dependency, fantasy, procrastination, dispersion, but the pain and impairment from her injury have brought on senility and the harsh, testing way of life in the desert has become too much for her. Yet she is unable to leave her house and its belated satisfaction, unable to live with her stuffy brother, unable to accept old age and death. Like her car, she is stalled at the crossing. Her plight whips her through the gamut of emotions—rage, resentment, regret, grief—and forces her toward the belated recognition of and remorse for the borrowed, jerrybuilt structure of her life: "I was never one single thing anyway,. . . Never my own. I was only loaned to myself." Wanting now to make a final act of self-possession, she sits down to make her will and give away her house. But soon drunk again, her mind staggering from one unsatisfactory beneficiary to the next, she leaves her house to herself.

Finally, there is "The Old System," Bellow's most recent story and one the high points in his career. Concerning an immigrant Jewish family, it is written with a force that enables its forty-odd pages to brush aside virtually all the banality that has accumulated over this subject. One Saturday, the traditional day of reentry into Judaism, Dr. Braun, a ranking geneticist, finds himself meditating on his two cousins from upstate New York, Isaac and Tina Braun, the one "born to be a man in the direct Old Testament sense," who trusted the old system of the patriarchs and became a millionaire; the other, a harsh, obese, rapacious woman who trusted nothing, hated her brother's success, and eventually forced him to bring $20,000 when she was dying of cancer in order to be reconciled with her. Now they are both dead. What did all that energy and effort and emotional tumult signify?

Dr. Braun carefully recalls and mulls over these family circumstance and events, looking for the patterns of causation, the general human implications "within the peculiar system of light, movement, contact, and perishing in which he tried to find stability." Heredity and nurture, cultural transmission, ego psychology, recent social history, even astronomy offer their perspectives, framing his idea that these two hostages he has given to death represented "Necessary existence." But the main revelation about their respective lives is their emotional structures: deep, solid, old-fashioned in Isaac; volatile, manipulative, modern in Tina.

"Oh, these Jews—these Jews! Their feelings, their hearts. He often wanted nothing more than to stop all this." But whether direct or devious, natural or undergoing the modern perversions, quietly spinning a destiny or making a circus out of dying, emotions are what Dr. Braun, having grieved, in his fashion, for his cousins and buried them again, finds himself left with: messy, uncertain data alongside the molecular processes, yet humanity's vague clue to "why life, why death," and its possible link to "the great begetting spasm billions of years ago" that cast the stars outward. As the cold-eyed but bitterly moved scientist puts it to himself: "Material details were of the greatest importance. But still the largest strokes were made by the spirit. Had to be."

So ends Dr. Braun's meditation and Bellow's collection of stories that reflect in their different ways their author's ability to lift the full weight of the human condition into the light.

(1969)

PART TWO

Alfred Kazin's America

Major critics tend to have a major subject, one which identifies them and is, in turn, marked by their imprint. What the liberal imagination was to Lionel Trilling, the social one to Irving Howe, the modernist one to Edmund Wilson, the moralist one to F. R. Leavis, so the American imagination was to Alfred Kazin. From the boy on the tenement fire escape in immigrant Jewish Brownsville reading his way into the American past to the old distinguished professor in his skyscraper office at CUNY pondering God's place in it, Kazin attended to the light that came from his favorite American writers and drew close to their native and individual traits and vibrations, even to those of their terrain.

There is a story told of his reviewing a book about the American West in which he went on a bit about the majesty of its mountains and rivers, something like that. "Hey, Alfred," Philip Rahv mocked, "What's this about *our* mountains, *our* rivers?" "What's this" was genuine, intensely so, starting early in his life:

> The day they took us to the Children's Museum—rain was dripping on the porch of that old wooden house, the halls were lined with Audubon prints and were hazel in the thin antique light—I was left with the distinct impression that I had been stirring between my fingers dried earth and fallen leaves that I had found between the paving stones of some small American town.

Kazin's sense of the American spirit continued to possess this visceral attachment. As he characteristically observed in one of his journals:

Every once in a while some token—a sentence in a book, a voice heard—will recall for me the fresh instant delight in American landscape and culture....The sentence this morning fresh as a spring wind comes from Constance Rourke's book on Audubon, on the sudden realization that his ornithology showed a national sense of scale, that like Whitman he was a great voice of American nationality.

The anecdote points up the difference between Kazin and most of the other New York Jewish writers associated with *Partisan Review* whose relation to America tended to be a position rather than a possession. In his later years Rahv, for example, became a significant Americanist—the framer of the famous classification of our writers as Palefaces (Irving, Hawthorne, James, et al.) and Redskins (Cooper, Mark Twain, Whitman, Dreiser, et al.). But what became a literary field to Rahv was a world to Kazin; and the Americanism that Rahv tuned into by his changing ideology and academic situation was to Kazin, in Henry James' phrase, a complex fate.

The complexity came partly from the implication of Rahv's teasing question—a Jew of their generation had not grown up in our pluralist society, but rather in one still sharply divided by custom and prejudice and governed by political coalitions, with a shaky tolerance clause. No matter how much one wished and dreamed otherwise, in Brownsville in the 1920s and 1930s, the feeling of being different, outside of and threatened by a society that proffered freedom and opportunity but remained exclusively Christian and mostly WASP in its culture, was inseparable from feeling Jewish, inseparable even from feeling authentic. "Why must it *always* be them and us?" young Alfred asks himself and then, typically, forecloses the issue by asserting his Jewish loyalty and solidarity.

As time went on, his anxious passage from home would take him far but not change him very much, being guided by his effort to fathom, like Whitman and Dreiser before him, the good and evil of American individualism and to live out "the bitter patriotism of loving what one knows."

2.

He grew up in the 1920s and early 1930s in one of the rawer ghet-tos—half Brooklyn, half Belz—at the end of the subway line. The firstborn of a house painter and dressmaker who had married out of immigrant loneliness and remained distant, Kazin was to be haunted by the image of his father weeping on their wedding night and by the cold barrenness between his parents that ensued, which he believed had chilled his own character until late middle-age. Fortunately his aunt Sophie, the family boarder, was a passionate woman of parts, a seamstress who brought books, art, music and two no less vivid friends into the house. Their Russian songs and stories at the weekly Shabbos dinner, as well as the nightly sense the boy had of ardent, manless Sophie lying close by in her room, gave his young sensibility the compensating glow and heartfulness that would go into his writ-ing. He was to remark that

> the best of whatever I knew as a child I got from this nearness to
> Sophie, lay in this brooding, dark, sultry arousement, this sudden
> brushing of wings, when I felt that it was Sophie, in her insistence
> on love, in the fierce sullenness with which an immigrant dress-
> maker no longer young lived for love, that made up the living con-
> trast to my mother's brooding carefulness and distrust.

One imagines that his characteristic positive adjectives—"burning," "fiery," "blazing," "furious," and their synonyms—were a primal link to her and through her to the headstrong Russian literature that part-ly shaped his sense of a literary vocation.

He also had both the lift and burden of being the fam-ily "Columbus"—as greenhorn couples referred to their firstborn ("What do *we* know?" their refrain); and also "the redeemer of the constant anxiety of their existence…the monument of their libera-tion from the shame of being—what they were." From the accounts in *Walker in the City* and *Writing Was Everything*, he comes through as a socially awkward, high-strung youth who keeps to himself but on whom nothing is lost. He was also a reader with a preternatural responsiveness. At twelve, he discovered Dickens and was never to recover:

> I felt I was in Dickens' head and could not get out... *Oliver Twist* was all around me and in me. I wanted never to get away from its effect... Why was Dickens compelled to write like that, and why did it work on me like a drug? .... That was how I started as a critic.

Walker in the City, from which most of the above quotes are drawn, is a memoir of images and scenes rather than events, of places rather than people, of rapid observation and impressions and very few stories: the experience of an intense boy who has no friends worth mentioning until he is sixteen. Living on a knife edge in school between triumph and catastrophe, he developed a stammer, perfect English being part of the right answer in the New York school system of the time. Sent off to the ignominy of speech therapy, he found that his impediment disappeared as he walked the streets, fluently mouthing the riffs of his inner voice. He became a walker, the loner's sport, and a Cortés of the near world of Brooklyn, with a passion to turn it into an outdoor museum of Americana and the museums themselves into intense communions.

The center of the Kazin household was the kitchen, not only by ethnic convention but because by day and far into the evening, it was his mother's dressmaking shop. Kazin's workaholic nature (his widow, Judith Dunford, has told me that there was hardly a flat space in their apartment not covered by books, journals, or manuscripts), his anxiety, and his social discomfort appear to have come from his mother, a woman who cooked for the family but was too busy or spent to eat with them; just as the incessant whirr of her sewing machine became the rhythm and emblem of the grinding, remorseless capitalist society out there in America. "Where is the day taking us now?" Kazin, "always so near to her moods," has her asking herself as she steals a moment to stare out the window into the Brownsville dusk.

The phrase soon echoes in the boy's own inner voice after crossing Brooklyn Bridge late one afternoon. He feels himself being picked up by the great American force of acculturation, of being whisked away from dreary, backward but secure Brownsville into the Great American Beyond, as Protestant as the austere brownstones on his journeys through Brooklyn Heights, and his mind spins with the question, "Papa, where are they taking me? Where in this beyond are they taking me?"

Also a loner and library haunter, Charles Kazin had started out in America by working his way westward. In his travels he had seen Sidney Hillman, the famous labor leader, working in a Chicago suit factory and had heard Eugene Debs speak at a rally. Taking a job painting boxcars, he had gotten as far as Omaha and been offered a homestead in Colorado. These were important events in the Kazin family romance that dictated to the boy's imagination. ("*Omaha* was the most beautiful word in the language, *homestead* the next one"), and help to explain Kazin's subsequent passion for the prairie novelists who provided a homestead of thousands of already mostly forgotten pages that he would settle in with, ten years later, to witness and write about the dawn of American realism.

Charles Kazin was an ardent socialist; his father, Abraham, had been an early one, a pieceworker with a rented sewing machine, who had tried to organize the "*forloiryne menschen*" (lost souls) of the terrible first years of the East European immigration. He died of the effort at twenty-five or -six, another important item in the family saga. The socialist legacy was also actively transmitted to Alfred by his aunt Sophie and her co-workers at the infamous Triangle Shirtwaist Factory. As an adolescent, he loyally went to meetings at the local Labor Lyceum, where he would gaze at the large photograph of Eugene Debs, who gave American socialism its human face; he had twice gone to jail for the cause, five times run for president. "Poor Parnell!" Alfred would say to himself. "Our dead king!"—Joyce having joined the other literary/spiritual rebels, Blake and Lawrence and Whitman, who were now his literary gods. Like the young Henry James, he wanted to be "just literary," but still it was socialism that he took into the street arguments of the 1930s along Pitkin Avenue where the radical factions were the Jewish mode of gang fighting. Brandishing their battle insult of "Sell out!," the Stalinists dominated the arguments, broke up the Socialist meetings, even got the girls. Opposing them in the Brownsville streets and later in the famed "alcoves" at City College, where it was always the period after Lenin's death and the right to the succession still in fierce dispute-Kazin developed his penchant for "strong argument" and for the dialectical dramatics that would characterize his criticism.

His main intellectual experience once he got out of Brownsville was the high-powered anti-Stalinist, eclectic Marxist circle around V.F. Calverton, the editor of the *Modern Monthly*, which Kazin helped him put out while still in his teens. The polymath Calverton embodied for his dazzled protégé, the libertarian spirit that was one of the better parts of the 1930s. So, too, was the intellectual intensity of Calverton's milieu where Kazin witnessed the arguments between such redoubtable figures as Max Eastman and Sidney Hook. For these and other reasons, the 1930s would remain a positive part of Kazin's background as the 1960s would for his son, the labor historian Michael Kazin. He would have no need to reject its ideals along with its illusions, no need to stalk himself and other radicals into the hard-line anti-communism of the 1950s and on to the neo-conservative chauvinism.

Kazin believed that literature was too important a personal and cultural resource to be left either to the modernist literati or the Popular Front. He had experienced it as the staff of his spirit and the better part of his aspirations in the wretched households in Brownsville where he went as a teenager early in the Depression to discuss works like *The Waste Land* and Blake's *The Marriage of Heaven and Hell*. The virtual hovel in which his older friend David, his first writing audience, lived with a dying mother and small brother, a few sticks of furniture, the photos of lynchings and the books of the international Left—Lenin and Frederick Douglass, Ernst Thaelmann and Henri Barbusse—conveyed to the sixteen-year-old writer "some deep, brave, and awful earnestness before life itself" and a "naked freedom of thought" that he would never lose and would soon come to write out of.

Another formative experience was the Group Theater productions of Clifford Odets's plays. Thanks to the authenticity of Odets's dramas and the revolutionary realism of this repertory company (Russian-Jewish-radical theater come into its own), Kazin discovered people occupying the stage "by as much right as if they were Hamlet or Lear." The "right" was hardly conferred by tragic stature but rather by the power of theatrical art to electrify the "crowded, tense, shabby Brooklyn life" and to present its soul while remaining insistently faithful to its coarse atmosphere, issues and idiom. The significance of such an experience is that it authorized as well as naturalized the sensibility young Kazin had developed in just such circumstances, giving the young writer the confidence to make use of who he actually was rather than willing a persona as many of the *Partisan Review* crowd did. It's not an accident, I think, that Kazin, Irving Howe, Paul Goodman, and Saul Bellow, its most productive members, were the ones who remained most connected to their early life.

At the end of one of the Odets performances, the exhilarated young writer from Brownsville thinks, "It was all one, as I had always known. Art and truth and hope could all come together—if a real writer was their meeting place." They indeed soon began to come together for him: the literary man's standards, the socialist aspiration, the Jewish respect for the hard facts but also for the soft ones, the working-class rebel's sense that his hour had come.

On the other hand, in every young writer there is a renegade yearning to break out into the land of otherness, all the more so in the immigrant Jewish family and community like Kazin's, whose ethos of possessiveness and solidarity made leaving it feel like a betrayal. One looks for models, and Kazin found two of his in the Solovey couple, whose arrogance and refinement weigh like lead in the rough sea of Brownsville survival. The enigmatic Soloveys' love and doom is the major episode in *Walker*, and one can feel in Kazin's fascinated retrospect of himself with the blond, French-speaking Mrs. Solovey and her bitterly aloof intellectual husband, the inchoate passion and independence they provoked as he hung around their failing drugstore.

So, too, in the remarkable section in *Walker in the City* where one sees the beginning of an insurgent spirituality with young Alfred's breaking a taboo of the Jewish mind when he all but falls into the prose of the Gospels and discovers in his intense excitement and shame "my Yeshua: the very embodiment of everything I had waited so long to hear from a Jew…." Kazin's Judaism was to be a religion he used rather than practiced. He prayed to his own, often elusive God and his spirituality as well as religious learning flowed most strongly, I think, when he was writing about another writer's, such as his superb introduction to William Blake.

The compact and nuanced narrative of Mr. and Mrs. Solovey is also a testimonial to the fiction writer Kazin didn't become, but who, locked away in his heart and active in his imagination, will make him the critic he became, one who writes about writers as gifted novelists and poets do: that quick assessment of the author's character and the work's texture—the life, or lack of it, on the page—and that ability to put a hand into the prose or verse and measure the strength of the current. Kazin wrote less as a literary critic than as a writer possessed by literature as moral testimony and lived history. He was not interested in literary theory or in what nowadays is called textuality; he didn't interpret the work; he explored and personified the mentality of the writer that is operating within the work and career, seeing him or her, in other words, like a character in a story or novel—an individual set against a social/moral ground or, often, two such figures to define and dramatize them against each other.

> Looking at [Sherwood] Anderson and [Sinclair] Lewis together, the drowsing village mystic and the garrulous village atheist, it seemed as if they had come from the opposite end of the world (or from the same Midwestern street) to meet in the dead center of the postwar emancipation and be stopped there, wondering what came next.

3.

Kazin's first work appeared in *The New Republic*, which he began writing for at the age of nineteen. He had been sent there by John Chamberlain, after he had barged into his cubicle at the *Times* to protest a review Chamberlain had written. Jewish sons in the 1930s did this sort of thing: the toughs had the unions, boxing and crime, the sensitives education and the arts as the ladder up from the ghetto; the reviewers' bench at *The New Republic* was crowded with them. The magazine had been founded at the height of the Progressive movement, and in the subsequent twenty years had become the leading national journal of political and social reform and innovation in the arts. Here Kazin began to develop his own tradition, to model his style on the intellectual dignity he admired in the early independent activist writers who sustained "the promise of American life," the title of a seminal book by Herbert Croly, its founding editor. The intellectual radicalism of the then Socialist Walter Lippmann, the democratic philosophy of John Dewey, the fiery reportage and social criticism of Randolph Bourne, the committed literary journalism of Edmund Wilson and Van Wyck Brooks all worked on young Kazin, inspired and authenticated his gift. During the Depression *The New Republic* was trying to restate Progessivism as Marxism—*To the Finland Station* was running in its pages when Kazin began showing up in 1934. Wilson himself was gone as literary editor, succeeded by Malcolm Cowley; who was then in his sophisticated Stalinist phase but was another brilliant practitioner as well as encourager of the review that dramatized the author and his book in the context of the issues of the times.

Young Kazin learned from him, too, but took his point of view from the less blinkered perspectives of Wilson and Brooks, whose book *America's Coming of Age* in 1919 had been the shot heard around the literary world for the next decade, a forthright indictment of America as a commercial civilization that acted like a plague on the careers of its serious writers and artists (Mark Twain and Henry James were subsequently to be his foremost examples). It was from the influence of Brooks's idealism that much of the literary ethos of the 1920s developed with its respect for craftsmanship, its resistance to "selling out" and its belief that literary criticism in America is compelled to become social criticism to preserve the human spirit.

To be sure, such a position was taken for granted during the Depression years, but the tradition of Progressivism with its positive blend of protest and faith in America, along with Kazin's own earlier socialism, would stand him in good stead by enabling him to maintain a coherent critical liberalism, like that of, say, John Kenneth Galbraith and Lewis Mumford who were also of the old *New Republic* stripe. But much as he admired Brooks, Kazin thought that in the hard times and hard light of the 1930s, Brooks's social program, derived from Ruskin and William Morris, was sentimental and anachronistic, and his style self-indulgently lyrical. Also I suspect that the the raw youth from Brownsville, standing on the edge of the Stalinist gin-and-lime and deck-tennis circle that gathered in the early evening at *The New Republic*'s brownstone in Chelsea, had a lot of resistance as well as fascination. Its cantankerous former literary editor, Edmund Wilson, was a hovering absence, and it was Wilson that he yearned to emulate, particularly his immense ability to dramatize literary and intellectual history by weaving a writer's character, work, career, and times seamlessly together; and he carried in his head the model of the final sentence of Wilson's chapter on Proust in *Axel's Castle*:

> Proust is perhaps the last great historian of the loves, the society, the intelligence, the diplomacy, the literature and the art of the Heartbreak House of capitalist culture; and the little man with the sad appealing voice, the metaphysician's mind, the Saracen's beak, the ill-fitting dress-shirt and the great eyes that seem to see all about him like the many-faceted eyes of a fly, dominates the scene and plays host in the mansion where he is not long to be master.

4.

Like everyone else, Kazin scrambled during the Depression—working as a researcher in the Federal Writers' Project and writing reviews wherever he could and anything else that paid, from vanity biographies to radio plays on WNYC based on Dickens and Poe. But though he was still writing on the kitchen table in Brownsville, the young freelancer had crossed the Brooklyn Bridge, his lifelong symbol of the linkage between his early and later self, and was beginning to make his way. One can easily sense his excitement from the momentum of the writing in his second memoir, *Starting Out in the Thirties*. *Walker* is situational—"The Kitchen," "The Neighborhood," "The Beyond"—an active reverie of the heart, the prose crackling with the tension of an anxiously venturesome young mind warmly hugged by Jewish solidarity and strongly tugged by the American prospect. *Starting Out* is relational—each chapter a year going by in rushes of mostly elated contacts, the prose picking up the beat of an eager, naïve rebel who is beginning to go places: to hang out with Otis Ferguson, sort of a Pete Hamill of his day; to go to the intellectual-studded parties of V. F. Calverton and ogle Calverton's ravishing young mistress; to meet other young minority writers from the slums or the sticks on their way up—Richard Wright, William Saroyan, James T. Farrell, Robert Cantwell. Then, in 1938, came the jolt of the big opportunity that would send a career into orbit. Carl Van Doren, the literary editor of *The Nation*, casually suggested to his young reviewer that a book was needed on the history of American modernism, and all the vectors of Kazin's development came together, all the bees in his bonnet began to buzz and head into clover.

Kazin has written in several places about the rapturous three years that followed at the shiny yellow desks in Room 304, the main reading room of the New York Public Library. His own graduate school—which he shared with his friend Richard Hofstadter, who was working on Social Darwinism in America—the reading room was also during those years the "asylum and church of the unemployed." What better place to launch himself into the mainstream of

American prose in the 1890s as it flowed strongly through another prolonged and bitter time of economic crisis and to do so directly at the point at which it bent widely left.

He went at the task whole hog: not just the complete works of Howells and Crane, Frank Norris and Upton Sinclair, Edith Wharton and Hamlin Garland et. al., but the whole archive of novels, stories, manifestos, studies, pamphlets by the ironic metropolitan realists, the lonely small-town individualists, the angry prairie naturalists. Kazin read them all, down to Joseph Kirkland's *Zury: The Meanest Man in Spring County*. His curiosity was ravenous, the literary immigrant possessing his newfound land, the ambitious young scholar-critic developing a background of minor writers against which to place the major ones and thereby write with the undertext of first-rate history—the silent reserves of what is left out that produce the aura of authority, the resonant hum of distinctions and implications. Finally, too, Kazin was driven by his own shock of recognition, his felt need to do justice to these "lone protestants of their time," these "Jeffersonian hearts plagued by a strangely cold and despotic America, some of whom lacked every capacity for literature save a compelling passion to tell the truth." Fighting or mourning for their land, their distinctively American voices and "elementary nationalism" were Emerson's prophecy come true—the "rank-rabble party" who uproot genteel cultivation and prepare the ground for "the newborn to frame their own world with greater advantage."

They were also pioneers of the new democracy of American letters that went hand in hand with the new realism that was springing up all across the cultural front from down-to-earth poetry to crusading journalism; from the pragmatism of Peirce, James, and Dewey to the revisionist history of James Allen Smith and the young Charles Beard that boldly questioned the class interests of the Founding Fathers and sharply distinguished between the abstract "juristic" republic and the actual rigged one. This broadly based realism also functioned as a kind of Greek chorus pointing out and lamenting the anarchy and brutality of rampaging industrial capitalism: John Jay Chapman summed it up as a railroad coming to a town and then dominating it, and as a "cruelty going on before you" that leaves the alternative of "interposing to stop it or of losing your sensibility." Liberal intellectuals and writers were made of sterner, more fighting stuff back then, and Kazin happily entered their minds and their fellowship.

With the 1930s' winds of change at his back and a whole, relatively unexplored field before him that began with Howells and ended with Faulkner; that ranged from the thought of Dewey, Steffens, Veblen, and Parrington to that of James Hunecker and Ludwig Lewisohn, Irving Babbitt, and John Crowe Ransom; from the turn-of-the-century aesthetes to the muckrakers across town; from the primitive realists and half-baked modernists to the sophisticated writers who put out *The Seven Arts* in the 1920s; from the Progressives who rose and fell with President Wilson to the Marxists and New Humanists and Fugitives and social documentarians of the 1930s—Kazin presented and evaluated them, connected them, and wrote on to the darkening end where everything came to an ominous halt as the new world war drew on.

A great story to be told. Supported by his wife, a young research bacteriologist, he had the time and stability as well as urgency to tell it, finishing it just before he received his draft notice in 1941. His heated imagination and cool judgment produced a tempered prose and a kinetic texture. The prodigious reading Kazin had done comes to seem like a great river and his capacious imagination like a hydroelectric plant steadily generating the images that bring power and light to his vast subject. And, to complete Auden's line, "a sovereign touch." The command of the subject at virtually every turn would be remarkable in a historian twice his age. Sixty years after its publication, *On Native Grounds* stands beside Perry Miller's *The New England Mind*, F. O. Matthiessen's *American Renaissance*, and Richard Chase's *The American Novel and Its Tradition* as landmarks of our literary history.

Basically, what Kazin did was lay the development of American realism and of modernism as parallel tracks on which to move his history forward, and to create perspective and argument by pitting the urgencies of expression of essentially a protest literature against

the exigencies of art as practiced and usually compromised by a succession of writers most of whom had virtually no native literary
models. In Europe, naturalism grew out of the literary tradition as
the counter movement to Romanticism; in America, naturalism was
mainly a weapon to assail the trusts. With a few nods to Zola, writers like Norris and Sinclair had to make up their literary culture as
they went along. Lacking a tradition other than the New England
one become genteel or the frontier one become obsolete, the more
imaginative writers, like Stephen Crane, Edith Wharton, Theodore
Dreiser, and Willa Cather, descended deep into themselves as Joseph
Conrad, another solo pioneer advised, to find the terms of their appeal. Otherwise, there were so many novels that were groping rather
than accomplished, so many careers that were topical, repetitious, or
brief.

Steering between the Marxists and the New Critics, Kazin early
set his standard by the career and practice of Henry James—itself a
pretty remarkable choice for a young radical doing his research amid
the human flotsam and jetsam of a reading room in New York City
during the Depression. What he drew from James was that human
character, social forces, and moral implications required a relentless
attention and a full consciousness of complexity as well as an artist's
intuition. By means of them James's art had "fastened itself to…sub-
jects, themes, qualities, events which the conventional assessment of his
talents were presumably closed to…but which by the slow, avid pressure of his perception he conveyed with devastating lucidity." Kazin's
case in point was *The Princess Casamassima*, the best American novel
of its era to portray the slow incubation of the revolutionary spirit as
it went on, in James's words, "irreconcilably, subversively, beneath the
vast smug surface." Stoutly resisting both doctrinaire modernism and
populism, the young critic held to the old Master's "standard of art—
perception at the pitch of passion and expression as embracing as the
air." In Fitzgerald, Cummings, Hemingway, and Dos Passos, modern
America finally produced the fiction writers who had led in varying
degrees of fullness the life and practice of an artist, who had stamped
their writing so that it could be read like Braille, as Fitzgerald put it,

and who had each written a chapter of the moral history of his age. And it is here that *On Native Grounds* reaches it own pitch of perception in Kazin's blazing account of Fitzgerald working his way deep into himself and into 1920s America to bring forth Jay Gatsby; of the remarkable surrealism of E.E. Cummings's *The Enormous Room*; of Dos Passos's slow development of his power and techniques of social observation; and of the rise and fall of Hemingway's practice of a "major art on a minor vision of life."

Throughout his book, Kazin's American pride and leftist sympathy leaven the text. Despite Stephen Crane's limitations, say, as a young journalist who was still "only half a writer" and who had no experience of war, Kazin points up the originality of his horrific landscapes of the Civil War battles and also observes how *The Red Badge of Courage* anticipates the future literature of war by focusing its boredom, havoc, and horror on the common soldier. Or again, though Anderson and Lewis each had only a couple of strings to their instruments, they nonetheless caught the tone and rhythm of the heretofore unsung private life of middle Americans and helped to create the first broad audience for serious fiction. Or again, he presents Dreiser transforming the wretchedness and disrepute of his family into the morally numbing force of circumstances in the new urban society and also introducing American literature to the sexual drive. You can pretty much tell a critic's literary politics by his take on Dreiser. Lionel Trilling, who came to see the liberal imagination in America as half-empty, regarded Dreiser as mostly a pretentious brute who is dogmatically praised to show up the artificiality and irrelevance of cultivated masters such as Henry James. Kazin regards Dreiser as a great folk artist like Knut Hamsun and Gorky—"the spirits of simplicity who raise local man as they have known him to world citizenship...."

The young post-immigrant radical tended to find isolation and alienation almost everywhere he looked, sometimes mistaking the novelist's necessary reclusiveness and quarrel with society for them. Also he gives short shrift to novelists like Hergesheimer and Cabell, who identified with the wrong class; he undervalues Edith Wharton's achievement because in snobbishly viewing society *haut en bas* she missed what Dreiser saw; and he faults the positivist Dewey for lacking a tragic sense of life. He writes about the literary South with a leftist brashness that makes the Fugitives into so many bitter nostalgists, if not apologists for slavery, and as excessive in their aestheticism as the Marxists were in their philistinism; and he will spend the rest of his career atoning for his underrating of Faulkner as a half-baked genius who let his social vision run wildly into rhetoric and solipsism.

Nonetheless, the literary and intellectual judgment in *On Native Grounds* is generally remarkable for its astuteness, and becomes amazingly so when you remind yourself that the author began writing it in his early twenties. Had the book been only a study of the fiction of its fifty-year span it would have been a major achievement. What made it a lasting one was Kazin's doubling its reach and interest and the evolution of its theme of the making of the modern American spirit by including its influential thinkers and historians, social and literary critics, and providing the background for these figures by his deft accounts of the leading movements. He also brings his narrative of the rise of the democratic mentality and its adversaries to a creative and appropriate climax by steering around the dreary dead end of protest fiction in the 1930s, save for Farrell and Steinbeck, to take up the rich and various documentation through all the arts, from poetry to photography, of the "new nationalism" that emerged during the decade, as the giant nation, on its knees, struggled to clear its mind and pull itself together.

5.

Kazin said that *On Native Grounds* was his easiest book to write because of the spirit of the times, his passion for the task, and the wide-openness of the field. Such favoring circumstances would not occur again in his career.

The book won him the position of literary editor of *The New Republic*, which put him in personal touch with other young Jewish prodigies such as Delmore Schwartz, Saul Bellow, Isaac Rosenfeld, and Paul Goodman, who energized him; with influential critics such as Trilling and Wilson, who certified his sudden reputation; and with such competitors as Philip Rahv and Mary McCarthy, who productively infuriated him. But *The New Republic* had fallen upon dull times during these war years, and he soon moved on to the staff of *Fortune*, which had become a sort of halfway house for disenchanted radicals who could use the money and stand the pretentiousness of Henry Luce. Rejected by the draft and eager to get overseas, Kazin ended up in England. Reporting on the British army's effort to educate its fractious working-class troops and absorbing on the spot, as it were, George Orwell's wide-ranging social vision and intellectual independence, Kazin found a more intense social consciousness than any he had known. He was also profoundly affected by the prophetic struggle of Kafka and then of the postwar European writers and intellectuals, notably Simone Weil, to pursue the philosophical and spiritual implications of the huge devastation of the war and its horrible aftermath of the death camps: a kind of cultural ground zero after the European twin towers of enlightenment and humanism had collapsed.

On his return to the States, Kazin found himself all dressed up for crisis writing, as it were, with no place to go. Just as it had after the First World War, the United States quickly resumed its pursuit of affluence and state power, much intensified now by the Cold War and the rise of McCarthyism. Having nothing to recant, Kazin stayed clear of the Committee for Cultural Freedom and the other former radicals who were making so much of a self-regarding alarm and so much of a good thing career-wise out of their anti-communism. Dubbing them the Upper West Side Hebrew Relief Association, he devoted the most blistering pages in his third and final memoir, *New York Jew*, to them as "total arrivistes" whose new notion of American society left them undisturbed by "what was really going on right before their eyes where the drug epidemic in Harlem, the massive Hispanic immigration, the flight of the middle class from the violence and crime was turning their own Upper West Side into a gilded ghetto and a violent one separated by Broadway.

Socialism being no longer even a hope to him, Kazin refrained from joining the saving remnant of it around Irving Howe's *Dissent* and went his solitary way—a progressive with a despairing sense of the future, a leftist who had gone from the deep-sea pressure radicalism of the 1930s to the thin air of liberalism in the 1950s, a humanist unhinged from his former faith in humanity by the Holocaust, a modernist who watched its rebels and iconoclasts being institutionalized by the pervasive New Criticism in the English departments. The literary scene was a lot thinner and blander, too, as one by one the last of the great novelists of the first half of the century declined and departed, and instead there were two young writers of major war novels, two new and accomplished black literary artists, a sprinkling of experimental work such as *The Recognitions* and *The Lime Twig*. The scene soon came to be characterized by Augie March knocking at the door of society, Holden Caulfield rebelling against prep school and phoniness, John Cheever asking plaintively why in this "half-finished civilization, in this most prosperous, equitable and accomplished world, should everyone seem so disappointed?" There was little awareness in America about the Holocaust until 1956 when Elie Wiesel, a young survivor writing in French and living in New York, published *Night*.

These would all become subjects for Kazin, opportunities to clarify and to discriminate, to take a position that lent support or put up resistance. But he had a hard time after the war in finding his way again. The trouble with sudden worldly success, particularly if you've been raised as far from it as he was, is that it badly throws off the default settings of your character which can take a lot of time, confusion and frustration to reset to your new program. The success of *On Native Grounds* appears to have gone directly to his libido. His supportive early marriage to the gentle biologist Asya was soon smashed by an all but predictable affair with one of those alluring young Villagers who live on air and for big ideas, and sleep with anyone who has them. After the war came a love affair, also pretty much in the cards, with a daughter of the Upper East Side German-Jewish gentry that ended in a trophy marriage *à deux*. This produced a son but soon fell apart from its own weightlessness. Kazin became a Central Park weekend father as well as an uneasy participant in the literary cafe society that had replaced his cafeteria one. After finishing his *Portable Blake* he collaborated with Henri Cartier-Bresson on a piece for *Harper's Bazaar* on New York, then began to write a book about walking around Manhattan in the postwar boom. But he couldn't bring it off, his prose fitfully dazzled rather than jelled, and for the first time he entered writer's hell.

He remained there for many months. He had written, "Every time I go back to Brownsville it is as if I had never lived there"; but, recording a family visit in his journal, he changed the last two words to "been away." The floodgate opened and the deeply held experience began to generate the intense prose of *Walker in the City*. He was back again to being the writer who would boldly title his third memoir *New York Jew*.

6.

I began to read him assiduously when I was a graduate student at Chicago during the late 1950s, mostly his reviews in *The Reporter*. By then he was teaching at either Amherst or Smith. The contemporary having breached the ramparts of the scholarly, the doors of the English departments in prestigious places were swinging open to Jews, and in the rapid expansion of the educated class and higher education, the New York intellectuals of the 1930s and '40s, who had lived mostly on their wives' earnings, joined the professariat. For a time it didn't matter very much: whether the prose was written in Northampton or Princeton, Minneapolis or Waltham, Massachusetts, it was coming to me like literary Care packages from New York. Try to imagine a Ph.D. student writing a dull, dutiful paper on "Two Recent Views of Emerson's Oversoul," opening *The Reporter* and reading:

> "I like," said Emerson, "dry light, and hard clouds, hard expressions, and hard manners." The writers who become our saints and sages,

the wise men of our tribe, they who help us to live—there is only one way by which we know them: their genius for compression. They are the ones who are always stripping life down to fundamentals and essentials, to aphorisms and parables and riddles, and if we ask what is holy about men whose life sayings often shock and hurt as much as they illuminate, the answer is that the final compression they get into their speech is a compression they have attained in their lives.

Such writing was not only sustenance but came to embody my hope that after I had done my time with academic jargon and got my Ph.D., I would try to write like that, the higher literary journalism that communicates directly and yet broadly, that rings like a hammer on iron, that revives the dead and positions the living. The point Kazin is making here reflects back on the prose making it, the pith and edge of a compression attained by a mind that goes to the core of a career and unwinds it in 2,000 words or less of high-intensity description, judgment, and context. Just as a first-rate short story is often like the nucleus of a novel, so a review of Kazin's typically read like the concentrate of a full-length study.

As with other young literary types during this time, Kazin became one of my go-to guys—the strong, accurate point makers at any range from the distant erudite to the close-in topical. Why was Bellow the preeminent novelist of the 1950s? Because, according to Kazin, he could calibrate so well the power of resistance in things at a time when society was losing its force and shape as a subject and becoming the mere backdrop of the hungry postwar self. Also because Bellow's prose was so wired with vision that a simple situation—the Viennese-style charlatan Tamkin carrying a plate of Yankee pot roast and red cabbage, two cups of coffee, and a slice of watermelon to a cafeteria table—made one see "multiple aspects of the human condition." Finally, because Bellow, like Melville, was a metaphysical writer who "identifies man's quest with the range of the mind itself." As Kazin observed, Bellow's heroes are so pulled and harassed by their need to understand their destiny within the particular problem of human destiny that taken together they constitute "the deepest commentary I know on the social utopianism of a generation which always presumed that it could pacify life, that it could control and guide it to an innocuous social end, but which is painfully learning...to praise in it the divine strength which disposes of man's proposals."

All of this is in the first few pages of a review of *Henderson, the Rain King*. What was most real for a fiction writer? What did he most love ("in the artistic sense of what fully interested him")? What empowered or weakened his work? How much of our life could he lift up and inspect? What made his work morally useful or useless? What distinguished his writing or made it all too typical of the age or one of its subgenres? Reading Kazin's answers corrected or enlarged my understanding of what was both original and distinctively Jewish in the work of Malamud: (1) his language: the cryptic expressiveness of a people who lived on the rim of existence, who wrote and spoke as if "the book of life were about to close shut with a bang." And (2) his transformation of traditional Jewish mysticism, where earth is so close to heaven and hell that the supernatural and the ordinary tweak each other. Malamud's principal limitation: the reliance on moral symbolism and allegory that make his characters less individuals than members of a depressed mystical repertory company.

Or again, what made *Prince of Darkness*, the first collection by J. F. Powers, so remarkable? His maturity. His stories were about a world, rather than diverse social situations and "constantly yielded literary vanity to the truth and depth of this world." His art also benefited from rising out of a long cultural tradition at a time most young American writers were standing on the dime of present-mindedness. With his rapid but deft touch Kazin put his finger on Powers's distinctive voice—fusing "intelligence and compassion to come out as humor"—and his main drawback—a tendency to let his stories of the workings of grace on worldliness and mediocrity turn into a formula. Why were James Baldwin's essays more powerful than his novels? Because his novels are willed, hypothetical, meant to prove he can write them, while the more open form of the essay enabled him to give his full attention and voice to the struggle in himself between the oppressed and the responsible man "'who had become an American,'" as Kazin lets Baldwin tell it, "'by walking right into the bottomless confusion both public and private of the American republic.'"

The bottom line of Kazin's judgment remained the standard of realism. However complex and nuanced his understanding of its possibilities, he remained committed to the power of the illusion of life generated by the human struggle against the force of circumstances in a life, a society, the world. In an essay on "the aesthetics of realism" Kazin used Dreiser's work to develop a model of what he calls "personal realism"—the assembling of the web of social images and facts spun from his varied experience and imbued with his own sense of wonder and bemusement at the strangeness of the real that both validates it and complicates it. Dreiser's personal realism achieves a depth of description that comes only to a writer whose imagination is fully inhabited by the social forces at issue, who has put himself in the way of being swept up by history, and in doing so is able to find a pattern in it that gives reverberating significance to his story. A good current example of what he means is the topical visionary fiction in the past decade of Don DeLillo and E. L. Doctorow or the deeply witnessed recent political novels of Philip Roth, work that points up the crying need for social vision in the contemporary novel, which continues to bear out de Tocqueville's prophecy that in modern society people become more alone and more completely preoccupied with a puny object—themselves.

This was already Kazin's complaint in the 1950s. In an important essay of that time, "The Alone Generation," he attributed the narcissistic malaise of most novels to the general condition of American culture:

> Our culture is stupefyingly without support from tradition, and has become both secular and progressive in its articulation of every discontent and ambition; the individual now questions himself constantly because his own progress—measured in terms of the social norms—is his fundamental interest. The kind of person who in the nineteenth-century novel was a "character" now regards him-

self in twentieth-century novels as a problem; the novel becomes not a series of actions which he initiates because of who he is but a series of disclosures…designed to afford him the knowledge that may heal him.

He realized that this wasn't the whole story, that the "queerness," as he called it, of society after the Bomb as well as the technology-driven universal of change that made the present seem more linked with the future than with the past had made the nature of America—the go-go, mobile, complacent consumer society on the surface, the stealthy superpower behind the scenes—that much more difficult to portray than the more ponderous and naked society of Dreiser's era. Despite his general dissatisfaction, Kazin continued to move with the times, to look for and to find writers as different as Ralph Ellison, Nabokov, and Flannery O'Connor who practiced a personal realism, who asserted values as truths rather than as options, who displayed the "unforeseen possibilities of the human—even when everything seems dead set against it."

7.

I first met Kazin in 1961, shortly after I began to work at *Commentary*. One of the first pieces I was given to edit was a lecture of his about the current state of literary criticism. It began by deploring the practice of teaching literature by issuing the New Criticism tool kit of tension, irony, paradox, symbol to open any text. He went on to argue for the old criticism that perceives itself as part of the general criticism of values that any humane society requires, and that is most itself when its account of a work, a writer, a career grows out of the critic's efforts to put his own thoughts and feelings about them in order, as does Randall Jarrell or F.W. Dupee. The essay concluded with the hope that criticism might yet regain the public function and force that it had had with Emerson and Matthew Arnold, Orwell and Eliot, Leavis and Trilling, might join itself to contemporary writing again, and might regain the élan and transgressiveness that had made modernism what it was.

I couldn't have agreed more. I had just come away from an English department that practiced its own analytic orthodoxy and was remote from current literature— my subject, Henry James, had barely qualified as ripe enough for scholarship. Moreover, I owed my new life in New York to an enthusiastic piece I'd contributed to the *TLS* about the impact of contemporary Jewish writers and sensibility on American letters, an essay written, I thought, to the risky specifications Kazin's piece was calling for. I didn't have much to contribute editorially to his essay, but I did give it its title, "The Function of Criticism Today," an allusion to Matthew Arnold's seminal essay on the quickening effect of fresh ideas in moving literature forward again. This pleased Kazin enough to invite me downtown for a drink.

It didn't go well. He quickly let me know that my essay was exaggerated and not well-informed, and the conversation was slow to recover, at least on my side. Riding back uptown in a cab, he asked me what I was working on. I said that I was editing a collection of posthumous literary pieces by Isaac Rosenfeld. He replied, "Why are you doing that? Isaac isn't important."

"He is to me," I said. I tried to explain why, even saying that Rosenfeld was just the kind of critic Kazin's essay was calling for. I reminded him that a famous piece of his in *Commentary* on the sexual implications of the dietary laws had almost shut down the magazine.

He said that was what he meant—the "clownish, Reichian squandering" of his gift. He had known Isaac well, he said. He had even sublet his apartment, sat in his crazy orgone box.

He was talking about someone I hadn't known personally but about someone other than the literary mensch I had read. I tried to tell him that. But as I talked, he mainly sniffed, a tic of his. Fully aggrieved by now, I said, "Okay, who do you think I should be writing about?"

"You should be writing about someone important. Like Willa Cather."

I looked hard at him. Was I being advised or insulted? Either way, his expression was deadly serious. When I got out of the cab, I took the adverb with me and let the adjective go.

That was the last time we had much to say to each other, but I continued to read and learn from him. A year or so later he brought out his major collection, *Contemporaries*, that covered the 1950s much as Edmund Wilson's *The Shores of Light* had done for the '20s and subsequent ones had for the following decades. By now Kazin had pretty much become Wilson's successor as the secretary of American letters, the one who best kept its proceedings, remembered its history, remained in touch with the outstanding writers abroad and the intellectual conditions at home, such as the sections in *Contemporaries* devoted to Freud and his influence, and to various recent books that bore on "The Puzzle of Modern Society." Part of the role Wilson passed on was that of acting as a public intellectual who brought a literary imagination to bear on American political and social issues, and in Wilson's case, according to Kazin, a character that "would be as ashamed to take the side of power as to write a bad sentence."

Kazin's judgment of Arthur Schlesinger Jr.'s history of the Roosevelt administration and of the Kennedy presidency around this time are typical of his criticism of the recurrent intellectual poverty at the center of American politics and hence the "tragedy of a diminishing democratic leadership" and the permanent crisis from the pressure of mass society, global power, and economic imperialism on an eighteenth-century system of government. Kazin regarded FDR's and JFK's extreme administrative maneuvering under the spell of personal charm and myth as a decline from the politics of Woodrow Wilson, which for all of his obstinate idealism, were still based on historical reasons and moral convictions for what he did and couldn't do and thus created a legacy of ideas for his party that none of his major democratic successors were to do. (He included FDR—rather perversely, I think—because of the meagerness of his presidential papers.) This judgment fell into place with Kazin's increasing despair of a society and culture "stupefyingly without tradition" and running more and more out of control of the immense power it generated.

My next memory of Kazin is at a public forum a few years later, following the publication of Hannah Arendt's *Eichmann in Jerusalem*. Led by Irving Howe, it had the air of an emergency meeting to deal with Arendt's thesis that the Jewish leaders collaborated in the destruction of their people. It was interesting to see so much fervor coming from several *bien pensants* who had hardly given any thought in their careers to Jewish concerns, and the rhetoric became more inflamed as each speaker tried to outdo the others in telling outrage. Finally, Howe introduced a survivor of the Holocaust and was happily translating for the audience his Yiddish testimony against Arendt when Kazin stood up, walked to the podium, and said, "That's enough, Irving. This disgraceful piling on has to stop." Something like that. He then said a few words about the great distinction of Arendt's thought and the complexity of her book and walked out.

I don't remember precisely what happened after that, except that a lot of the energy went out of the room and the meeting ended soon after. When he'd left I noticed that Kazin had the same obdurate expression on his face as when he'd told me to write about Willa Cather. So I saw that it wasn't personal, that he'd spoken his mind in both cases because he knew no other way and cared not a fig what people thought of him.

8.

By the 1970s he had taken his sensibility about as far into the present culture as it cared to go with the publication of *Bright Book of Life*, his energetic and wide-ranging study of the postwar fiction writers from the later Hemingway and Faulkner to Pynchon and Nabokov and of categories such as war, Southern, and urbane social fiction (from O'Hara to Updike) as well as the new ones that had emerged, such as the contemporary Jewish novel, the absurd novel, the nonfiction novel, and the oeuvre of Nabokov, which constituted a kind of one-man genre of Euro-American fiction. As with *On Native Grounds*, whose coverage of American fiction he was bringing up to date, *Bright Book of Life* derived its strength from Kazin's ability to capture the tone and issues of an age through a writer's interaction with them and through his or her vitalizing take on life itself—the fateful operation of sin and error in Flannery O'Connor; the drifty, porous reality through which subversive fantasy streams into John Cheever's suburbia; the émigré's past-haunted self and sharpened eye for Americana in Nabokov; the antagonistic mutations of history in Pynchon; the new social mobility in Updike; the new Jewish outspokenness in Philip Roth. The writer who preoccupies him as the most fully cognizant of the increasing anarchy of power and the most responsive to the "voraciousness of American life…its fury of transformation" is Norman Mailer. He appears in three separate profiles in *Bright Book*: the most politically aware and purposeful of the war novelists, the most ambitious and effective in becoming a cultural force among the Jewish ones, and the most able of the practitioners of the new journalism to impose his perceptions of the psychic effects of our multifarious age: the nuclear, space, information, racial integration, sexual liberation, and feminist age. As Kazin puts it, Mailer's characteristic vision of the shock and simultaneity of diverse new experience, of "different orders of reality to be willed together did in fact reflect the imbalance between everyone's inner life and the constant world of public threat, as well as the seeming unlimitedness of national and personal ambition." Alluding to a well-known remark of Philip Roth, Kazin observes that Mailer would never regard America as an embarrassment to the meagerness of one's own imagination.

What Kazin shared with Mailer was a heavy investment of psychic energy in that precarious vantage point of the mind between close attention and foreboding, from which the devil could be glimpsed at work in Washington and Watts and Vietnam, in the jockeying for advantage at the edge of mutual assured destruction, in the horrors of the century that were still alive and latent behind the scenes of multiple coexistence with the inhuman. In 1943, while he was at *The New Republic*, he had reprinted in its pages with his own commentary a letter from the *New York Times* written by Shmuel Ziegelboim, an official of the Polish government-in-exile, explaining why the continuing indifference of the West to the destruction of his people left him with no other recourse than to join them by taking his life. Heartbreaking in its calm despair, the letter lodged in Kazin's memory as the voice that personalized the six million, as his cousin in Poland who refused to flee and was shot dead on her doorstep personalized their image. From then on he kept close track of "the murder of my people" and found that "nothing had so unhinged me from my old 'progressivist' belief."

The Holocaust remained the abyss on whose edge he felt that we lived. But during the postwar era he found himself virtually alone among the New York intellectuals who, he said, found it easier to think about Alger Hiss and Whittaker Chambers; and he drew close to Hannah Arendt and her husband, Heinrich Bluecher, who insisted that a decisive break in human history had occurred. Later on, though he defended her at the *Dissent* meeting, he thought her thesis about Jewish responsibility was a willfully misplaced attack on the Jewish leaders that she had always scorned, like most other assimilated German intellectuals. He also regarded the lesson she drew from the Eichmann trial of the banality of evil as appalling German intellectual swank. Nonetheless, he continued to think of her as an "everlasting consolation" because of her spiritual depth and her abiding concern for the public realm as the basis of civilized life that she adapted from classical political thought and that led her to cherish John Adams as the most tutelary of the American Founding Fathers. It was this theory of the *polis* that became the foundation of the *Origins of Totalitarianism* and enabled her to understand and dramatize the unprecedented nature of the two states that had produced the limitless European catastrophe. She and Bluecher were his most kindred spirits after Richard Hofstadter died in 1970, and the strongest influence, I think, on his thought after World War II, reinforcing his view of a new dark age of humanity and complicating his sense of himself as both a leftist and a New York Jew.

9.

By 1975 he had settled down, as much as he ever did, into being a distinguished professor at CUNY and was going through the final years of a notoriously hostile marriage. I heard his beautifully apt eulogy at a memorial for Josephine Herbst, and afterward went up to him to tell him it was. He gave me a perfunctory nod as if to say, What else did you expect from me? Then, toward the end of the '70s, two decades of marital obsession and strife ended for him when he met the writer Judith Dunford. Reading his journal for that year, one sees the sun finally stay out in his life:

> If Judith didn't exist, I could never invent her, ever hope for some-one like her...How to describe her plainness and openness of soul, the honesty, the absolute purity in the smallest details of life—the long-cherished pieces from Chaucer through Yeats to Lear always gushing out. And the fun. "Of course I look like a Latin teacher." Her letters run the blood through me, there is such a fearlessness to her loving.

"There is a God," he said immediately after meeting her for the first time, and she proved to be a godsend in the crisis years that fol-lowed through a divorce whose terms were no less upsetting and onerous than the marriage had been. Moreover, he was now in his mid-sixties and struggling with the condition in which everything begins to decline except the anxiety of ambition and the sense of the distant summons. In his journals, he observes himself turning increasingly to prayer:

> When I lie awake at night, afraid that I am walking though the valley of the shadow of death, I feel that I am still the entangled Brooklyn boy who all his life has depended on His will. . . When I pray to You to give me some peace, to cease this endless clamor of anxiety... I am really asking for relief from my overstrained will, from the determination to do and even to do over what is expected of me. That is what secularism is—the triumph of the individual

will, no matter what the cost to everything crying out in you for another realm of living and being.

Just a thought away from this prayer is the big book he is trying to write, having turned away from the dizzying present to travel back to the first great age of American letters before the Civil War and then come forward once again to the end of the second one in the 1920s. He envisioned *An American Procession* as the assembling of the great tradition of literary individualism and selfhood responding to a century of mounting accumulation of wealth, power and demagoguery. Or, to put it the other way around, he wanted to explore the remarkable phenomenon, often unremarked by those who didn't know America from the inside, that the most dynamic society in Western history had produced as its major characteristic writers, ones so intently concerned with the inner life, who vested so much power and truth in the self, whether Emerson or Hawthorne, Melville or William James. His main companion of this dialectical route is Henry Adams, the firsthand witness of the American dynamo, who as political scion, historian, Washington insider, and autobiographer saw the beginning and thought he saw the end of the accumulation, acceleration, and explosive dispersion of American power as a "planetary event."

An American Procession is Kazin's least coherent book. He not only places Emerson at the head of the line, as Whitman did, but seems to be sometimes under the spell of the cryptic style of Emerson's *Journals*. Instead of the prose of Kazin's literary journalism and memoirs, which generally hangs together despite the pressure of his rushes of thought and feeling, the sentences of *Procession* sometimes do not make a point so much as by free-association encircle several at a time. I quote almost at random:

> Dickinson's poetry must be taken, initially, as a young woman's rebellion. There are obvious cries of frustration, a sexual kittenishness and bravado from the round corner room (her first image of "circumference") in the house on Main Street. She was very late in

accepting restriction on her destiny; it was a game to make restrictions on herself when her brother, Austin, and Susan Gilbert were married and lived next door. Amherst was "old," sedate, churchy, assured. The Dickinsons were important people. The life of an unmarried young woman in the family setting was traditional. Whatever her often self-mocking cries of protest she accepted the setting and the life that came with it.

The final sentence seems to have lost touch with the first one in this very busy account. There is a kind of dispersion of Kazin's own mental energy in these staccato sentences—his mind running full tilt between objective and subjective, fact and inference, explication and implication, biography and criticism, Dickinson's mentality and Kazin's own. Previously he was personal; now he is subjective. Also the book as a whole has a curious bend in its shape and perspective that comes from Kazin's holding the material very close to himself, letting his elderly preoccupations into the design and vision of the book. Thus it begins with the Adams of 1918, an old man in his airy Washington study, warplanes flying nearby, as he contemplates with "his special dryness of heart and mockery...the century of improvement" that is ending in the chaos of world war. Similarly, Kazin begins the first of his two chapters on Emerson with him on his deathbed, his sonorous voice and fragmented mind still working away. The chapter on Thoreau begins with Queequeg's coffin and the chest Thoreau built himself to house the journals that had been his main residence on earth. Hawthorne, too, is first taken up in his frustrated closing years, obsessed with several "tales" he couldn't bring off. The marvelous chapter on Melville comes to rest on his mostly silent, anonymous later years as a New York customs inspector. They are presented less as the authors of specific works than as Emersonian representative men viewed at the point where their shadow lengthens into America's moral history as it resides in Kazin's mind. As such the portraits themselves have an impressionistic effect, the perspective diffused through the details and examples, comparisons and allusions, images and symbols that crowd Kazin's mind and often require a second reading and much contemplation for the figure to come to-gether. This is a book for a patient reader prepared to do a lot of the integrating himself

What most enables one to do so is Kazin's still unfailing instinct for the mentality of a writer and his ability to dramatize it by means of its force and crises. With Thoreau, the turning point comes when his genius for self-completeness and transcendental harmony is over-taken by the reach of the state and the gathering forces of the Civil War; instead of the inspector of snowstorms he becomes the fiery defender of John Brown and of pacifism in the war—a disconnect that can weaken and even kill a man of Thoreau's integrity, which is what Kazin feels happened. With Melville, the great metaphysi-cian and voyager of American literature, there is the long aftermath of his disastrous career: the customs inspector in New York banking the fires of his imagination of the negative, destructive universal and of proto-American imperialism to write his lapidary poems and his final testament in "Billy Budd" of the dark enigma at the heart of things for which only a code of duty provides a little direction. With Mark Twain, there is the immensely successful literary entertainer and entrepreneur turning the nineteenth-century American passion for books about larky youths (the national sentiment) into the discovery of *Huckleberry Finn* in himself and the recovery of his soul in the re-lationship of Huck and Jim.

The radical or at least progressive light that steadily fell across America in *On Native Grounds* is, for the most part, already dimming by the 1840s in *An American Procession*. Instead of the democracy that earlier was producing Emerson's brave new audience of "men and women of some religious culture and aspirations, young, or else mystical," Kazin emphasizes the Emerson who found himself, on his frequent lecture trips, surrounded by a society in which people as-serted the most primitive self-interest and self-importance as "rights," and portrays him as increasingly alarmed that the "multitude have no habit of self-reliance or original action." Twenty years further along in the national destiny, he announces that "the calamity is the masses." Until the Dred Scott decision forces Emerson to think otherwise, the

American problem is not slavery but mediocrity.

Emerson is hardly alone in this respect in Kazin's "great procession." Thoreau could just barely abide his Concord neighbors, whose industry was much less apparent than their alcoholism (one of the well-kept secrets, Kazin notes, of the national mythos). Hawthorne loathed the debased taste of the popular audience. Melville had a highly developed contempt for American society in general and the New York rabble in particular. Mark Twain's view of the democratic populace is pretty much that of the cowardly, gullible crowd that Colonel Sherburne addresses in Huckleberry Finn and is so readily swindled in "The Man Who Corrupted Hadleyburg." And so on to Mencken's boobs and Faulkner's Snopeses, Eliot's carbuncular young man, and the aging Henry Adams's Washington insider's contempt for "the degradation of the democratic process." With the notable exception of Whitman, who identified his genius with American democracy itself, most important modern American writers, including the elder Kazin, himself, are unable to forgive it for the loss of the hopefulness it had inspired. Fitzgerald, for example, has his spokesman, Nick Carraway, turning away from his "crowded, sprawling, disordered, increasingly pointless country" to his solitary vision of "the West's last magic island before the people came."

So ends *Gatsby* and so, too, is soon to end the forward-looking direction of the public American imagination, with its waning legends of a unique and positive destiny, its faith in the individual having turned into the theology of capitalism. As Kazin concludes, the skeptical novelists of the 1940s and thereafter no longer felt the need to wrestle with the huge embracing American subject that one still finds in a writer like Thomas Wolfe; the great subject for them, as John O'Hara had advised, was no longer the rise of modern America. Even before Hiroshima, with writers like Nathanael West and Faulkner, the American dream had edged into the nightmare that anticipates the skeptical literary view of America as an impinging mass society like any other.

Though a good deal of the material in *An American Procession* was pulled together and revised from earlier published essays and lectures (another reason for its unevenness), it still bears the mark of being completed during the early Reagan years, which Kazin regarded as the rock bottom of American politics, and it left him, I think, all the more under the influence of the acerb Henry Adams and his woeful/cynical view of American power rather than of Walt Whitman's democratic vistas of a progressive destiny for its people and fellowship with their poets, which had formed one of the themes of *On Native Grounds*. Or, perhaps, some of the recent exhaustion, diffuseness, and ambivalence of the post-Vietnam American spirit had crept into Kazin's own point of view, and it is hard to know whether to read his book as an American version of the "great tradition," as he began it, or as a "redoing" of the perspective of *On Native Grounds* as it developed.

Reviewed respectfully but quizzically—notably in *The New York Review of Books* by Denis Donoghue, who found it more moving than thought through, *Procession* did not have anything like the impact and staying power of *On Native Grounds*. Bitterly disappointed, Kazin found himself in the late-life crisis of What Then?—confronting in his four A.M. awakenings not only the terror of death but also praying "to get beyond myself to indicate to this believing unbeliever that there is a territory beyond this bundle tied up so angrily in the night. I pray to be relieved of so much 'self,' I asked to be extended."

As his journals show, his turmoil led to the effort to think religiously as well as socially. Not so much about Judaism, though occasionally that, too, but rather about what his favorite American writers had made of religion as, in Whitehead's words, "the vision of something which stands beyond, behind, and within the passing flux of immediate things; something which is real, and yet waiting to be realized...."

As such Kazin wasn't looking for faith so much as company in his own quest: his working title for his next and last major book, *God and the American Writer*, was "Absent Friends." Each of his subjects had used his or her freedom of thought to arrive at a characteristically idiosyncratic spiritual position. As Emily Dickinson, America's greatest religious poet put it, "We thank thee for these strange minds that enamour us against Thee." At the same time, in typical fashion, Kazin pitted their religious individualism against another, opposing American tendency. America was not only the home of the free man's worship but also the nation which, as De Tocqueville saw, had effectively applied the most radical theories of eighteenth-century government, including unlimited free speech without making any headway against the influence of religion.

Kazin began this time with Hawthorne, wanting to see the paradox *ab ovo*, as it were. In the early chapters, however, one feels from the writing that he is going mostly to his mental hard drive for his material, the text sprinkled with familiar themes, pet phrases, allusions, etc. The chapter on Hawthorne makes the interesting point that American individualism begins with the Calvinist view of man steadily fixed in God's scrutiny, but the discussion then becomes mostly an adaptation of a previous introduction to *The Scarlet Letter* and all but ignores the central biographical question it raises of why Hawthorne, who became a full-bore skeptic in his own life, should have been so haunted by the Calvinist/Puritan absolutism. One feels that the real story is being missed, that Hawthorne's preoccupation with the permanence of guilt as the core of religion derives from his own relation to the Puritan subject, which steadily drew his imagination back 150 years, when two of his ancestors, bearing his name, had been leaders of the Salem witch hunts. One feels the pressure of Hawthorne's guilt on his imagination particularly in the closing pages of the novel, when Hester, the life-force in this dismal world, returns to it after leaving her daughter in England and resumes her penitence.

It is only when Kazin gets to Lincoln that the "do-over" machinery stops and fresh biographical and spiritual insight flows in. Carefully and subtly, Kazin builds up his portrait of Lincoln—the firm Unionist slowly giving way to the morally tormented Emancipator; the agnostic, proudly rationalistic lawyer—who had rejected both his parents' old-time religion and the "living Scripture" and battle hymns that North and South drew around their cause—coming very late in his presidency to attach God's will and justice to his own mystical faith in the Union. Like Eric Auerbach in *Mimesis*, developing a paragraph or two of Machiavelli or Stendhal into a ramifying study of the writer and his age, Kazin unpacks from the Second Inaugural the mentality of Lincoln and the climax to the whole terrible course of his ordeal as president that produced the probing, humble, but positive belief that only God's own purposes could account for the horrendous cost of His justice. Thus, by the ordeal of his conscience, will, and humility was Lincoln brought to the extraordinary tone and texture of the address in which he labors both to bind up the wounds of the nation and also to rededicate it to the scourge by the Union sword of the slaveholder's lash.

Some of the same intensity of focus enters Kazin's chapter on Emily Dickinson, who domesticated the last of the Calvinist legacy and dramatized the mystery of death from the household and pew to interplanetary space. So, too, does Kazin bear down firmly and freshly on William James's use of religion that developed out of the terror of life he experienced in himself and witnessed in others. So, too, with Mark Twain, who finally canceled the last of his boyhood Methodism by giving the devil the sensible last word.

As Kazin concludes, the religious side of American writing emerged from a multiplicity of contending theologies, faiths, and sects, and he believes that some of the spiritual aggressiveness of its writers was owing to the contentious circumstances of their rearing as well as to the sovereign uses of the unlimited freedom that as American writers they put them to.

I don't know how much direction his own spirituality received in these years he spent with his "absent friends." What does come through clearly in his other late book, *Writing Was Everything*, is the writers he seemed to draw closest to toward the close of his life were two Europeans whose mind, like Hannah Arendt's, had gone through the fire of the "radical evil" of the age.

The first was Simone Weil, who ministered to the night sweats and lamentations of his overdriven ego by her beautiful thought, among others, that attention without object is the supreme form of prayer. The other was Czeslaw Milosz, the extraordinarily measured witness of both totalitarian regimes in Europe. Along with the Holocaust and "the captive mind," as he called it, of Communism, Milosz brought Kazin back to Blake by his book *The Land of Ulro* (1984), the name Blake had given to "the inhuman, material world," as Kazin puts it, "from which the spiritual imagination leads us to poetry, with its revelation of another order of being." There is nothing more lucid and moving in all of Kazin's writing than the closing pages of *Writing Was Everything*, when he takes Milosz's arm, so to speak, to walk together through the contemporary version of the land of Ulro—not only the poverty, racial conflict, homelessness, drug addiction, remorseless "downsizing," but also, as Milosz remarks, the "very strong feeling of opposed forces of good and evil," the moral relativism that marks "a profound change of mentality and imagination." Reading Milosz's words and Kazin's commentary one senses the latter's profound recall of his own lived experience of what is left of faith "after credulity has vanished from our practical, issue-tormented world," abetted by "our endless defenses and explorations of the ego."

The old issue of "alienation" comes up again, though now in a different form. Where the two briefly part company is Milosz's belief that the East European writers achieved an elemental strength by virtue of their sharing and expressing the burdens of their communities, while the Western writer continues on his "alienated" course of self-involvement, Kazin now puts the matter otherwise: the contemporary writer's alienation is not from society so much as from American literary culture itself that is "content to curse dead white males and rejoice in the loss of tradition." Where they rejoin again is in the shared belief expressed by Milosz's words: "Nothing could stifle my inner certainty that a shining point exists where all lines intersect." Nothing could be more removed from the acid vat of radical skepticism in which postmodernism immerses itself. Nothing could be more essential than their shared certainty that imaginative writing, the making of connections between the facts and the imponderables of existence, is an act of faith that can make the world shine again. What he wrote in his journal in the midst of researching his first book, he believed in to the end:

...To think of Albert Pinkham Ryder and Henry James, of Emerson and Whitman and Dickinson in the same breath, as it were, gives me extraordinary satisfaction. Makers and movers and thinkers-observers in the profoundest sense. I love to think of America as an idea, to remember the adventure and the purity, the heroism and the *salt.*

About a year before Kazin died, there was a celebration of his career at the Center for the Humanities at CUNY. After two days of lectures and readings in his honor (he insisted that the invited writers talk about their work, not his), the event drew to an end with his appearance. As he took the podium, one settled back to receive the heartfelt, valedictory words appropriate to the occasion. There were none. As though he had just stepped out of his office, Kazin began talking about what was on his mind: the thwarted purpose of the Founding Fathers who separated church and state to protect not only the state from religion but also religious belief from the rampant politicizing of it today that was riding roughshod over the separation and debasing the values of both.

That's how I best remember him now: Emerson's American scholar standing up there—civic-minded, forthright, independent, incandescent.

(2003)

V. S. Pritchett:
Autobiography as Art

We seem to be in the middle of a literary age in which the autobiographical impulse is as catching as a virus. In recent months there have been, for example, *The Double Helix*, *Making It*, *North Toward Home*, *Stop-Time*, and *The Armies of the Night*, books of varying purposes and qualities but whose lines of inquiry rely heavily on self-documentation. Meanwhile the contemporary novel has been taking on more and more subjective cargo as the realism of character and place gives way to the spontaneities of improvisation and fantasy, and contact with the world mainly intersects the arc of the novelist's obsessions.

Why there should be this sudden traffic in the revelations and imagery of the self is anybody's guess. Mine is that the faith in the news media, in what one might call certified public reality, has reached an all-time low. This has opened the way to the belief that the only truths worth communicating about human affairs are those perceived in a personal, even idiosyncratic way, the more subjective the point of view, the more unconditioned and therefore valid the report.

Regularly conned as we all are by the agents and media of public reality, which is already difficult enough to grasp as it is, it is not surprising that writers should fall back on sincerity as the ground of truth. Autobiography gives direction to the enterprise, and witnessing—in both senses of the word—confession, and other modes of individual testimony are brought to bear. Directly behind cant, writers seem to be saying, lies the honest truth. Although such writing develops its own cant, a ready esteem for the offensive and daring,

117

the aberrant and perverse, no one loses readers on that count since it then ministers to the kind of psychic voyeurism which, thanks to pop psychiatry, we confuse with insight.

In any event, the result of all this coming clean in print has been a mixed bag of edification and skepticism that would take the rest of this review just to begin to sort out. But, in brief, it has sprung and given new scope to comic talent such as Philip Roth's and has fostered a firm, clear note of contemporary pathos in a writer like Frank Conroy. It has beckoned Mailer on to create an immense checker board of perceptions and distractions in his account of the Pentagon demonstration. Carefully restrained, it can produce the pleasantly personal cultural journalism of *North Toward Home*, and, recklessly pursued, it can lead to the tendentious and purblind self-caricature of *Making It*.

If there is any immediate moral to be drawn, it is that candor does not necessarily provide instant conviction or relevance. An exhilaration to one writer, it fosters doublemindedness, as Kierkegaard would say, in a second, and is clearly a burden to a third. And, like garlic, a little goes a long way, a truth that former ages, less preoccupied with candor and more with inwardness, were willing to accept, without appreciable loss to their knowledge of human nature. This was not just a matter of good taste and an unwillingness of readers to forgo their dignity in being addressed, a right that many have abandoned to keep up with literary fashions. Besides all that, candor is a very tricky motive: the counter-product of malaise, as much as anything else, it is particularly vulnerable to the mutterings of those two conspirators of the ego, guilt and vanity, that establish the "line" we hand ourselves and others. As such, candor requires a great deal of the complexity and effort of art to support its claims to truth.

All of which is prologue to my admiration for V. S. Pritchett's *A Cab at the Door*, the best 250-odd pages of autobiographical writing that I know of by a living author. What makes it so good is that Pritchett is, first of all, a master of the natural, direct style. As with Thoreau or Shaw, open any page and you are immediately in touch with the man. Or, as Pritchett has said of E. M. Forster, when he begins to speak the machine stops.

A Cab at the Door is written with plenty of candor, but it is also written with something even better, which is artistic tact. Reversing the customary procedure in contemporary autobiography—heavy on the self, light on the world—Pritchett places at the center of his memoir a solid and deliciously detailed commentary on lower-middle-class English life in the first two decades of the century, based on his family, educational, and early business experience; meanwhile he modestly lays around the rim the account of his own troubled development as a person and of his inchoate intentions as an artist.

The effect is a beautifully sustained priority of interests in which the depiction of concrete social conditions and forces, of manners and mores, stands almost by itself as a portrait of an age and a class, while serving as the ground that brings out the development of his character. This places the emphasis where most readers would wish to see it—on the way things were rather than how they felt, on the individual life seen less through its accidents than as common experience. This approach also enables Pritchett, both as writer and as subject, to exist naturally and unselfconsciously among his interests and feelings. The result is a splendid montage of persons and places fixed in their individual being, casting their representative light, and suggesting the evolving personality of the author through his relations to them. By this kind of artistic strategy an autobiography turns into a life.

In his criticism, no less than in his fiction or travel writing, Pritchett's great gift has been for characterization, the overflow of relevant, vivid, surprising detail that actualizes a person, a place, a book. Pritchett among the hallowed dead of literature is like Odysseus in Hades: a little of the blood of his critical vitality, and even as spectral a figure as Samuel Richardson immediately begins to speak again and cast his light. Still, one is unprepared for the dramatic sketches of the Pritchett family and the full, dominant portrait of his father. Moreover, if Pritchett brings to his autobiography the gifts and aims of a social novelist, he also belonged to a family that seems especially designed for this enterprise: a veritable treasure trove of individual types. Thanks to the adventurism of his father, whose field of wild oats was commerce—"one of nature's salesmen," as Pritchett delicately puts it, "he was even more one of nature's buyers"—the family lived in a good many different places and circumstances, one step ahead of its creditors. And since the boy was regularly being farmed out to relatives, he led as picaresque a youth as David Copperfield's.

His formative influences began with the austerities of the English north and the laxities of the south:

> On my mother's side they were all pagans, and she a rootless London pagan, a fog worshiper, brought up on the folklore of the North London streets; on my father's side they were harsh, lonely, God-ridden sea or country people who had been settled along the Yorkshire coasts or among its moors and fells for hundreds of years. There is enough in the differences between North and South to explain the battles and uncertainties of a lifetime.

So it proved, at least in the twenty years recounted in *A Cab at the Door*. Family crises sent Victor frequently into his paternal grandfather's household. A man who had pulled himself out of poverty with one mighty lunge from the army and bricklaying into the ministry, he "looked like a sergeant-major who did not drink." His guides were Carlyle and Ruskin as well as the Gospel; a somewhat mellowed authoritarian by Pritchett's time, he urged his iron aspirations on his grandson, and the will to learning and self-improvement and independence Pritchett was to live out began with the influence of this solitary and hardheaded Dissenter. There was also his great-uncle Arthur, a cabinetmaker in York, who had literally taught himself to read with Burton's *Anatomy of Melancholy* and had made himself into an amateur naturalist and antiquarian. From these two resolute figures and their industrious households, one gets a feeling for the powerful religious and economic forces that had created mobility at long last in the working class and enabled it to make its first significant inroads into English culture.

Still, there was a long way to go, and Pritchett speaks of his grandfather as being like an immigrant, so strange to him was his place in the middle class. Exhausted by his early climb and devitalized by the vocation that had enabled it, he was eventually dominated by his fastidious and stuffy wife and by his own dream of status. Pritchett's father inherited the dream and the fastidiousness; in full flight from the rigidity and repressiveness of the minister's household, he became a premature gentleman, addicted to fashions and comforts that his exaggerated sense of opportunity and his superficial resourcefulness never quite earned for him and that had to be purchased at his family's expense. A softheaded business man, a fantasist, his mobility was mostly circular, now tilting upward toward respectability, now downward into sordidness. His religious upbringing led him into various denominations, which he tried on for style, and eventually his obstinacy, expansiveness, and self-righteousness found an abiding stay in the teachings of Mary Baker Eddy, the "other woman" in his life. His relation with his wife, as Pritchett puts it, was "like a marriage of the rich and the poor." A sly, imaginative ex-shopgirl, she vaguely followed with her four children in the turbulent wake of her husband's career, wryly singing to herself "At Trinity Church I met me doom."

Needless to say, Pritchett grew up with deeply ambivalent feelings toward this flashy and unreliable father who still dominated his family in good Victorian fashion ("Until 1918," Pritchett remarks, "England was a club of energetic and determined parricides"). Early on, he can only helplessly accept his father's nutty glory: "We have no desire to see things like the pantomime or Peter Pan; other children see such shows, but we prefer to send Father there on our behalf; it will be one more chapter of his fantastic life." Victor wears cut-down striped morning trousers to one of his slum schools, imbibes his father's myopic view of reality, even takes for a time to Christian Science. "No one else had (I was sure) our dark adventures. We were a race apart, abnormal but proud of our stripes, longing for the normality we saw around us."

But eventually he found he had his own singularities to cultivate.

The first good teacher he encountered led him directly into literature and painting, a deviation which his father, hot for emulation, met with open contempt and secret jealousy. So began Pritchett's long struggle to work himself free of his father's ego, from commerce and religion, from the family mania for "getting on." Visits to his more stable and enlightened relatives helped. So did his busy life in the streets and schools of London and environs, a boy's first line of escape from a neurotic home.

His family settles for a time in Dulwich, Ruskin's neighborhood, and this patron saint of lower-class aspirations beckons him on. The great novelists also begin to offer him some solid ground. One day, in the peace and quiet of the countryside, a sense of purpose forms: "Money would have nothing to do with it...The important thing was to be alone...and always walking and moving away." Prescient but still sad. He remarks on his poor performance in school, on his being "self-burdened," on "the dirty cunning and flightiness of my priggish nature"—that is to say, on being his father's son and suffering from two generations of the Nonconformist vertigo. That he will grow up to be V. S. Pritchett is only a little more surprising at this point than that that he will develop at all.

Yet his brother, who adored his father and therefore remained suitably dull, springs to life once he leaves home and returns from France a success in business. Such is the resilience and toughness of the human stuff. After four years spent in the relative sanity of the leather trade—here the book rises to the most sustained and luminous level of social observation—Pritchett is ready at nineteen to begin his own life in France. His father puts him on the boat train, still self-importantly fussing over him, the elder Pritchett's portly, almost sumptuous manner the mark of the dreamlike appetite that had seduced his own father and perverted himself. Exhausted by their anxieties, hatreds, conflicts, Pritchett has little to say to him; they watch two Italians, father and son, passionately embracing each other.

It is a moment of pure revelation: the profits and losses of the family's long climb into the middle class registered by the contrast. In his modest, unsentimental way, Pritchett quickly passes on to other matters and feelings, but this detail in its setting leaves behind for the reader, as does the memoir as a whole, a very clear sense of the difference between writing as self-display and writing that enables the self, through the tactics and tact of art, to tell its story.

(1968)

Stanley Kauffmann's Albums

In an age of narrow self-interest (both kinds), with memoirs falling from the press like autumn leaves in a high wind, Stanley Kauffmann's *Albums of a Life* is virtually unique. As the title suggests, his purpose in writing about himself, his ways and means over a long lifetime, has no higher, or lower, purpose than to collect memories that fall together around a person, place or subject. As such he is not overtly telling us his inside story or delivering his career, whether for the public record or the annals of gossip, or bending his experience to make some large political or cultural point. Instead of the typically heated prose of the private memoir or the typically flat style of the public one, his tone is crisply genial, warmly objective, the prose of a writer who does not try to dig into or inflate or argue his experience but to commemorate it in an exact, felt, uncoercive way. Like an album of carefully selected photographs that span a lifetime, they are unassuming and they matter. Open any of these discrete, ad hoc remembrances and you touch a rich life.

The axial lines of a life or a career that the conventional memoirist labors to reveal and sustain are mostly left by Kauffmann to the reader's intuition and insight. The precocious city kid, three grades skipped, who submits himself each summer to the hard, exigent routines of farm work becomes father to the writer who rises at 5:30 each morning to grapple with the task at hand, whether a novel or a play or even a Western, who is still sustaining his phenomenal weekly performance as the film critic of *The New Republic* as he enters his 90th year. So, too, the Stanley Kauffmann who spent his coming of age years, ten of them, as the can-do manager of a repertory theater stands behind the later man of many parts—magazine and book editor, both mass- and class- market; major theater as well as film critic; television host of notable figures of the stage and screen; and later one of the mainstays of the Yale Drama School. What is remarkable to me about Kauffmann's accounts of his work life is how little fuss and muss he makes of the literary vocation, most accounts of which are typically redolent of storm and strife, bitching and exulting. The emotional overlay that attends writing on either side of the editorial desk, or performance on either side of the footlights is brushed aside by him, the better to portray what is objectively before his eyes and hence ours. He casts his light rather than standing in it; his prose is a polished window rather than a mirror.

Feeling is the detector that the personal memoirist employs to tell him where in the boundless terrain of memory his ore is and how to tap into it by the tone that the feeling engenders. This tone can be the terse, resonant ambivalence of Kauffmann's album of his mother, a good woman who was confined to her life rather than free to live it, whose reticence comes across as an ache in his soul. Or there are the yearnings and lessons of adolescent desire that flow through Kauffmann's album of the three older woman who introduced him to them, notably the vignettes of the warmly chaste Irish chemistry teacher and of the cooly experienced French proctor, who taught him that "romance was a male invention, licensed by women and sometimes pitied by them."

Except for a passing comparison to the publisher Alfred Knopf, whom Kauffmann worked for, his father is a kind of haunting absence in his gallery of portraits. The more so in that the elder Kauffmann is the evident link to his son's ancestral German past that provides one of the ongoing themes of his identity and of his relationship to the history of his times. Instead there are two albums, the longest and most nuanced in the collection, of father figures. The first is the director, known as CD, of the theater company that was to be Kauffmann's existential home from the age of fifteen until he was well into his twenties; the second is Mister Cohen, as he liked to call his father-in-law, whose strong, challenging character all-but presided over the early years of the marriage. Though markedly different in certain ways—for one, CD was gay and and Mr. Cohen intensely virile— they were both among nature's aristocrats, men who from unprom- ising beginnings—CD from the rural sticks, Mr. Cohen from the immigrant Jewish sweatshops—had turned themselves into models of civilized deportment and intellect: CD "wise, skilled, stoic, courteous, Roman"; Mr. Cohen a businessman whose main interest was read- ing, who joined the workers he managed on a picket line, who "had forged an ethics, intellectual and humane, in the narrow space that the traffic of life had given him." It is hard to separate influence from affinity with respect to values, but the effect of Kauffmann's formative years with CD "who had touched the receding past and who wanted to keep it from receding" is frequently apparent in Kauffmann's inter- ests and taste, particularly so in his attachment to traditional European culture which informs his account of his two deepest and most du- rable friendships—with the aristocratic English writer Giles Playfair and the Hungarian actress Lili Darvas. Indeed, one might say that the animating motive and spirit of *Albums of a Life* itself was born in CD's passion and practice in his stagecraft to touch the past and keep it from receding.

There is nothing like serious love in the memoirist's kit of feelings. In writing as in life, we have much more to say about those who have deeply mattered. We remember more about them quantita- tively and also qualitatively (vividness, complexity, nuance) because they fund our memories with imagination, strong emotion, and care- ful discrimination so that in writing about them we are most keenly writing about the better part of ourselves. (Hate can have a similar excavating power but generally it is driven by one attitude rather than love's medley.) Moreover, a serious early love tends to wax and wane over the course of time which provides the memoirist with a natural dramatizing element, a source of power and complexity. This, too, makes the albums of CD and Mr. Cohen particularly striking and subtle as Kauffmann assiduously details the coming apart as he did the coming together of both relationships, the wages of time and temperament, tacitly adopting and adapting the role from the model, turning wide-eyed admiration into circumspect judgment, eventually leaving Kauffmann to sustain their mutual "mettlesome" manliness in his own life.

And so he does, through thick and thin. Whether he is telling us about his stint as the drama critic of the *New York Times* or as a play doctor of Broadway trash, as the editor who discovered Walker Percy at Alfred A. Knopf or handled three comic books at Tappan Publications, who volunteered as a hospital orderly during WW II or literally loved to kill hogs as a summer farmboy—there is the same simple, expensive black dress of his prose, the same gift for telling description, the same moral attentiveness that has made his weekly film column in *The New Republic*, as Susan Sontag put it, "a national resource" for four decades and counting. With his characteristic tone of matter-of-factness underpinned by self-confidence, Kauffmann attributes his career to his discipline, and one of the interests of reading these albums in order, which I recommend, is to watch the career of a stout-hearted professional writer adapting to the vicissitudes of this life.

His consistency of behavior and morale flies in the face of the modern and, even more, the post-modern notion of character which views integrity, both psychological and moral, as a dissimulation, floating on the swamps of the self where our real motives breed their energies and conflicts. Kauffmann doesn't deconstruct himself, he doesn't provide the low-down, as we aptly call it, that is the staple of the contemporary memoir and that earlier ages had little interest in and taste for. His album of working on a book with Marilyn Monroe has the same composure as the one of the sadly unlikely women he interviewed to be his assistant. The suicide of Mr. Cohen is foretold not only as a narrative strategy but to eschew any possibility of melodrama.

The one experience which shakes Kauffmann's sturdy sense of himself is the trip he made to Germany with a group of American writers. Since World War II and the Holocaust, he had been mildly troubled by his German-Jewish ancestry, by his being spared the fate of those whose families didn't emigrate in time. This had been reinforced by his exemption from service in World War II in which he might have confronted the Nazi nemesis and is joined to the more general feeling of "being only distantly connected to the core of my century . . . an [unmarked] visitor, observer, escapee." It is only when he finds himself bowled over by a German professor of philosophy, a world-class mind, who had formerly worked on the atom bomb for Hitler that he comes to grips with this shadow fate in a remarkable passage in "Album of My Germany." Instead of being appalled by this man who "had been laboring to kill me," Kauffmann finds himself admiring him not only for his warm civility and intellect but for what had been "harrowed, sickened, transformed" by a shame that Kauffmann "incomprehensibly," as he says, wishes to share. Literally frightened by this jolt of consciousness, he wishes it to remain incomprehensible. But to my mind it is perhaps a manifold outcropping of character—not only the tribute that the spared pay to the participant, particularly the participant in what he has been spared, but even more to the point the characteristic tribute that the Jew pays to the German in the *yekke* mentality which Kauffmann had, to some degree, inherited and which has only now come to the fore. Finally, it is the tribute that one classy intellectual pays to an even classier one, the more readily so in this case because Kauffmann's sensibility eagerly crosses borders, is essentially cosmopolitan, though his effort to start a new career in London ends by confirming that his place is in America.

One will read this book for its evocative portraits—large, small and diverse; for its tours of different walks of life, both rough and smooth, for the happenstance and assiduous making of a gratifying life with his wife Laura, who is discreetly present virtually throughout it, turning up every so often as its guarantor and guardian. As I turn through these albums in my mind, it comes to rest on the word *refined*, a mentality and deportment, steeped in the past and quietly active in the present, which our two post-immigrant generations, Kauffmann's and mine, were brought up to aspire to and whose currency has dramatically and dismally fallen. Catch and savor it while you can in the following pages.

(2007)

The Cheever Chronicle

A writer who maintained an intense privacy through most of his career, John Cheever has been transformed in the decade since his death into a kind of Exhibit A of hidden damage in the trial of the literary life before the bar of publicity. In Cheever's case, the skeleton of his problems and misdeeds has flung open the closet door, with no little assistance from his family. His daughter, Susan, has expanded her cool exposure of him in *Home Before Dark* into an acerbic tour of three generations of "the family jungle" in *Treetops*, while his older son, Ben, has eagerly filled in the blanks of salacious information and innuendo in his edition of Cheever père's letters. Now we have *The Journals* in which Cheever himself is thrust upon the stand to provide full disclosure of the dissolute life he bled into his fiction.

About five years ago, when the journals were put on the market, a colleague and I from Harper & Row visited Ms. Cheever to look through the twenty-eight thick notebooks that constituted the last remains of her father's vocation. Given the growing notoriety of his secret life, his relationships with such figures as Malcolm Cowley, Eleanor Clark and Robert Penn Warren, Saul Bellow, John Updike, Philip Roth et al., his frequent stays at Yaddo, his long association with *The New Yorker*, as well as his own significance as a fictional craftsman and social observer, I thought his journals might be very valuable, though hardly worth the cool one million the family was asking.

What these badly typed, misspelled and often unstrung entries contained was mainly a monotonous account of the Westchester round of visits and parties and a naked but less-than-riveting one of the at-home dissipations and marital distress of a mostly depressed and money-driven man. Now and then a trip into New York or elsewhere, a good morning's work at the desk or an afternoon of yard work, touch football or the opportunity to "have my way" with his wife would raise his spirits and eyes to the world and some interesting and moving passage would result. But these were few and far between: The image of Cheever that settled in my mind was of a writer who had just masturbated (he kept a record of that), doodling in the margins of his despair or boredom or occasional euphoria while waiting to hit the bottle. After a couple of hours my colleague and I shrugged to each other and prepared to leave. I asked the noncommittal Ms. Cheever who would be editing the material and was told that she and her brother would. Well, I thought, a woman had to be pretty tough to have survived the shambles of the home life I'd just glimpsed. Walking back to the office, I thought of Owl-Eyes' remark about the dead Gatsby, which Dorothy Parker repeated as she gazed at Fitzgerald's bier—"The poor son-of-a-bitch."

So I was very surprised and not a little crestfallen to find myself fascinated by the excerpts of the journals that began appearing in *The New Yorker* last year. By the magic of editing, his daily life had shed its monotony, the suppleness and precision of his style had been detected and restored, triumphing over his "forlornities," as he put it, and his moments of joy, perceptiveness, circumspection and courage had been brought out to light and lighten the reader's journey. Now we have a full version of the passages that the editor, Robert Gottlieb, has carved out—about 5 percent of the total wordage—and my admiration for his editing is even greater since he has turned it into a cohesive text that presents Cheever's inner life in what might be called a final draft: concise, lucid, moving, and brimming with implications. Not since *Look Homeward, Angel*, as far as I know, has there been an editorial feat like this one.

There is one important aspect of Cheever's personality that I picked up in my reading of the original journals that has been omitted from the published one except for some discreet references to the "dream girls" he was wont to summon once or twice a day or to his "sore cod": His compulsive masturbation contributed a good deal to his sense of being unmanned and unstrung. Since I looked at only about one-fourth of the journals, I can't say how steadily and intensely it persisted. Nor do I raise it to darken his image further. The compulsion is common among writers, the last of the loves that dares not confess its name. As one novelist recently put it, "Writers jerk off more than anyone else because they're alone so much and it's such a convenient fix for all the anxiety and frustration." Its characterological and vocational significance of course, varies from one of us to the next. In Cheever's case his intense shame points up the struggle between the adolescent and the adult in his nature that is often apparent in *The Journals* and that kept him standing on a dime, psychologically speaking, for much of his career.

The popular view of Cheever these days is that he was tormented by his bisexuality and that the drinking was his way of assuaging the frustration and anxiety it bred. There is little evidence for that in *The Journals*. His bisexuality often turns up in the more ramifying context of the standoff, embalmed in alcohol, between the boy and the man. The following passage comes at a point when Cheever was in his mid-50s, going through one of his brief periods of psychotherapy and yet another marital crisis:

> I drink heavily because I claim to be troubled. We talk about the shrink at the table, and I expect I talk with drunken rancor. We go to a third-rate movie and, leaving, I cry. "Why, when I asked if the bulk of our life had not been happy, did you not reply?" "My look," she said, "was my reply."...I have one drink, no more, and sit on the stone steps. I think myself youthful, even boyish in my misery. I stretch out on the stones, sobbing, until I realize that I am exactly in the position of a doormat.

There is much of Cheever's plight in this entry. His frequent mood swing from resentment to self-pity pivoted on his fast dependency on Mary Cheever, which was cemented by her emotional and sexual aloofness. His term for it was her *maldisposta*, which runs through *The Journals* like a leitmotif of plaintive resentment or resignation. This adhesiveness to her moods was actually a compound, one part of which came from his relationship to his mother, who was also an independent and baiting woman named Mary, and, in the words of Cheever's biographer Scott Donaldson, "not given to shows of affection." Because of his father's alcoholism and improvidence, she became the family breadwinner, running a gift shop that enabled the family to hang on to its shabby respectability by its fingertips, which were to remain sore and exigent in John's case—the Westchester squire even though he was renting the coach house of the estate. His mother resented doing the housework, which often fell to him, another early experience that he sometimes bleakly refers to in *The Journals* in the course of grumbling about his role in his marriage as a househusband. When Mary Cheever took up college teaching and began to go her own way, the two sectors of Cheever's twice-born life, which he had labored to keep separate since leaving home for good at 18, came together and locked.

The passage I quoted above continues:

> I sleep in my own bed, although this seems to be an indignity. I wake at dawn, crying, "Give me the river, the river, the river," but the river that appears has willows and is winding and is not the river I want. It looks like a trout stream, so I cast with a fly and take a nice trout. A naked woman with global breasts lies on the grassy banks and I mount her. She is replaced by Adonis, and, while I fondle him briefly, it seems like an unsuitable pastime for a grown man. . . . I take a pill this morning, and it seems best for me to take full responsibility for everything that has gone wrong. There is no point in recounting to myself rebuffs, wounding quarrels, etc. One has come through much; one will come through this.

Readers of *Bullet Park* will remember the young and stricken Tony Nailles crying out in his sleep, "Give me the mountains, the mountains." The passage represents a characteristic move of Cheever's spirit from childishness to maturity and from despair to determination along the sure route of his feeling for the natural world and the tricky one of his hyperactive, dual eroticism, he regarding his gayness as immaturity, his straightness, when requited, to feeling like a man.

Donaldson raises the possibility that Cheever and his older brother Fred may have been lovers, following hints from Cheever himself. What is indisputable is their unusual intimacy. Unwanted and unloved by his feuding parents—"I have the characteristics of a bastard," he writes at one point—he improvised a succession of father figures, but his main resource was the care and support he received from Fred. After he left home they lived and traveled together, and it was Fred's money that enabled him to begin a second life as a writer. But there was a crucial lacuna in his adolescence when his brother was away at college that continued to haunt him and that he was condemned to refrequent psychologically. He writes of the "galling loneliness of my adolescence" that was still assailing him at the height of his career: "the sense of the voyeur, the lonely, lonely boy with no role in life but to peer in at the lighted windows of other people's contentment and vitality."

Cheever's adolescent fixations, his "damaged consecutiveness of growth," appear in various contexts. The day that his second son, interestingly named Federico, was born, he writes: "I don't ever remember loving a child so much"—but though filled with paternal well-being, he finds himself gazing at some young men in an open car and "coveting their freedom." So with others—a male washing himself from a bucket or pulling off his swimming trunks or taping an oar would be glimpsed for a moment and remembered for years. The furtiveness and daring of early sexuality also played a large role in his homoerotic excitements: his attraction to boys and men would often disappear as soon as any more normative social connection was made. Watching someone cunningly expose "his whatsit" in the men's room in Grand Central Station, he is tempted to throw himself into an "erotic abyss" as well as to "make some claim for man's wayward and cataclysmic nature." Then, true to form, he returns home, takes Federico swimming and is restored to the manly virtues—"Decency, courage, resoluteness."

His relationship to Federico also has an adolescent cast, as though he were more like a big brother than his father. His son Ben received a good deal of his anxiety and guilt in the name of discipline and criticism; his daughter is typically either annoying or mystifying. But as the younger son, like Cheever himself, Federico was a piece of perfection: "How my whole love of life seems to gather around his form; how he fills me with the finest ambitions," and so on for the next fifteen years, the person, besides himself, for whom he remained married and mostly home-bound. His terror of loneliness was such that he viewed divorce as a life sentence to some sordid furnished room, and even in the worst stretches of Mary's *maldisposta* and his own immobilizing depressions, he could "count on touching my younger son at breakfast as a kind of link, a means of staying alive."

Read in the light and shadows of *The Journals*, Cheever's fiction tends to take on a certain unity until *Falconer*, his final novel, when he kicked his alcoholism and the adult in him finally triumphed over the anxious, lonely and subversive boy. Through most of his career the conflict between them informed his work as a kind of tense lyrical moralism in which the inner waywardness and discontent beat against the bulwarks of propriety, responsibility and well-being. In many of the stories his virtually interchangeable protagonists carry the haut-bourgeois burden of obligations which when put down results in a pratfall of panic or humiliation: a child is temporarily lost, an adulterer is shamed, a liar is exposed, a failed businessman reduced to house breaking is terrified—before the beneficence of life, often borne in by the natural world, intervenes and the moral order reasserts itself, "the obdurate truths before which fear and horror are powerless," as he put it, whistling in the dark of his melancholia. Cheever's lesser stories are emotionally constrained and typically settle for a kind of wry headshake over the vices and follies of human nature, the strain of its social arrangements, the ironies of its providence. When he is bearing down hard in his stories, the family man forsakes his burden, the family pathology is exposed, the stupidity and cruelty of the ad agency or other genteel commerce assert themselves. When the destructive element Cheever knew so well is given its full say, one gets the surrealism of the Fall through the amenities and assurances of polite society into the hell that lurks in his best stories—such as "The Housebreaker of Shady Hill," "Torchsong," "The Swimmer," "Goodbye My Brother," "The Death of Justine"—where the punishments of guilt are let loose, nightmarish-like, in the daily world.

His own best critic, the Cheever of *The Journals* worried about his "confined talents." Alongside the magnitude of *The Naked and the Dead*, "my autumn roses and winter twilights seem not to be in the big league." Or there is Bellow's "big, wild, rowdy country. . . and here I am stuck with an old river in the twilight and the deterioration of the middle-aged businessman." As time went on he increasingly deplored his lack of development. Compared with writers who are much closer to him in milieu and temperament, such as Updike or William Trevor, his power of invention seems cruelly curtailed and his exploration of modern life hugs the shoreline of a small homogeneous community of the privileged and ungrateful, who re-enact his "wanton disappointments" ("Why should so many of us struggle to forget our happy lot?") as viewed by the old-line moralism of his New England upbringing ("Is it the ineradicable strain of guilt and vengefulness in man's nature?").

Seldom has such a sensitive and subtle observer, as evidenced by *The Journals*, written so patly so much of the time in his fiction. One could say that his money problems drove him to write for magazines that wanted mostly small and not-too-bitter doses of social and personal conflict. But when Cheever gave himself more autonomy and scope, as in the two Wapshot novels, his imagination shows little questing power, his narrative ability weakens over the longer haul, and one gets a series of incidents and ruminations connected by a mood. *The Wapshot Chronicle* (1957), though much praised in its time, reads today like an exercise in nostalgia, paper-thin in its social texture of the thirties and forties, a regression to the dawn of the modern novel in its technique. *The Wapshot Scandal* (1964) is also a mood novel, this time a vehicle for Cheever's mordant but mostly esthetic response (shopping malls, subdivisions) to the rootlessness and barbarism of postwar America. Its structure reminds me of a man trying to hold together a bead necklace whose string has broken, and its bewildered characters portray the emptiness of the American scene mostly by lamely imitating it.

In *Bullet Park* (1969) Cheever returns to his base, and much of his earlier ease and conviction concerning the Westchester gentry are again in evidence in the first part, though hardly deepened. But structurally and dramatically the novel then becomes a botch: two novellas in different modes joined by an attempted murder that comes out of the blue. Written in a period when Cheever's alcoholism and marriage were hitting bottom, its principal interest and poignancy is in Cheever's objectification of his twin demons of drink and melancholia in the characterization of Hammer and of his guardian spirit of rectitude embodied in the troubled, addicted but upright Nailles. The absurd ending, in which Nailles rescues his son Tony with his chainsaw (Cheever's favorite tool) from Hammer's mad clutches, only adds to the inadvertent pathos of the fable.

While giving much richer and more harrowing expression to his understanding of how "the force of life is contested," *The Journals* have some of the same hemmed-in narrowness of Cheever's oeuvre. For years at a stretch not much changes except the hour at which he begins drinking, which grows earlier and earlier. "My best hours are from five to six," he writes at one point, by which he means a.m.. However much personal nuance there may be to a life at bay, it inexorably repeats itself and one begins to long for the kind of material of literary and social interest that the journals of an Evelyn Waugh or Edmund Wilson provide. The fifties, the sixties, the seventies go by with seldom even a nod in the direction of the public dramas of McCarthyism, the civil rights movement, the cultural revolution, the Vietnam War, Watergate and so forth. The hoax of Updike's death draws forth a splendid impromptu eulogy that makes one regret all the more Cheever's reticence about other writers. He mentions an author he is reading such as Borges or Nabokov or Hemingway, drops a tantalizing opinion and returns to his self-reflections, his local and travel notes, his family's behavior, his "chains formed by turf and house paint," his flings, his moral temperature-taking. After a couple of hundred pages one begins trying to keep track of the initials by which most of the people he encounters are identified, simply to stay interested.

However, there is a change of tone and a more objective focus in the last years. His love life finally stabilizes in a guilt-free association with the devoted M., he and Mary stop relating to each other like two hostile porcupines, the wealth and fame he has been craving come with *Falconer* (1977). The sobriety of the recovering alcholic enabled him finally to sustain an entire novel and to venture deep into "the stupid pageantry of judgment" that prison life represented and enacted—his personal subject at last finding a new and challenging home. Writing with the liberation from his played-out stamping grounds (except about Farragut's wife), Cheever displays the same passion and empathy in *The Journals*.

His record of his last year lived in the world of cancer is a remarkable document in itself, climaxed by a stunning incident when he and other chemotherapy patients are joined by a beautiful bald woman with "a look of absolute victory on her face." Cheever's joy in her "air of having bested the tumors and carnage of the disease" became in this reader's mind a recognition of his victory over his own psychic tumors and carnage. Or again, he talks to his dogs of the first snowfall of his life that he will not be able to work or sport in, and their imperturbability prompts him to ask himself, "Whatever made me think that I would live forever?" This is Cheever giving up the narcissism of a lifetime, an outcropping of the steady manliness he was always asking of himself and which, in his last years, he made come true.

(1991)

A Witness of Vietnam

In April, 1969 I was invited to Honolulu as one of the guest speakers of the Young President's Organization. The honorarium was the opportunity to live like the head of a multimillion-dollar corporation for five days. Just down the way from the Waikiki Hilton was the Army's R & R center, whose beach was filled with young men on their five-day furlough from Vietnam. Though I found myself wandering down there a lot, there wasn't much to feel about these soldiers. Sunbathing, playing touch football, chatting up girls, or lying quietly with their wives, they seemed more like the college crowd at Jones Beach than the temporary survivors of a vicious war.

On the final evening, I ducked out of the banquet and went for a walk. It was around midnight and the road took me past the Army center. A line of green buses was drawn up there, and they soon were filled with soldiers and drove off, leaving behind a small group of young women. One of them walked away ahead of me, and I watched as her shoulders began to shake.

Though we were then four years into the war this was the first time its effect on the lives of the other America had come home to me. It was not only that weeping girl but those buses returning their passengers as surreptitiously as possible to the carnage, while six hundred yards away another group of Americans lived it up, some of them no doubt on profits from the war, and remained as oblivious of the human costs as the Army authorities meant them to be. As the government meant the rest of the country to be.

Though this little epiphany stayed with me, I wasn't much changed by it. I quickly went back to viewing the war through the abstracting lens of my politics, which readily converted the soldiers, marines, and pilots I saw on TV into the sacrificial dupes or violent zealots of Nixon and Kissinger. The only servicemen who were real to me were the veterans who opposed the war; they and, of course, Lieutenant Calley, who confirmed the worst. Then the war ended and, like most Americans, I put it out of mind, except when the Watergate revelations provided an oblique kind of retributive justice.

Which brings me to *A Rumor of War*, whose title expresses the remoteness I have been trying to characterize but whose pages steadily obliterate it. The author, Philip Caputo, achieves this by the relentless immediacy of his descriptions of this "war of endless dying" (quite equal to the World War II writing of Mailer and very little since); by the acuity of his comments on the psychological and moral devastation of fighting a "people's war"; and, most to the point, by placing himself as a marine lieutenant directly before the reader and giving the American involvement a sincere, manly, increasingly harrowed American face.

If you've had much contact with the upper reaches of blue-collar America, you'll know Caputo right away. Though he went on to become a foreign correspondent for the *Chicago Tribune*, he is still closely in touch with the earthy, hot-blooded, ambitious, adventurous kid who grew up with a fly rod or a .22 in his hands in a tract-house development out on the prairie west of Chicago. He doesn't tell us much about his background, but it's easy to imagine him as the hard-nosed player who wants the ball when the game is on the line; also as the English major who now and then asks a question that cuts through the literary cant. In short, to use David Halberstam's phrase, Caputo was among "the best and the brightest" of the social class that fought the war. As such he is an excellent witness and interpreter of men, much like himself, who came from the "ragged fringes of the Great American dream," who embodied its "virtues as well as flaws: idealistic, insolent, generous, direct, violent, and provincial." And from being their articulate and troubled spokesman he draws much of his fierce will to make you listen and much of his authority.

His career in the Marines was no less representative and expressive. In the early 1960s he signed up with the Marine ROTC because he was sated with "security, comfort, and peace" and "hungered for danger, challenges, and violence" that would test his manhood. Hence the Marines. At the same time he was full of the altruism of the Kennedy years and was eager to respond to the ringing exhortation of the Inaugural Address. Hence his thrill in March 1965 to be an officer in the first combat unit sent to Vietnam. After about a year, most of it spent in the field, Caputo was charged with ordering the murder of two Vietnamese civilians, of which he was ambiguously, understandably, and, by then, almost inevitably guilty.

A Rumor of War is thus the true story of the transformation of one of the "knights of Camelot," whose "crusade" was Vietnam and whose cause could only be "noble and good," into a vindictive, desperate, and chronically schizoid killer in a war that he had come to realize was futile and evil. As Emerson put it, "the lengthened shadow of a man is history": the course and character and damage of America's involvement was registered on Philip Caputo's body, mind, nerves, and spirit.

The causes and stages of his transformation form the spine of his narrative. It begins with his account of his summers at Quantico, where reserve officer training differed little from the fabled sadism of marine boot camp. Along with the physical ordeals and mental abuse, there was the brainwashing in the classrooms and mess halls: the voices chanting in unison "Ambushes are murder and murder is fun," or a litany about the Marine Corps' invincibility, ending with "Gung Ho! Gung Ho! Gung Ho! Pray for War!" All of which, as Caputo observes, was "designed to destroy each man's sense of self-worth…until he proved himself equal to the Corps' exacting standards." Though he saw through much of this cult of "machismo bordering on masochism," he was also driven to embrace it by his overwhelming desire to succeed as a marine officer. His most significant experience was being chewed out for smoking during a maneuver, which he believes lastingly reinforced his fear of criticism and his yearning for praise. "By the time the battalion left for Vietnam, I was ready to die…for a few favorable remarks in a fitness report."

Though lean and mean, his head filled with the jargon and tactics of "counterinsurgency," adapted from the British success in Malaysia, Caputo was not prepared for Vietnam—not for its climate or terrain or its phantomlike enemy. As soon as his company moved away from guarding the airfield near Danang and began to practice its "spirit of aggressiveness," what had been "a splendid little war" became miserable, terrifying, and absurd. Their search-and-destroy missions were mostly in the Annanese Cordillera, mountainous rain forests which "the Vietnamese themselves regarded with dread." There the heat was awesome, "a thing malevolent and alive," capable of inflicting a stroke by raising a marching man's body temperature to 109 degrees. The jungle was all but impenetrable: elephant grass that cut through field uniforms; bamboo thickets and vines that had to be hacked through with machetes; barricades that were likely to be mined; trails made deadly by almost invisible trip lines, sniper fire, ambushes. Into this nightmare green world where, as Caputo remarks, the whole NVA could easily have been concealed, the helicopters would fly in a couple of rifle companies. Moving at the torturous rate of three or four miles a day, they might, if successful, flush out and kill a handful of Viet Cong and have only that many marines hit or blown apart. The mental strain, if possible, was worse than the physical: a file of men desperately bunching up, despite the danger of an ambush, because "even the illusion of being alone in that haunted dangerous wilderness was unbearable."

It took only one such mission for Caputo and his company to revert to the primal fears and lusts that Hobbes described as the state of nature. At the outset, when a platoon of VC, heavily outnumbered, is spotted and shelled, Caputo feels sorry for them: "I [still] tended to look upon war as an outdoor sport and the shelling seemed, well, unfair." But once they attack the ridge, one man shoots a wounded VC in the face, another slices off ears, and Caputo himself, having picked up a VC's bloody spoor, suddenly realizes that he doesn't really want to take him prisoner. "All I wanted to do was kill him—waste the little bastard and get out of that dank, heat-rotted ravine." Afterward, he remarks, "we felt like ghouls."

Murderous rages followed by guilt and remorse and the sense of degradation continue to stalk Caputo. On staff duty for a few months, he finds himself mainly keeping track of the casualties on the American side, the "kill ratios" and "body counts" on the VC's. Identifying the shattered bodies of men he served with, receiving a report on the fatal wounds of his best friend, he begins to dream of leading a platoon of resurrected corpses and suffers hallucinations in which a man's dead face peeks through the living one. His mind begins to split under the pressure of his obsessive fury, grief, guilt, as the casualties and atrocities steadily mount during the NVA offensive. Finally, he manages to return to line duty, but the monsoon season has begun and the torments of the summer campaign are but a prologue to those that follow.

With each month he appears to have more fury to burn, more moral numbness to account for in needlessly destroyed villages and hamlets. He wrestles with the mockeries of the "rules" of engagement: "it was wrong for an infantryman to destroy a village with phosphorus grenades but right for a fighter pilot to drop napalm on it." He concludes that military ethics seemed to be a matter of killing people at long range with sophisticated weapons. But the actuality was the official American strategy of "organized butchery." In his final month of duty, the commander of his half-decimated company is offering a can of beer "and the time to drink it" for any enemy casualty.

Caputo's book is not as relentless as I am making it appear to be. It is not meant to be one long damning indictment of a war that demoralized and brutalized him. There is the humane as well as the sadistic, sometimes together: two grunts rubbing salve on a baby's jungle sores while their officer threatens to pistol whip the uncooperative mother. There are the frequent accounts of the loyalty and concern of American troops bonding together not only for survival but to preserve their humanity. There are Caputo's close, brilliant accounts of the exhilaration and tension of combat: the heightening of the senses and mind to a pitch of acuity. There is his almost "orgasmic" pleasure of leadership when his company responds perfectly under the stress of battle. There is the transcendent moment when Caputo's fear of death disappears: "I would die as casually as a beetle is crushed under a boot heel....My death would not alter a thing. I had never felt an emotion more sublime or liberating."

But this moment also marks a further stage of numbing. Indifferent to his own death, he is still ravaged by anxieties and deliriums of violence about his steadily dwindling company. When a village boy reports that he knows of two VC in an adjacent hut and when nothing is done about it, Caputo frantically decides to capture them. He sends in a team of his most reliable sharpshooters: "If they give you any problems, kill 'em." As he then admits, "In my heart I hoped Allen would find some excuse for killing them and Allen had read my heart." When the two bodies are duly brought in, one of them is the boy who gave the information.

What was Caputo's degree of guilt? By the time one reaches this culminating incident, one believes him when he says, "Something evil had been in me that night." One also believes him when he says, "The war in general and U.S. military policy in particular were ultimately to blame for the death of Le Du and Le Dung." One wants to see Caputo exonerated, which he was. For the ultimate effect of this book is to make the personal and the public responsibility merge into a degreeless nightmare of horror and waste, suffered by young men like Caputo, ignored and concealed by the policy makers. Out of the force of his obsession with the Vietnam War and his role in it, Caputo has revealed the broken idealism and suppressed guilt of America's involvement. And listening to his honest voice, one's own conscience begins to stir again though more complexly than it did ten years ago.

(1977)

The Young Camus

When the Greenwich Village Independent Democrats decided to support Humphrey after all, a spokesman dignified their retreat by quoting...guess who? "'In this absurd world, the only thing one can do is make choices.' Hubert Humphrey is not my choice. But..." One hardly needs Camus for that kind of reasoning. But if he speaks now from the grave, as he does virtually every day, it is usually to confer some sort of moral authority on other men's positions or prose. His reputation seems more and more fungible; his work has been carved up into quotations—a kind of *Bartlett's* of liberal piety, which now only awaits an edition. During their famous fight, Sartre said that Camus carried a "portable pedestal." It was partly true, just as it is partly true to say that Sartre has carried a portable barricade: high and mighty writers, after all, need something to mount; generally it is the image of their self-esteem as spokesmen. Be that as it may, Sartre's remark has proved prophetic. If it is hard to know what to think about Camus, it is partly because one has lost sight of the man inside the statue.

A good way to begin seeing Camus himself again is by reading a new collection of his prose titled *Lyrical and Critical Essays*. The "lyrical" part contains his first two books—*L'Envers et l'endroit* (*The Wrong Side and the Right Side*) and *Noces* (*Nuptials*)—which he wrote in his middle twenties after a recurrence of tuberculosis, and which are often so bleak or ardent in feeling, despite their diffuseness, that they immediately begin to reveal the human clay beneath the bronze. Written at times in imitation of the self-commemorative, sentencious meditation which is virtually a genre of French prose ("If it is true that the only paradises are those we have lost, I know what name to give the tender and inhuman something that dwells in me today"), *The Wrong Side* and *Nuptials* also show a hard hand inside the stylish glove. The essay that begins on the above note ends on this one:

> But I must break this too limp and easy curve [of the absurd]. I need my lucidity…—It's men who complicate things. Don't let them tell us any stories. Don't let them say about the man condemned to death: "he is going to pay his debt to society," But: "They're going to chop his head off." It may seem like nothing. But it does make a little difference. There are some people who prefer to look their destiny straight in the eye.

The last statement is no mere gesture. At twenty-four, Camus' "destiny" was staring coldly back at him, and even his elegant paradoxes were bitterly true. Not much has been written about Camus' youth, but he appears to have been one of those vital, able, manly kids who somehow manage to raise themselves in the slums. His father had died in World War I; his mother supported him by working as a maid. His revolts began early. From his family's poverty and sadness he escaped to the Algerian beaches, whose sunlight and surf, as he claimed, molded his spirit. A talented swimmer and boxer, he was also the goalkeeper on a crack soccer team by the time he was fifteen. Despite his family's illiteracy, he was a star pupil, moving from scholarship to scholarship until he became the protégé of the philosopher and stylist Jean Grenier. When he was seventeen he came down with tuberculosis and rebelled against that too: he completed his course in philosophy, married at twenty and also became the lightweight champion of Algiers. But at twenty-three his tuberculosis recurred. This harsh confrontation of so much vitality and apparent fatality lies directly behind the life-death dialectic that forms the theme of these first two books.

From the start, as throughout his career, Camus felt more lucidly than he reasoned. His ideas were the home truths of his experience, linked less by logic than by their emotional fit and weighted by their existential consequences. "I have never seen anyone die," as he put it, "for the ontological argument." Just as his theme of the absurd came directly from his life, so did its resolution—the conquering indifference in which he had been raised. His emotions had been shaped by his mother's detachment and solitude as surely as his physical élan was nurtured by the climate and mores of Algiers. He writes of her as weak-minded and inarticulate. She apparently had been brainwashed by her own mother, who raised Camus and who liked to make him say, in company, that he loved his grandmother more than his mother. Loving his mother so passionately and hopelessly ("she has never hugged or kissed [me] for she wouldn't know how"), Camus always felt himself to be enclosed within her isolation and indifference. In the 1957 preface to *The Wrong Side*, he writes that his real work will begin only when he has rewritten this first book and placed at its center "the admirable silence of a mother and one man's effort to rediscover a justice or a love to match this silence."

All of which gives a seriousness and poignancy to these youthful meditations on the divided aspect of being. His first essay, "Irony," presents three stark descriptions of the "horrible and dirty adventure of dying," as he later puts it: a moribund, clinging old woman whom her daughter and boyfriend desert to go to the movies, leaving her in the darkness that is "her only hope" and with the "God she loves so poorly"; an old café chatterer who realizes that the end has come because there is no one left in the world who wants to listen to him; and, finally, Camus' grandmother, who is rudely overtaken by the death whose imminence she has been feigning. Her death redeems nothing about her; the only thing about it that moves him is the radiance of the winter afternoon on which she is buried, whose serene and remote sky points up the sordid negations he has been describing.

Throughout *The Wrong Side*, Camus continues to think against the grain of sentiment, to station himself in the "steady breeze blowing in from the dark horizon of his future" that his Meurseult discovers only as his life is ending. Struggling for an affirmation that is completely free of hope, he views himself as the uprooted stranger he discovers during a week of utter solitude in Prague, climaxed by a man dying alone in an adjacent room in his hotel, and during a week in Italy, whose warm, bare countryside revives his love of life and connects it to his despair. Nothing of his daily existence in Algiers is allowed to intrude, for he wishes to strip himself of the familiar and secure, of the little acquiescences and illusions on which he, like other men, study and work and marry, on which humanity gets by. Thus, he is drawn to the inhuman: his mother's "animal silence," the depraved gleam in the eyes of a cat that has been eating the litter she could not feed, the moment at the bottom of a night of fever when the world "has melted away, taking with it the illusion that life begins each morning." In the inhuman he finds both his terror and his peace; the majestic indifference of the earth supplements his mother's "lesson" as the model for his own point of stillness between no and yes, between the wrong side of the world and the right. "The great courage is still to stare as squarely at the light as at death." His strength lies in his power of acceptance: not of death but of responsibility for the attitude in which he approaches it, for the whole individual who exists until the next trauma tears him apart. Despite this strength, despite the moments of joy that sustain it, *The Wrong Side* is the bleak book of an invalid, as lonely in the writing as in the subject. Its disjunctions of mood are more convincing than the rhetoric that connects them: the author's voice becomes potent only when it is ironic.

In the year or two between the composition of *The Wrong Side* and that of *Nuptials*, his health revived, his unfortunate first marriage was dissolved, and he experienced an "overwhelming sense of life." The two books are as different as night and day. He no longer views the sun from the pit of despair or through the bars of estrangement. Rather than as a condemned man, he writes as a celebrant of his marriage with nature, of the "simple agreement," as he says elsewhere, "between the earth and the foot," and of his companionship with the Mediterranean "race born in the sun and the sea, alive and spirited." Written at a pitch of sensuousness, two of the essays, "Nuptials at Tipasa" and "The Wind at Djemila," contain the most imaginative prose that Camus was ever to write, as rich as D.H. Lawrence's in

The *Sea and Sardinia*. Even such statements as "the loving understanding between the earth and the man delivered from the human"
are justified by the intensity of the communicated experience that
embodies them. Thus, he writes of the beach at Tipasa, the wild
scent of absinthe and roses, pine and cypress, the taste of a peach, the
consummation of the skin with the sunlight and water, the "joy that
descends from sky to sea." Coming from the sea, he throws himself
down among the plants and inhales their scent. "I am fulfilling a truth
which is the sun's and which will also be my death's." At Djemila the
stone ruins of a Roman colony, the heavy, unbroken silence, and the
tearing desert wind slowly evoke his sense of man's nakedness and
vanity, which annihilates the mind "so that the truth which is its very
denial may be born."

In "Summer in Algiers" Camus for the first time places the terms
of his dialectic in a social context. He describes his city under its aspect of carnality, a city enamored of the body and its intense, violent,
and brief pleasures, where the haste to live borders on the extrava-
gant, where "a man has played all his cards by the time he is thirty."
Under the spell of his own hedonism, Camus even views the absence
of culture in Algiers as an augury of its future greatness and creativity. Here the dull brain neither perplexes nor retards: here people live
without the usual hopes, myths, or consolations. In the lush Algerian
landscape, ravished by the sun, he realizes that "only one thing is more
tragic than suffering, and that is the life of a happy man." In a review
of *Nausea*, written about this time, Camus faults Sartre for failing
to realize that the true source of the absurd is that which exalts life
rather than impugns it. "Without beauty, love, or danger it would be
almost easy to live."

The concluding essay in *Nuptials*, "The Desert," applies the cult
of the carnal to art. In Florence he discovers that the Tuscan masters are not concerned with the flickering play of consciousness but
with the essential expression of a face—"the shape of its bones and
the warmth of its blood. What they have expelled from these faces
molded for eternity is the curse of the mind: at the price of hope.
For the body knows nothing of hope," etc. The work of art, like the

unmediated life, is a stripping down to truth: the Franciscan monks of Fiesole who live among flowers and meditate over human skulls, the sun worshippers on the beaches of Algiers, even the incest and rapacity of the Italy of the Borgias, all testify to the same "fierce and soulless grandeur," the same "resolve to live" that Piero della Francesca places on the face of his risen Christ. Full living and expressing begin with beauty and lead past the far side of morality to a point of awareness at which "the heart is closed" and the mind "feeds on nothingness." It is in this "desert," the one that Rimbaud found in Abyssinia, that the healing springs of indifference begin to flow.

On this pure nihilistic note, *Nuptials* ends. As the rest of the essays in this volume demonstrate, it is as far as the young Camus was to go. He had reached the limits of his essentially positive nature: the point at which the inhuman demands more of man's creaturely existence than it can provide and the will of a Caligula begins its experiments. The essays in *Summer*, spanning the next fifteen years, represent a retreat from these demonic paradoxes. Dionysus gives way to Prometheus, nature to culture, the inhuman to the unjust, death to the death camps. The prejudice against mind becomes a prejudice in its favor: the mitigable suffering of men, the plague of violence that has overtaken Europe, desperately require it. Like Tarrou, the traveler who makes his sacrifice and stays in Oman during the plague, Camus found in the Resistance and in his work for the newspaper *Combat* an allegiance to the party of humanity that ended his long estrangement and redirected his temperament as an opponent of nihilism: the vocation on which he, like Gide, eventually based his pride in being a man. Thus the noble savagery of Algiers is displaced by the rationality, moderation, and "tragic optimism" of classical Greece as the center of the "Mediterranean culture" that Camus brought north with him to Paris. Finally, his literary criticism, like his prose itself, grows progressively more austere and conservative; as though everything since Greek philosophy and drama represented to him either inspired imitations of their circumspect, measured approach to the great themes of human destiny, or else a falling away, the final collapse being the cult of personality and improvisation found in the writing of his time.

The civic stance and burdened tone of the later Camus, the excessive *mésure*, the clear loss of sensuousness are paralleled in his criticism. He rejects the perversities of modernism: "if the words 'justice,' 'goodness,' 'beauty,' have no meaning, then the world becomes absurd and men can tear each other to pieces." Language is not meant to express what is most personal in men but what is most strictly impersonal and closest to their common experience. If the novel is to revive, if it is ever again to present men in "their flesh and their duration," it will need to recall itself to this "higher banality." Similarly, the freedom of the artist, like that of the political rebel, lies in his recognition of limits. The secret of a Stendhal or a Proust or, for that matter, a Sade is not originality but fidelity: an obstinate hewing to "a certain tone, a certain constancy of soul, and a human and literary knowledge of sacrifice."

We are back again with the familiar, public Camus. But we will be in much better touch with him if we keep in mind the young, solitary explorer of "the desert," who was no stranger, after all, to the author of *The Stranger*, *The Fall*, or the stories in *Exile and the Kingdom*. His final rebellion, against the power of the inhuman, began with his own character, and from it he acquired his own "knowledge of sacrifice." Or, as he wrote in the later preface to *The Wrong Side*: "In order to be created, a work of art must first of all make use of the dark forces of the soul. But not without channeling them, surrounding them with dikes, so that the water in them rises. Perhaps my dikes are still too high today. From this, the occasional stiffness…"

(1968)

PART THREE

One of Us:
The Poetry of Hayden Carruth

In his literary career, Hayden Carruth has been as resourceful and steadfast as the Vermont hill farmers he lived among for many years. He is a people's poet, readily understood, a tribune of our common humanity. But he is also a poet's poet, a virtuoso of form from the sonnet to free verse, from medieval metrics to jazz ones. Carruth has also been, to my mind, our most catholic, reliable and socially relevant critic of poetry in an age of burgeoning tendencies, collapsing standards and a general withdrawal of poets, except during the Sixties, from the public to the private sector of consciousness. Finally, he has worked as much in the American grain as any writer of his generation, and his anthology, *The Voice That Is Great Within Us*, is the best presentation of American poetry that I know of.

Although Carruth's career has been of inestimable value, his reputation has remained marginal. This is partly because his varied *oeuvre* eludes the trends and schools that fix reputations; partly because the spare directness of his characteristic work does not have the aura of big-time postmodern poetry and so has not received the attention of the Helen Vendlers and Harold Blooms. Nor has he been part of the circuit of readings and conferences, of gossiping and networking that the poetry establishment uses to constitute ranking and to keep score. So the MacArthurs and the poetry chairs, the slots at the American Academy of Arts and Letters and Library of Congress, have passed him by. As with other notable poets of his generation, the quality crunch in trade publishing has relegated most of his recent work to the small presses. His broad, deep river of criticism has been channeled into small, dispersed reservoirs (*Working Papers*, University of Georgia; *Effluences From the Sacred Caves: More Selected Essays and Reviews*, University of Michigan; *Sitting In: Selected Writings on Jazz, the Blues and Related Topics*, University of Iowa). As he once said to me, "Well, it's a goddam shame."

Of course, not even seminal writers are promised justice in their lifetime, and there are other reasons why Carruth's career has unfolded in a kind of counter-famous way, from the center to the periphery. When he was in his late 20s he became the editor of *Poetry* magazine, still the journal of record in the decade after World War II, and a few years after that, he was an editor at New Directions, which was then at the height of its importance. He was also writing and publishing the kind of culturally ambitious and accomplished poetry that enabled him to win a prominent place among the New Poets, i.e., the generation that came after the modern masters:

> Fortunate land, that Egypt, where
> From time to time the phoenix comes
> And wheels among the temple domes,
> A golden circle in the air,

And so on in its measured, skillful, magisterially nostalgic, Yeatsian way. There are similar distinct traces of the influence of Pound and Williams in the early Carruth of *The Crow and the Heart* (1959). The difficulty is not that the poems in his first collection are derivative, though some are; it is that most of them stand so resolutely apart from the times and man who wrote them that they seem not only autonomous but virtually anonymous, psychologically unsigned. From this kind of practice some art can come but not much emotional reality. I'm thinking not just of "Cappadocian Song," "The Buddhist Painter Prepares to Paint," etc., which are remarkably sensitive transcultural experiments, but of poems like "Lines Written in an Asylum" and "On a Certain Engagement South of Seoul," in which the smooth texture and decorum of the poetry stand like a scrim over the terror of madness and battle respectively, that they seek to render. Like many writers in that daunting twilight of modernism, Carruth was more sure of the force of its literary values—complexity, order, self-detachment—than he was of the force of his own experience.

Well, that was to change. In Carruth's case as in some notable others—those of Robert Lowell, John Berryman, Delmore Schwartz, Sylvia Plath, Theodore Roethke, Anne Sexton, Randall Jarrell—he cracked up and was institutionalized. Much has been said and written about the seeming contagion of madness among many of the best poets of the postwar generation. Perhaps it is glib to say of their poetry that the stately mansion they had internalized had to be leveled for the new road could go through, but that is what I think happened to him and to the others. His illness, which was to last in a modified form for the next twenty years and forced him to live an isolated and mostly impoverished life in rural Vermont, must have made the fashion he had first adopted of the autonomous poem and the poet whose identity consists mostly in its refinement seem like a terrible joke.

The change is immediately apparent in the difference between "Lines Written in an Asylum," (1959) which ends:

> The mind is hapless, torn by dreams
> Where all becoming only seems
> A false, impossible return
> To a world I labor to unlearn.

and "Ontological Episode of the Asylum," published six years later in *Nothing for Tigers* :

> Many of us in there would have given all
> (But we had nothing) for one small razor blade
> Or seventy grains of the comforting amytal.

In the first poem the poet's suffering has left his persona intact. His mind may be hapless but you wouldn't know it from the firm control of the thought and poetics. In the fashion of the time, he presents his predicament in a tightly wound paradox, but there is little current going through its circuit. In the lines that end the first stanza of the later poem about living on a mental ward, Carruth's persona has lost its decorum and been reduced to its membership in the company of the suicidal: the language is nakedly direct in its anguish; the rhyme is as bluntly functional as the overdose. In short, the poetry has become genuinely authentic: the voice and the desperation are inseparable, the one liberating the other from the merely conceptual and rhetorical, the incompletely felt, the secondhand. The poetry has also become potent and serious, changing and indelibly marking our consciousness of its subject.

It continues:

> So I went down in the attitude of prayer,
> Yes, to my knees on the cold floor of my cell,
> Humped in a corner, a bird with a broken wing,
> And asked and asked as fervently and well
> As I could guess to do for light in the mists
> Of death, until I learned God doesn't care.
> Not only that, he doesn't care at all,
> One way or the other. That is why he exists.

After such knowledge, what detachment? In finding his own voice for his own life—spare, plain, unliterary speech that is even willing to risk a cliché because the pain of the lines reactualizes the image of the bird—Carruth also began speaking for his age. One of the reasons that the reign of the autonomous poem came into question is that the idea of art as a higher life, a supreme reality, not unlike the religious one, was hard and dangerous to maintain in an era that was trying to fathom Auschwitz, Hiroshima, the Gulag, the Cold War. His growing antipathy for this irrealist art became one of the central themes of Carruth's criticism as well as the agent of change in his poetry. Henceforth he tended to praise poetry and to write it that accepted the responsibility of immersing itself in the life of its time.

Under the influence of Eliot, Pound, Tate, et al., there had been a marriage of poetry and religion as part of the conservation of high culture against the vulgarity of the age. However, as the supreme reality became that of Walter Benjamin's frail human figure in a field of lethal or dehumanizing forces, the only recourse for many writers was that of existential engagement by which one accepted the responsibility of creating his or her own freedom, fortifying his or her own selfhood. This had a profound effect across the culture, from Abstract Expressionism to crisis theology, but it was particularly felt by poets, some later than others, who had been lulled into a kind of spiritual fellow-traveling with their mentors. Lowell's recusancy not only from Catholicism but from the elegance of his first two collections and his re-emergence in *Life Studies* (1959) as an inmate of his life and times in poems like "Memories of West Street and Lepke" is a similar example of the acceptance that was taking place in the rockbottom paradox of the final lines of Carruth's poem.

In 1963, writing against the self-complete poem, Carruth put the position of moral realism about as well as it's ever been put. If it reminds you of Thoreau and Twain as well as Williams, you'll see what I mean in saying that Carruth is one of the hewers of the American grain:

> Such self-completeness is only the dream-product of a deeply divisive mania. The truth is that things and ideas and poems are realities among many realities, conformable to the general laws, not opposable in any useful sense. But reality (whatever it is) is intractable, and usually ugly and boring as well, with the result that some people will always try to escape it by one means or another. You can't blame the poets more than the rest. Beyond this, reality consists of Right and Wrong; and since Wrong is by nature always immanent if not ascendant, Right is continually tempted into sanctimony and unction (to say nothing of bigotry), and the effort to resist these temptations is difficult and tedious—another reason for escaping. It is all a misfortune, the whole business, so great a misfortune that people lately have taken to calling it an absurdity. God knows it is absurd. But putting a name on it cannot extricate man from reality,

or relieve him, as long as he is alive from the necessity of thinking
about it, of having ideas about it.

Carruth's prescription of existential rather than artistic autonomy
was one that he had to take himself. His illness, which left a residue
of agoraphobia so that he could not teach or give readings, took him
away from "the social machine" of poetry from which he'd made his
living. He saw that poets were getting by better than before, "provided that they teach, recite, perform, expound, exhibit—in short
that they tickle the institutional vanity of the age." He believed that
this new version of "the scrimmage of appetites behind the hedges of
privilege," in Delmore Schwartz's words, had destroyed the life and
much of the later work of his friend. In his tribute to Schwartz, he
wrote:

> I wish that somehow he had gone away when he was about twen-
> ty-five, had gone out West perhaps, to live on the desert or in the
> mountains. He wouldn't have liked it, he was too much a city boy.
> But if he had been forced to stay until he learned to like it, until he
> learned to recognize the strength he possessed within himself..."

These words were written in 1967. By then Carruth had been
living for years on a small farm in Johnson, Vermont, where he supported himself, his wife and son mainly by reviewing books of poetry. During this period I thought he had the hardest life of any
well-known writer I knew. But he had also found the strength he
possessed within himself that enabled him to be creative in his piece
of the real world. Revitalized and stirred by his love for his family,
by his attentiveness to the intense phenomenology produced by rock
and soil, cows and loons, and by making a place for himself in a community where hardship and usefulness were taken for granted, he also
found his master theme. A poem from the early seventies, titled "The
Ravine," begins:

> Stones, brown tufted grass, but no water,
> it is dry to the bottom. A seedy eye

of orange hawkweed blinks in sunlight
stupidly, a mink bumbles away,
a ringnecked snake among stones lifts its head
like a spark, a dead young woodcock—
long dead, the mink will not touch it—
sprawls in the hatchment of its soft plumage
and clutches emptiness with drawn talons.
This is the ravine today…

One notes immediately the nearly total reliance upon a hard, clear, natural language that draws heavily upon its Anglo-Saxon origins. Similarly, the steadiness of vision is here not a contrivance of tone but an outcropping of character. Carruth sees the hawkweed, the mink, the snake, the dead young woodcock evenly, holding the subject through its physical mutations: the barely and fully sentient, the harsh and the gentle, the quick and the dead, the hardy and the futile. The figurative language—*spark, bumbles, hatchment*—is so nearfetched that it seems to have its own literalness. This evenness and terseness of vision creates a texture as expectant as a new spiderweb. It looks simple but takes great moral concentration and imaginative strength as well as verbal and syntactical resourcefulness to spin it. Carruth's handling of genuine experience has become like his neighbor Marshall Washer's handling of an ax: "rolling the post / under his foot in the grass: quick strokes and there / is a ringed groove one inch across…" After commenting quickly on the seasonal changes he has seen in the ravine, the geological ones he envisions, Carruth continues:

…These are what I remember and foresee.
These are what I see here every day,
not things but relationships of things,
quick changes and slow. These are my sorrow,
for unlike my bright admonitory friends
I see relationships, I do not see things.
These, such as they are, every day,
every unique day, the first in time and the last,
are my thoughts, the sequences of my mind.

I wonder what they mean. Every day,
day after day, I wonder what they mean.

The allusion to William Carlos William's famous dictum, "No ideas but in things," does not refer to Carruth—his tutelary spirit joins Carruth's in the first stanza—but to Williams's "bright admonitory" followers for whom writing poetry is a discrete activity rather than an endless, daily quest for lived meaning. He indicates something of what he means by "relationships" in his essay on Muriel Rukeyser, in which he speaks of lyric poetry as a form of prayer which in a secular age requires an absolute honesty. "Suppose, in the straits of reason and experience, you must deny the supernatural but assert the ultranatural, those extreme susceptivities of consciousness which govern our spiritual and moral lives." In poem after poem in Carruth's middle period there is an ongoing struggle of those extreme susceptivities for the absolutely honest, affirming relationships that can be wrested from "the conspiracy of the natural and the human."

One finds them structuring and empowering a poem like "August First," in which a weary and tattered moth, a drying-up brook and a burgeoning geranium plant growing from a 19-cent seedling present themselves to a poet who quietly tells us he is down to nothing, and then the force of the flower begins to assert itself. Brooding on the relatedness of such "things," Carruth creates a naturalism of the spirit, so that the poems in *From Snow and Rock, From Chaos* (1973), *Dark World* (1974) and culminating in *Brothers, I Loved You All* (1978) form something like an anarchist's bible. There is the missing great elm in the meadow in "Once and Again" that evokes Carruth's love of England, a place that he has never been, and the God "who does not exist"—belief in whom is "a heroism of faith, much needed in these times." The poem rises in the trumpet of Hopkins, with a New England mute, as it returns to nature:

....To discover and to hold, to resurrect
an idea for its own sake. Ah my heart, how you quicken in
    unrecognized energy

as hard little pellets of snow come stinging, driven on the
   gray wind.

The deep-down relatedness of things continued to conduct Carruth
through his green pastures and his valleys of the shadow. It informs
his love poems to Rose Marie, a refugee of the Nazi occupation:

Liebe, our light rekindled
in this remoteness from the other land,
in this dark of the blue mountain where only
the winds gather
is what we are for the time that we are
what we know for the time that we know
How gravely and sweetly the poor touch in the dark.

Or again, he draws upon his characteristic vision of life's metaphors
to summon and mourn the spirit of Paul Goodman. Reading his
friend's "sweet and bitter" poems, Carruth suddenly feels the heat of a
chunk of beech blazing up in the woodstove of his cabin; he dampens
it with a shovel of snow and then goes outside and sees a plume of
steam rising "straightly" from the stovepipe: a simple perfect eulogy
for another spiritual naturalist. His trust in his sense of relationships
when it is absolutely honest enables him to bring off a poem as risky
as "Emergency Haying": Hanging onto the side of a haywagon in a
cruciform position, his side pierced by kidney pain, Carruth rides in
from a brutal day in the fields. This leads to thoughts about forced labor under the Nazis and sugar barons that rise to a furious prophetic
note struck in the name of a rehumanized Christ. "My eyes / sting
with sweat and loveliness. And who / is the Christ now, who / if not
I . . . woe to you, watch out / you Sons of bitches who would drive
men and women / to the fields where they can only die."

In the 1980s, being able by then to teach, Carruth was at Syracuse University, where he became a poet of the outskirts—the ruined
lakes and fast-food strips, the uprooted values and fading chances of
the local blue collars. His work, like his life, had its ups and downs.

Whose didn't, in the Reagan decade that was the antithesis of art and spirit? His major work became mostly his love poetry: the greatly ambitious *The Sleeping Beauty* of 1982 (the one book of his I edited), which invokes the troubadour tradition of male feminism and gives it various historical, erotic and ecological settings for both good and evil; also his collection *Sonnets* (1989), which wittily, tenderly, acutely record the arrows to the heart of a late-in-life love affair and which also rejuvenates and tempers the sonnet form. The other three collections of the past ten years seem to me uneven. Perhaps goaded by neglect (particularly of *The Sleeping Beauty*, which I felt he regarded as his masterpiece), he said at one point that from then on he'd write in the way he damn well pleased; but this has sometimes unsprung his structure and line and taken some of the finish off his texture, i.e., his sense of significance. His character studies and short narratives of bar and diner life around Liverpool, New York, don't have as much moral and emotional resonance as their earlier Vermont "cowshit farmer" counterparts: the indomitably capable and doomed Marshall Washer; the morally androgynous "Lady" who both farms and nurses in the state hospital; the aphasic Marvin McCabe, the pathos of whose life becomes so eloquent in Carruth's liberation of his near-strangled voice and feelings. Carruth's gift of empathic intelligence and natural language seems to be too readily proffered in the life-story poems in *Asphalt Georgics* and *The Oldest Killed Lake in North America* (both 1985). Also, the depressed element that he could earlier manage to hold in solution with his other extreme susceptivities of consciousness tends to precipitate out into the bitter sediment of the Septic Tank poems and others.

One can infer from Carruth's recent essay on suicide that there were some terrible years in which any poem he could manage to finish was a gift and its publication a confirmation. I can wish he had done more winnowing in selecting from the recent collections and the new poems. But part of the purpose and justice of the spacious *Collected Shorter Poems* is to allow a poet as embracing and undervalued as Carruth generally has been to receive a full hearing, as well as to commemorate his continuing efforts to reconstitute himself. That the Copper Canyon Press people, who are otherwise to be congratulated for producing such an ample, handsome and affordable book, have scrambled the Table of Contents seems like a final reminder of the grimly mixed and contingent conditions of this career and quest it recapitulates.

Carruth says somewhere that his father, the editor of a socialist newspaper, once told him never to take a job that wasn't socially useful. Well, if there is a social use for poetry, this is the man whose poetry and criticism have embodied and husbanded it. As he said of William Carlos Williams, Carruth has been, more than any other poet of our time, "one of us, committed to our life, our reality, our enigma."

(1992)

Captain Bly

Gore Vidal once remarked that instead of politics Americans have elections. One sees what he means, but it's not quite on the money, because elections matter mostly to the politicians, their PAC groups and their dwindling party loyalists. For the rest of America, elections are a peculiar form of TV entertainment in which the commercial has become the program. The affiliations and ideologies people care about are elsewhere, in what Theodore Roszak termed "situational groups," the politics of the personal. "In less than a generation's time," he wrote, "every conceivable form of situational belonging has been brought out of the closet and has forced its grievances and its right to exist upon the public consciousness." He was writing about the mitosis of the counterculture, but his observation was no less prescient about its opposition—the pro-lifers, creationists, apocalyptics, neoconservatives, school vigilantes, et al. There are also the expressive therapeutic groups: The most influential ideology of change in America today is probably that of A.A., not only because it works so dramatically but because it provides a model of psychological and spiritual community, which is what the ethnic, racial, gender, sexual and other situational groups are partly about. The most interesting recent example is the men's movement, a complex phenomenon that appears to derive from A.A., feminism, New Age religion and therapy, environmentalism and the culture and charisma of Robert Bly.

That a poet is the spokesman of a broadly based movement as well as at the top of the charts with his book *Iron John* has struck many people as strange but not, I imagine, many poets. They are used to Bly the group leader, publicist, ideologist, translator, mythologist, guru and scold, he having played these roles in the American poetry of the second half of the century, much as Ezra Pound did in that of the first half. Poets are also used to Bly the showman, his hit performance on Bill Moyers's program, which sent the men's movement into media orbit, having been preceded by hundreds of his sold-out poetry readings and seminar star turns.

Like most literary careers that last, Bly's has been formed from the ongoing play of oppositions, but his have been particularly intense: Lutheran and pagan, rural and international, reclusive and engaged, austere and grandiose. These contending traits and inclinations have generated Bly's high energy and also created a certain rhythm to his career that makes his present celebrity and function almost predictable. Also they are compacted into a strongly lived life that personalizes the mythopoeic structure and idiosyncratic counsel to males of *Iron John*, and gives the book, for all of its discursiveness and high-handedness, an overall staying power and a kind of charmed ability to hit paydirt about every third page.

Iron John is less about male identity than it is about what Jungians, following John Keats, call "soul-making." Much of Bly's soul has been forged and refined by his relationship with the Wild Man, his favorite name for the tutelary figure in the fairy tale that he unpacks and unpacks, embroiders and embroiders to tell the reader how boys psychically become men and men remain psychically boys.

Bly grew up, as he says, as a "Lutheran Boy-god" in Minnesota, being his mother's favorite, and in good Freudian fashion, drawing from that a heightened sense of entitlement as well as a tendency to see the world through her eyes and feel it with her heart, which means he didn't see or feel very much on his own. In Bly's terms his soul or psyche had a lot of conducting "copper" in it, which would come in handy as an editor, critic and translator, and not much of the "iron" of autonomy that he would later have to extract on his own from the mines of the archetypal warrior king in himself. In short, he grew up "soft," like the males of today to whom *Iron John* is mainly addressed. Bly's brother appears to have been his father's son, the one who took up the family occupation of farming, the hairy Esau to his tent-dwelling Jacob. His father was strong, kindly, intensely moral, and alcoholic, creating a particularly poignant remoteness that broods over *Iron John*, as it does in some of Bly's later poetry: "the man in the black coat" who appears only to turn away again and whose haunting absence, along with his mother's haunting presence, has created Bly's lifelong project and process of fathering one's soul, which has led him to become a founder and leading spokesman of the men's movement.

For the rest, Bly was a well-raised product of Madison, Minnesota, a small plains community with a Norwegian cultural accent. He was properly clean and godly, cheerful and repressed, "asleep in the Law," as he puts it in his major autobiographical poem, "Sleepers Joining Hands." A Lutheran Boy-god who remains in this state is likely to become a minister, his grandiosity put into the service of interpreting doctrines and counseling the flock. Bly has, of course, taken the opposite road, "from the Law to the Legends," as he puts it in *Iron John*, but the deal he apparently made with his psyche is that the nascent preacher would go with him and adapt to his various stages and purposes.

Bly doesn't talk about his Harvard experience in *Iron John*—he seldom has in a career otherwise rich in self-revelation—but it was a determinate stage in which this wounded Boy-god and naïve "ascender" was both endowed and banished, a literary version of the prince of his fairy tale. Here he is as an editor of the *Harvard Advocate*, reviewing a collection of British poetry edited by Kenneth Rexroth. One sentence tells the tale:

> Perhaps it is unfortunate that Rexroth should have been let loose on the Romantics; there is, I think, a difference between the desire to express personal emotion by increased direct reference to the world of nature, and the desire to overthrow all external discipline of morals, of government.

This is a typical getting together of one's T.S. Eliot act, as did many young writers in the postwar era who thought they were putting themselves on the cutting edge of modernism. In Bly's case, it suggests that he was turning over in his sleep from the Lutheran law to the Anglican one. The literary atmosphere at the time was thick with "external discipline" and high churchiness. It had an archbishop, Eliot; a set of bishops, the New Critics; a martyr, Pound; and lots of acolytes, who were becoming semi-paralyzed by the dogma that poetry was a hieratic vocation, that the imagination lived and worked best within The Tradition. As Eliot had laid it down, the Tradition was mostly Dante, the metaphysical poets, and the high Anglicans like himself. The dogma came equipped with Eliot's emphasis on the impersonal, objective image and with a set of literary heresies and fallacies that were meant to nip any revival of Romanticism in the bud.

To subscribe to this ethos typically led a young writer to graduate school or to the pits. Bly chose the latter, having become committed to what he was not, as Erik Erikson would say, and badly needing to find his way to his own "inner tradition." He ended up in New York, where he spent the next three years being mostly blocked, depressed and poor: the state of "ashes, descent, and grief" that forms a major early stage in his mythic prince's initiation. According to Bly, life reserves this "katabasis" particularly for the grandiose ascender, putting him in touch with the dark, wounded side he has tried to ignore and evade and ministering to the naïveté, passivity and numbness that comes with the apron strings of his entitlement. The road, in short, that leads "from the mother's house to the father's house."

The one poem that Bly published from this period, "Where We Must Look for Help," is based on three types of birds that were sent forth from Noah's ark into the flooded world: the glamorous peaceful dove and the graceful swallows find no land, only the crow does:

The crow, the crow, the spider-colored crow,
The crow shall find new mud to walk upon.

As Bly was to tell Deborah Baker, who has written an excellent biographical essay about him, "It was the first time...I ran into the idea of the dark side of the personality being the fruitful one." After a year at the Iowa Writers' Workshop, Bly went to live on a farm his father had bought for him, and a year later, while visiting relatives in Norway, he discovered his new mud lying adjacent to his inner tradition.

In primitive societies, as Bly tells us in *Iron John*, the male initiation is viewed as a second birth, with the elders acting as a "male mother." Bly's were first Georg Trakl, a German, and Gunnar Ekelöf, a Swede. From them he began to grasp the subjective, intuitive, "wild" side of modernism as opposed to the objective, rationalist, "domesticated" one. In their work as in that of the French and Hispanic surrealists—Char, Michaux, Jiménez, Vallejo and Lorca, among others—Bly sensed the missing irrigation, the unconscious, for lack of which he believed Anglo-American poetry was suffering vastation. Increasingly dry, ironical, exhausted, remote, it was itself The Wasteland, while the European poets were still fecund, passionate and present. Returning to the family farm, Bly started a magazine, *The Fifties*, to say so as aggressively as possible and to provide translations of the European and Latin American surrealists in three or four languages, as well as to give welcome to his contemporaries who showed signs of new life and to put down those who were dead on their feet. Flying a woodcut of Woden as his logo, Bly almost single-handedly led the charge against the reign of the "Old Fathers," joined by the New York School on his right and the West Coast Beats on his left. Neither wing was anywhere near as relentless, reductive, and brutal as Bly. He was out to deauthorize as well as replace the Eliot-Pound-Tate tradition, stamping on it well into the next generation—Lowell, Berryman, Delmore Schwartz, Jarrell, Karl Shapiro, whomever. In *Iron John* he chides himself for contributing to the decline of "Zeus energy," attributing it to the demons in his father-wound; but this seems like a false note from someone who has repeatedly insisted that literature advances by generational strife and deplored the absence today of adversarial criticismamong poets.

Be that as it may, in the late fifties Bly entered his warrior phase, developing the strategy and service to a cause that, as he says in *Iron John*, distinguish the warrior from the soldier. Though his magazine became notorious for its demolition jobs, it also blazed, paved and landscaped a new road. Bly wrote many essays that developed his concept of "leaping" and "wild poetry," both in concept and prosody. In an essay, "Looking for Dragon Smoke," Bly hooked together a countertradition to the Christian-rational-industrial one that provided a kind of culture of the Wild Man. It begins with *Gilgamesh*, in which the "psychic forces" of an early civilized society created the hairy, primitive Enkidu as the adversary and eventual companion of the golden Gilgamesh (the first harbinger of *Iron John*). After *Beowulf* (Bly's Nordic touchstone) the "dragon smoke" of inspired association with primal memories is not much in evidence until Blake arrives to give the lie to the Enlightenment, as do the associative freedom and "pagan and heretical elements" in his German contemporaries Novalis, Goethe and Hölderlin. With Freud and Jung the unconscious is back in business again, and the romantic/symbolist/surrealist wing of modernism provides Bly with a whole range of leaping, dragon-smoke poets from Scandinavia south to Spain and across to Latin America to translate, publish and emulate.

Compared with Trakl's images ("On Golgotha. God's eyes opened") or Lorca's ("Black horses and dark people are riding over the deep roads of the guitar"), Bly's own early leaps as a poet did not take him very far inward. About a horse wandering in the moonlight, he wrote: "I feel a joy, as if I had thought/Of a pirate ship ploughing through dark flowers." The poems of his first collection, *Silence in the Snowy Fields*, are noticeably restrained, wishing to be admired for the integrity of their mood, mostly a meditative one: a young pastoral poet updating the tradition rather than appearing with snakes in his hair or as a messenger from the deeps.

Then, in the mid-sixties, Bly got caught up in the antiwar movement. He became a leading mobilizer of the literary community and provided one of the great moments in the theater of demonstrations when he gave his National Book Award check for his second collection, *The Light Around the Body*, to a draft resister on the stage at Lincoln Center. Auden said of Yeats, "Mad Ireland hurt you into poetry"; the Vietnam War hurt Bly into writing the kind of poetry he had been calling for and that in places matched Neruda's in its creeping balefulness. Evoking the fallout of evil that has settled in Minnesota, he ends:

> Therefore we will have to
> Go far away
> To atone
> For the suffering of the stringy-chested
> And the short rice-fed ones, quivering
> In the helicopter like wild animals,
> Shot in the chest, taken back to be questioned.

In the course of writing these poems and of editing a collection of antiwar poetry, Bly developed his concept of the intuitive association to reconnect literature with politics, two realms that most criticism and most experience of their "bloody crossroads," in Lionel Trilling's phrase, counseled to keep apart. Bly's position was an early version of the statement, long before it became cant, that the personal was political. As he put it, "A modern man's spiritual life and his growth are increasingly sensitive to the tone and content of a regime." Since much of our foreign and domestic policy comes from more or less hidden impulses in the American psyche, and because that psyche is in the poet too, "the writing of political poetry is like the writing of personal poetry, a sudden drive by the poet inward."

Along with strengthening his own poetry, Bly's involvement turned him into a performer of it. His high-visibility poetry readings developed into a countercultural event, the Lutheran Boy-god and warrior now reappearing as the bard. I first caught his act in the early seventies, when he entered a symposium on literary editing dressed in a Mexican serape and tapping a Tibetan drum, as though he were a cross between Neruda and Chogyam Trungpa, the meditation guru Bly studied with. After his poetry reading, complete with primitive masks, the other Bly, the literary caretaker, appeared on the panel of editors—sharp, shrewd and no less dominating.

He supported himself by his public appearances; otherwise he remained on his farm, tending to his chores as an editor, publisher, critic and poet and using his solitude to nourish "the parts that grow when we are far from the centers of attention." Through the writings of Jung, Joseph Campbell, James Hillman and other psychic/cultural explorers he developed his encyclopedic command of the great heuristic myths, legends and folklore that understand us, concentrating on prose that involved the female side. He gave lectures on Freud and Jung, as well as on Grimms' Fairy Tales, in the church basement in Madison, his trial by fire in making the esoteric vivid and meaningful to a rural audience. He turned from America's shadow to his own, producing eleven collections of poems, most of them inward, associative, naked—Bly fully joining the tradition he had been staking out.

He put out only one issue of *The Seventies*, a noticeably temperate one. The warrior was giving way to the gardener and lover, two roles that Bly lived through and that noticeably "moistened" his poetry in the eighties. They also provided two more stages in the process of male initiation that he carried into his work with the men's movement. So did certain personal experiences of shame, guilt and loss, along with the aging process through which the holds that a father and son put on each other can turn into a yearning embrace. So, too, did his awareness that the young men in the literary and New Age circles he visited and who visited him on his farm had been weakened by the feminism of the era, and that male consciousness was in short and despairing supply. It was time, as Bly would say, to do something for the hive again.

Iron John, then, grows not only out of Bly's experience during the past decade in the men's movement but out of the central meanings of his life. If he has bought into the confusion and anxiety of many younger men today, caught between the new sensitivity and the old machismo, he has done so with the capital he has earned from his own growth as a man, a poet, a thinker and a husbandman of the culture. The souled fierceness that he prescribes for staking out and protecting the borders of male identity has provided much of the motive energy for his career as a literary radical. By the same token, his devotion to asserting and cultivating the primalness and primacy of the imagination in a highly domesticated and institutionalized literary culture has led him to view the condition of men in similar terms and to apply the learning he has acquired in the archeology and anthropology of the imagination to remedy it. This authority is finally what makes *Iron John* a serious, groundbreaking book.

The startling public response to Bly's masculinist sermon is not hard to fathom. Based on Jungian psychology, it takes a much more positive measure of human potential for change than does the Freudian model, whose Great Father and Great Mother are pretty strictly one's own and give not much quarter to altering their influence: a foot or two of freedom here, a pound less grief there. Bly's pagan godspell is that the gods are still around and within each of us, able to be mobilized or deactivated, as the case may be. Like Rilke's torso of Apollo, they search us out where it aches and command us to treat it and thereby change our lives.

Also, *Iron John* has a lot of specific insight and lore to teach men and employs a very effective method. It takes an old story and gives it a new spin, thereby enlisting the child in us who is still most open to learning and the adult who is keen to escape from his own banality. Along with combining therapy for men, or at the very least clarity, with a course in the world mythology and ethnography of male initiation, *Iron John* is also a spiritual poetry reading in which the words of Blake and Kabir, Rumi and Yeats and many others join Bly's own poems as a kind of accompaniment to the text.

The prominence of poetry in the men's movement is perhaps its most surprising feature; none of the other situational groups seem to be particularly disposed to it, and most poets would tend to agree with Auden that poetry "makes nothing happen." Perhaps it's only an aspect of Bly's influence, but I see it as part of the same reviving interest in the imagination signified by the increasing popularity of poetry readings.

Some people say that the men's movement will have to move

into national politics, as the women's movement has done, if it is to survive its trendiness and become socially significant. I'm not so sure. As the bonanza of the Reagan era recedes and the midlife crisis of its favored generation draws on, there are a lot of men in America who have mainly their imaginations to fall back upon. As a social analysis of male distress, *Iron John* is pretty thin stuff; but that's not why it is being read. It's not the *Growing Up Absurd* of the nineties but rather a deeply based counsel of self-empowerment and change. Like the men's movement itself, it offers the sixties generation another crack at the imagination of alternatives they grew up on, right where they most inwardly live and hurt and quest. This is the imagination that they turned in to become Baby Boomers; if it can be let loose in America by this broad, influential and growing situational group, there's no telling what can happen.

(1991)

Passing It On

The novelist John Keeble told me this story. He was living in Seattle and working at an industrial job when he found out that he had been accepted at the Iowa Writers Workshop. It was a last-minute thing, classes were starting in a week, he was just scraping by and had no money to move his household. An older friend of his at Boeing offered to give him a hand. Working straight through the weekend, he built a frame for Keeble's pickup truck to make it into a small van, then helped him to pack and load all his movables. By Sunday night the job was done, in time for Keeble to be on his way to his new prospects. His cup running over, he said to his friend, "I don't know how to repay you." "You can't," he replied. "You'll have to do it for someone else. Pass it on."

The story has meant a lot to me. It has reinforced the motive I began with as an editor and at times has lifted me out of egotism and other modes of narrow-mindedness in my writing by reminding me of the obligation we all have to pass on the good that we have received. The story reaches into a part of the self that is not for hire and to another part that attaches one to the rest of humanity, and it makes a connection between them. It also provides a counter to the calculation and greed that well up in a society awash in self-interest and consumerism.

But I've recently come to see that the story goes well beyond the uses I've made of it. It's like a cutting from a vigorous, complex, and beautiful plant whose roots go wide and deep into the earth: in this case, the strata of human nature and experience. They go back to societies whose whole way of life was built around gift exchange and to a folk wisdom contained in a global literature that deals with the nature of material and interior gifts, and to the religions, including our own, that began with offerings and sacrifices. Some of this wealth of customs, sentiments, insights, and creeds survive in and illuminate our own gift exchanges; they also can be found at the heart of the highest mode of gift exchange that remains with us—the creative process itself. I've been learning about all this from a splendid new writer named Lewis Hyde, whose book *The Gift*, with its esoteric but apt subtitle, "Imagination and the Erotic Life of Property," seems to light up every thing it touches, including the reader's mind.

I imagine that Hyde and Keeble and his friend would understand one another immediately. They come from the same place, morally speaking, and share a similar background, Hyde having worked as a carpenter and electrician and a counselor on an alcoholic ward to support his literary interests. He also comes out of the 1960s, the foolishness and smugness of the counterculture stripped away, its articles of faith in nature, community, and spirit presented in an enlightened and tempered form; he seems like a young Robert Bly or Gary Snyder. His words and tone are those of a man who has come his own way, traveling far, but who is glad to have your company. He will show you the wider vistas of otherness and credence to which we still belong once we get away from what he calls the "small ego" and the "commodity society."

Hyde tells us at the start that he came to his subject in an existential way. As a self-employed poet, translator, and scholar, he had gifts that the society he lived in didn't support and barely valued. Indeed, in its increasing reliance on forms of work that are highly codified, routinized, impersonal, and in its awarding of status not so much to what one contributes but to what one consumes, America today can be viewed as the antithesis of art. Sensing, too, that poetry and scholarship are gifts that must be bestowed, that the work of the imagination and the documented intuition are not completed until they are carried over, as he puts it, into "the real" by means of publication or its equivalents—that is, by public validation and use—he came to perceive the problem of the market for his work as doubly onerous, making him feel trivial as well as deprived. Trying to think his way out of this impasse, he became interested in the anthropology, theology, and folk literature of gift exchange as a commerce within and between tribes, as well as with the natural and spiritual realms that completed and guaranteed the flow of the cycle.

He was particularly struck and instructed by the literature on the "spirit of the gift": the generative principle or "eros" that provided the increase and whose exchange and worship provided the "feeling bond" in the members of the group, the bond that protected the source, fostered solidarity in the group, and conducted its members beyond the personal and tribal ego, beyond nature itself, and into the mysteries of creation. Thus the Northwest Indian tribes treated the first-caught salmon as a visiting chief, then ate it, and then returned the bones to the sea to ensure the supply and its return; so, too, the Maori hunters gave some of their birds to priests, who brought them back to the forest to feed its "hau" or generative spirit; so, too, the Israelite priests burned the fat of the firstborn male sheep and cattle on the altar "as an odor pleasing to the Lord." The person or group that feeds the hau and is fed by it thereby enters a realm of life that underlies creaturely existence and consciousness and endures beyond it. Hyde draws upon the distinction in Greek between its two terms for life: "Bios is limited life, characterized life, life that dies. Zöe is the life that endures; it is the thread that runs through bios-life and is not broken when the particular perishes."

From this principle of generation and generosity in cyclical exchange, it is but a step to the creative cycle of the source gift (both natural ability and cultural heritage) of the artist's generous and grateful labor by means of his imagination to shape and enliven it, and of its bestowal on his or her community, tradition, faith, and the race itself:

A circulation of gifts nourishes those parts of our spirit that are not entirely personal, parts that derive from nature, the group, the race, or the gods. Furthermore, although these wider spirits are a part of us, they are not "'ours'"; they are endowments bestowed upon us. To feed them by giving away the increase they have brought us is to accept that our participation in them brings with it an obligation to preserve their vitality.

The artist, then, wishes to nurture, develop, and bestow what he has been given: the gifts of his sources and of his talent. What he has to pass along are the fruits of this intercourse, the images, as Hyde finely puts it, which enable the rest of us to imagine our lives. Or, in the famous words of Joseph Conrad, which Hyde quotes twice as a kind of ur-text:

> The artist appeals. . .to that in us which is a gift and not an acqui-sition—and, therefore, more permanently enduring. He speaks to our capacity for delight and wonder and to the sense of mystery surrounding our lives; to our sense of pity, and beauty, and pain; to the latent feeling of fellowship with all creation—to the subtle but invincible conviction of solidarity that knits together the loneliness of innumerable hearts, to the solidarity...which binds together all humanity—the dead to the living and the living to the unborn.

As Hyde develops his vast array of sources to provide an ethic/aesthetic for the situation of the creative artist, a fascinating and com-pelling perspective comes into view. On the one hand, it functions as an incisive and startlingly fresh critique of the commodity-exchange society that separates and alienates its members from each other, that despiritualizes life and denatures the world, that fosters the greed, envy, competitiveness, and callousness by which in getting and spend-ing we lay waste our powers: in short, that exploits the essence and maldistributes the increase. At the same time, Hyde takes literature out of the hands of the various elites in which it has been languishing and losing identity and restores it to its rightful place in the human community, the agent of its moral memory and faith, the mover and movement of its spirit. He does so without loss of complexity and subtlety: his understanding of the creative process is phenomenal, his portraits of Whitman and Pound as the culminating examples of art understood as gift exchange are models of critical imagination, sympathy, and acumen. *The Gift* is a book about life and art by someone who know and knows.

My one disappointment is that it doesn't come fully forward into the present and deal with the actual situation of art in a commodity society and culture. At the end Hyde tells us that he has come around to believing that the artist, if he watches his step, can make his way without sacrificing his gifts. For sure. But the way is much more problematic than he suggests and I would like to have seen Hyde address it. For example, he writes that there are three primary ways in which modern artists have resolved the problem of their livelihood: They have taken second jobs, found patrons, or placed their work on the market. His notion of a secondary job is "some work more or less unrelated to his art...so that when he is creating the work he may turn from questions of market value and labor in the protected gift-sphere." But the way most contemporary writers support themselves is by teaching their practice, and as anyone knows who has had much to do with the writing programs and workshops that proliferate like outlets for a profitable new product, there is precisely the temptation to "exploit the essence" that distinguishes commodity exchange from gift exchange. In my experience the publishing industry today is not that much more dispiriting, devitalizing, isolating, and corrupting than the MFA one.

On the other hand, Hyde overlooks the development of a place in the literary environment today that comes close to the old gift society that he describes. I'm thinking of the emergence of a poetry community that operates pretty much outside the literary marketplace, and is responsible for the substantial increase in poetry readings, magazines, chapbooks, and volumes, as well as in the generosity and solidarity among poets and with their audience. Like that of its ally, the small-press movement, the situation of poetry today provides as good a context for exploring the gift culture as the practices of advertising does of the commodity one.

I fault Hyde not so much for ducking these matters as for depriving his readers of the clarity of vision he would turn on them. As is, his book has given me more to think and feel about and to try to put to use than anything I've read in a good while. His words, like the saying of Nachman of Bratslav, which he quotes, "'have no clothes. When one speaks to one's fellows, there arises a simple light and a returning light.'"

Buy two copies of this book: one to nourish you and the other to pass on.

(1984)

PART FOUR

The Diasporist

Many years ago, when I was an editor at *Commentary*, I was invited to a reception to meet Shimon Peres. I hadn't been to Israel yet or seen its official face, but I'd met a number of Israeli intellectuals, who all seemed to play in the first division of the arrogance league. So I went there with my guard up, prepared to be unintimidated. Yet before long, I felt awed and diminished. It wasn't from listening to Peres, who was ironic and a bit wistful as well as tough, a kind of Jewish Mario Cuomo who inspired more respect than confidence. No, what intimidated me were his bodyguards: attractive young men with more or less Jewish faces but who had an aura of alert, steely confidence. The collective face they showed was new to me: the cold face of Jewish victors. This would have been in the mid-1960s, when the truths of the Holocaust and the Hannah Arendt indictment of Diaspora passivity were sinking in. O, brave new world that had such young Jews in it! But what was going on behind those inscrutable gazes?

I've since had more complex and negative feelings about Israel, but this remained the gut one. It was confirmed by the Six-Day War, which altered my mindset for good: from *Oy vey iz mir* to Never again! Mine and most of my American-Jewish landsmen. When I was growing up, the primary sense of being Jewish was of being a marginal American; today it is that of being a kind of honorary Israeli. What else organizes the Jewish community, caught up in its own dispersion through assimilation and pluralism, besides Israel? It's where the money goes, where the political action is directed, where the main source of controversy lies. Check it out in the pages of *Com-*

mentary and *Tikkun*, which have relocated the infighting of the hawks and doves of the Vietnam War, along with their attendant subcultures, to the West Bank and Gaza Strip. Between these two positions most American Jews have been hunkered down, taking for granted the rightness if not the righteousness of the Begin-Shamir hard line, not wanting to know more than is good for their pride, solidarity and peace of mind. To wit, the Jonathan Pollard affair, which amid whispers and shudders was swept under the rug with the same dispatch as it was disowned in Israel, leaving Pollard to serve a life sentence for sending documents from the Naval Intelligence office where he worked to Israel. His sentence was as severe as the Walker brothers received as Soviet spies, though Pollard was spying for a leading ally and his actions are well within the self-imagination of many American Jews.

Enter Philip Roth, one of the few and the latest Jewish-American fiction writer who has gone where the new action is and who is once again disturbing Jewish minds and hearts. Jerusalem and the West Bank have become for him what Newark and Short Hills were in the 1950s: not only where the interesting Jewish material lies but where his early master theme has reemerged like a broken spring in a newly upholstered couch.

In the postwar era, the tension between American and Jew in one's identity expressed itself as mainly a struggle between the generations: the elder concerned about its security and devoted to a lingering ethnic loyalty and sense of moral superiority, while the younger, declaring its independence, found the concern exaggerated, the loyalty stifling and the moral superiority infuriating. This conflict wired most of the stories to one another in *Goodbye, Columbus* (1959) and led to the dynamite: the charge that Jews were addicted to outmoded forms of groupthink, particularly a tendency to both flatter and intimidate themselves. The aftermath of the explosion could be seen as late as Judge Wapter's letter to Zuckerman's father in *The Ghost Writer* (1979). The generational conflict meanwhile branched out into other modes of control and resistance, such as the Oedipal comedy of *Portnoy's Complaint* (1969) and the family trauma of the Zuckerman trilogy—the scandal produced by Zuckerman's "Carnovsky," *Portnoy*'s fictional counterpart. Roth's most recent book, *Patrimony* (1991), is a more circumspect and sympathetic re-envisioning of the generational theme. A memoir of the bond between Roth and his father, as it comes to be revealed in the final years, the book is also a kind of secular Kaddish not only for Herman Roth but also for his generation of immigrant sons, whose heavy-duty work-and-family ethic put in the foundation of the American Diaspora.

In the second section of *The Counterlife* (1986) Roth began a new stage of his career by sending Nathan Zuckerman to Israel to retrieve his brother, a gilded ghetto dentist, from his new life in a West Bank settlement. The conflicts between and within the good Jewish son and his maverick brother enact themselves with so much more impact and significance in the Judaen hills that they eclipse the ones in South Orange and Manhattan, where the issues are mostly heart surgery, mid-life potency and second marriage. Judaism doesn't attend even the funeral of Zuckerman's brother, but it grabs Nathan by the lapel at the Wailing Wall and leads Henry and his midlife crisis into a study house in Mea She'arim and then into the West Bank settlement of Mordecai Lippman with his keepah and his assault rifle. Nathan visits there. Instead of the vestigial fears and new hustles of American Jews, in Israel Zuckerman encounters fiercely articulate points of view that overpower and instruct his own. The journalist Shuki Elchanan, formerly a war hero and aide to Ben-Gurion who has turned into a sardonic apostate of Zionism, reveals to Zuckerman the core irony of the Jewish world: contrary to popular American-Jewish sentiment, Israel is not the second coming of David's kingdom but the new "homeland of Jewish abnormality," while America has become Theodore Herzl's promised land. "We are the excitable, ghettoized, jittery little Jews of the Diaspora, and you are the Jews with all the confidence and cultivation that comes of feeling at home where you are." He sums up the new Jewish ethos that has developed in Israel: "if the humane approach fails, try brutality."

This view, if no other, is shared by Zuckerman's other reality instructor, the equally aggressive, bitter and eloquent Rabbi Mordecai Lippman who makes his points the way a pile driver makes holes. According to him, Elchanan and the rest of the Tel Aviv cafe intellectuals, "the nice, humane" Jews, are just a new version of the Jewish loser and secretly envious of the Palestinians: "'I am sad and hopeless and lost...how *dare* he steal my touching melancholy, my Jewish softness!'" The American Jews are living on borrowed time before the Gentiles let the blacks drive them out; their only experience with violence is in the fantasies of writers like Norman Mailer. Which leaves Jews like himself, who face and fight real violence, who are not afraid to rule in order to survive: "If this is a game that only one can win—and those are rules the Arabs have set...*then somebody must lose*. And when he loses, it is not pretty—he loses *bitterly*. It is not loss if it is not bitter! Just ask us, we are the experts on the subject. The loser hates and is the virtuous one, and the winner wins and is wicked."

Is that why those bodyguards of Shimon Peres looked so cold? And where does Zuckerman stand in this cross-fire? Mostly he keeps his head down, though it is clear he is not uncomfortable with Elchanan's views and responds to a typical American booster of Israel with the thought that there has been more Jewish self-transformation in the United States than in Israel. On the plane home he begins to counter Elchanan's belated fear that he will screw up American military aid by writing about extreme characters like Lippman, who will be taken by American taxpayers as representative Israelis. Ironic shades of Judge Wapter! But before Zuckerman can defend himself against this return of the repressive, he gets into a sadistic farce instigated by a young admirer of his who wants Israel to get out of the Holocaust business before the "little Eichmann in every Gentile" allows Israel to be annihilated in order to shut off its relentless guilt machine. The rich new material of the previous section suddenly goes off the rails, as though Roth were abruptly exiting from a subject he can't handle any further in the kaleidoscopic series of autofictions that make up *The Counterlife*.

Whatever the reason, these two sections are prologue to *Operation*

Shylock, or, perhaps better, unearthed ore that Roth has now refined and alloyed with the carbon of a vigorous, tormented self-drama and the chromium of his lustrous later style, all of it heated in the furnace of a masterful Mossad scam to trap the Philip Roth who narrates the book into spying for it. The result is a novel as shining, tempered and strong as stainless steel, which it needs to be to cope with the outer and inner pressures of its subject: the fateful psychopolitics of the Israel-American-Jewish connection: intimidation working on vulnerability.

This is an extremely risky and difficult subject because (a) so much is riding on it both politically and subjectively for an American Jew and (b) so much of it has been repressed as well as concealed that it takes a major crisis to swing it up to the light, which in turn freights the issues all the more. Roth's strategy is to write his indictment of Israel and defense of the Diaspora as a dark comedy that exaggerates and even travesties its own thesis but whose plot, sprung by a personal identity crisis, confirms it. Far from being the questioning observer, he puts his own persona in the center of the action and on both sides of the issues.

As most readers of book reviews know by now, the agent of this strategy is Roth's namesake, impersonator and goad, whom he calls Moishe Pipik—i.e., a twerp with chutzpah. As for the other two Roths, I'll call the author Roth and the story's agonist Philip. Pipik is trading on his uncanny resemblance to Philip to promote in Roth's name, the new cause of "Diasporism," which seeks to throw Zionism into reverse gear, repatriating the European Israelis and leaving the Sephardic ones to settle down with their fellow Levantines in a now roomier and more accommodating land. According to Pipik, a nuclear-armed Israel run by people like Shamir and Sharon (the novel is set in 1988) is a menace not only to itself, the Arabs and the moral foundation of Judaism but also to the Diaspora. His Exhibit A is Jonathan Pollard:

> [Pollard] enacted no more, really, than the Israelis demand of
> Diaspora Jews *all the time*...Israel, which with its all-embracing

> Jewish totalism has replaced the goyim as the greatest intimidator
> of Jews in the world which today, with its hunger for Jews, is, in
> many, many terrible ways, deforming and disfiguring Jews as only
> our anti-Semitic enemies once had the power to do.

He is also alarmed by the possibility of a second Pollard turning up.
Rightly so.

Diasporism is Shuki Elchanan's view of an outmoded and dysfunctional Zionism taken around the bend. Why, then, doesn't Roth
strengthen his case by making Pipik's destination the American
Diaspora, which would be about 90 per cent more plausible than
the European one? Probably the best answer is provided by Louis
B. Smilesburger, a Mossad spymaster, in the course of explaining to
Philip the literary side of espionage:

> There is the dense kernel, the compacted core, and how to set
> loose the chain reaction is the question that tantalizes, how to pro-
> duce the illuminating explosion without in the process mutilating
> oneself....You do as the writer does...you begin to speculate, and
> to speculate with any scope requires a principled disregard for the
> confining conventions. . . a daring to tamper with the taboo, which,
> he added flatteringly, had always marked my best work.

As Smilesburger goes on to say, it is often a ridiculous gag or something equally foolish that creeps in and points the way. In Roth's
case it is the loopy idea of returning the Jews to Europe that opens
the vista of possibilities by immediately engaging his wit, which calls
in his nerve, which together make up the R&D department of his
imagination. It's no accident that this most audacious and pioneer-
ing of his novels since *Portnoy's Complaint* is also his funniest. Also,
the European component provides a satirical cover for Pipik's points
against Israel. These largely go unanswered while the novel takes pot-
shots at Pipik's idea of resettling the Jews in their European graveyard,
attended by the recovering members of his Anti-Semites Anonymous:
"And what a historic day for Europe, for Jewry, for all mankind when
the cattle cars that transported Jews to death camps are transformed

by the Diasporist movement into decent, comfortable railway car-
riages carrying Jews by the tens of thousands back to their native
cities and towns." The embarrassing fantasy of a new European Jewry
being proffered under his name drives Philip himself halfway around
the bend, where Smilesburger is waiting for him.

Impersonating an Israeli man-on-the-street—the street of disillusioned irony that runs from Jerusalem to Tel Aviv—the frail, crippled
Smilesburger poles himself to the table where Philip is lunching with
his friend, Aharon Appelfeld, and announces himself to be a Holocaust survivor who has come from New York to be miserable in Jerusalem. He informs them that the crazy Jewish God, who "from
the very first day He created man. . . has been irritated with him
from morning till night," is getting ready to visit a new catastrophe
on this country of "Jews without souls." He then proceeds to hand
Philip a check for Pipik's Diasporist cause, and it turns out to be for
one million dollars. Spurred on by his own talent for deceit, spite
and Jewish mischief—"how some Jews get involved in living," as Appelfeld tells him—Philip takes on Pipik's persona and position like
a young socialite slipping into a hooker's outfit. Diasporism gets a
new American slant and comic lift as Philip, filled by "the lubricious
sensation that is fluency," delivers the now-famous spritz on the great
Diasporist Irving Berlin, who made Christmas and Easter safe for
American Jews by turning one into a celebration of snow and the
other into a fashion parade. Also, it is the role-playing Philip who
soberly tells a troubled Israeli army captain (who wants to emigrate to
study film at N.Y.U. before he falls apart from his duties in the West
Bank) that he is an unknowing Diasporist, whose "*authenticity* as a Jew
means living in the Diaspora, for whom the Diaspora is the normal
condition and Zionism is the abnormality."

The barrage of raillery and sententiousness that Pipik and Philip
direct against Israel from their abstract base in Europe and secure
one in the United States, respectively, is so much fun and games beside the heavy artillery of invective that is wheeled into position by
George Ziad, Philip's Palestinian friend from their University of Chi-

cago days. George's ammunition is his father's confiscated house in Jerusalem, a military court in the occupied territories, and his own family's wretched, fearful existence in a hovel in Ramallah. George is the real thing, the voice of a Palestinian intellectual, sharpened by humiliation and propelled by rage:

> Jews who use clubs to break the hands of Arab children—and how superior they feel to you Jews incapable of such violence! Jews without tolerance. Jews for whom it is always black and white, who have all these crazy splinter parties, who have a party of *one man*, they are so intolerant one of the other....Here they are *authentic*, here, locked up in their Jewish ghetto and armed to the teeth? And you there, you are "inauthentic," living freely in contact with all of mankind?. . . .Oh, what an impoverished Jew this arrogant Israeli is! Yes, they are the authentic ones, the Yehoshuas and the Ozes, and tell me, I ask them, what are Saul Alinsky and David Riesman and Meyer Schapiro...and on and on and on and *on*? Who do they think they *are*, these provincial no bodies! Jailers! This is their great Jewish achievement—to make Jews into jailers and jet-bomber pilots! And just suppose they were to succeed... what would they have here fifty years from now? A noisy little state of no importance whatsoever. That's what the persecution and the destruction of the Palestinians will have been for—the creation of a Jewish Belgium.

George is one of the three great character creations in *Operation Shylock*. Fat, white-haired, shlepping after the *Intifada*, he is a far cry from the slim, debonair graduate student Philip watched seducing young women with bits of Dostoevsky and Kierkegaard, or from the Boston-area version of Edward Said that Ziad subsequently became. When Philip first meets him in Jerusalem and asks what he's doing there, George replies, with a touch of his old suavity, "Hate." He leaves the stone throwing, broken hands and brain damage to the young. "I oppose our masters with ideas—that is my humiliation and shame. Clever thinking is the form my capitulation takes." The irony of this generation's history has turned him into a genuine personification of

Dostoevsky's underground man—all heartache, self-spite and bile—as well as of Kierkegaard's divided man, whose whole being "shrieks in contradiction against itself."

George also bears the burden of "the shaming nationalism that the fathers throw on the backs of the sons, each generation…imposing its struggle on the next." This becomes a theme of the novel, connecting the Diaspora to Israel, the Israeli to the Palestinian. George's personal life is a wretched tangle of family sentiment and contempt knotted by guilt as he tries to atone for his youthful rejection of his father's politics both by professing them (when the Israelis will let him teach and write) and by inflicting them on his adolescent son. Meanwhile, he continues to tear himself down the middle of his spirit, his useless and damaging political commitment at perpetual odds with his nostalgia for the cultivated life he once lived among American Jews.

Against the fury of George's words and the pathos of his existence, *Operation Shylock* offers little in the way of rebuttal. Indeed, Louis B. Smilesburger, the one strong Israeli counterfigure, agrees with him: "They are innocent, we are guilty…they are the violated, we the violators. I am a ruthless man working in a ruthless job for a ruthless country and I am ruthless knowingly and voluntarily."

After he retrieves the check for Pipik he had given to Philip—which unleashes a chain of unnerving events that deliver a freaked-out Philip into his hands—Smilesburger has many more words for Philip. He is a powerful and subtle mindfucker who has penetrated more deeply into Philip's psyche even than Pipik has. Not since Bellow's Tamkin in *Seize the Day* has there been an intellectual rogue with the presence and presence of mind of this Mossad official who has been controlling Philip by using Pipik and Jinx Possesski, Pipik's shiksa extraordinaire, to draw out Philip's two consuming interests—self-impersonation and the Jews—to bind and deliver him. As a prospective mole, Philip manages to resist the seduction and indirect chastisement of Smilesburger's learned, charming lecture on Jewish self-hatred, which draws upon the teachings of Chofetz Chaim, the saintly authority on *loshon hora* (evil speech), which the Jews practice unduly among and against themselves. That failing, Smilesburger delivers a rhetorical slap in the face, a cutting comparison of the Israeli Jew, who does, without justification or apology, what Levantine reality demands—a reality whose scale of violence and duplicity the famous novelist has barely begun to grasp—and the Diaspora Jew who clings to his blameless politics and unprecedented liberation as he retreats into his studio, where his only reality is himself.

Philip resists this intimidation too. The words that he discovers he has no resistance to, that implicitly lead him to sign up to spy on George Ziad and his Jewish friends abroad, are the homely, banal, matter-of-fact ones of Leon Klinghoffer, the crippled tourist murdered by PLO terrorists on a cruise ship. Philip reads them in two travel diaries that have been thrust upon him just before he is picked up and detained by the Mossad in a Jerusalem schoolroom, where a regression to his happy Jewish childhood has been arranged to further soften him up. On the blackboard is a sentence in Hebrew script that is both as evocative and inscrutable as the past two days have been. Pipik's increasingly weird impersonation has been just the beginning of it, and Philip's spiteful impersonation of Pipik has been far from the last of it. Close to a recurrence of the terrifying loss of himself he had experienced a half-year before, Philip desperately addresses Pipik less in the spirit of Aristophanes, as he had been doing, and more in that of the Yom Kippur liturgy. He even agrees to share his name. Then, to maintain contact with his foundering self, he begins to read the Klinghoffer diaries and take notes for an introduction to them he had previously refused to write. He learns that the tourist was another typical Jewish business and family man, but one who happened to be chosen to enact and bring home to his bemused reader "the incredible drama of being a Jew." Later, when Philip has managed to wriggle free of Smilesburger's proposal and stalks out of the classroom, he leaves the diary behind. Smilesburger tells him he has forgotten something, and returning it to him, tells him it is a forgery. This proves to be a distinction without a difference. The patrimony in which Philip's Jewish loyalty is wrapped is thicker than even a Mossad spymaster's deceit. Or so the reader is left to infer from his subsequent participation in Operation Shylock.

Along with being the first international contemporary Jewish novel, *Operation Shylock* is also a brilliant novel of ideas, a distinguished genre that is practiced in the United States today about as widely as the epic poem. Listening to George Ziad's alternately apt and maniacal analysis of contemporary Jewish history as a prolonged case and manipulation of survivor guilt, Philip remarks, "I studied him with the cold-hearted fascination and intense excitement of a well-placed spy." This is precisely the texture of the narrative itself: everyone who walks into this dark, high-strung yet firmly controlled comedy is placed under intense surveillance—from John Demjanjuk, the Cleveland automobile worker and good family man who is on trial for his actions as Ivan the Terrible, the sadistic foreman of the Treblinka gas chambers, to Jinx Possesski, Pipik's nurse, mistress and first "recovering anti-Semite," who has led as many different lives as Jane Fonda and turns up in Philip's hotel room, supposedly in desperate flight from a crazed Pipik, in a ravishing little dress from her singles-bar nights. The amazing Jinx delivers an account of a terminal cancer ward and its oncologists from the point of view of a caring nurse that all but shakes in your hands as you read it.

For all of its zaniness, compounded by its author's post-publication insistence that it's all true, that he was turned into another Pollard, *Operation Shylock* is a panorama of intense scrutiny. Roth has assembled a gallery of characters, most of whom can't open their mouths without making a trenchant point or speech. This is an Israel where a religiously Orthodox civil defense lawyer, who is also a Shin Beth agent, rolls out a mordant lecture on *taqia*, the indigenous code based on desert scarcity that has created a binational politics of deceit and treachery; where an Israeli bookseller fills Philip in on the terrifying performances of Shylock on the English stage as he hands over the Klinghoffer forgery. The most articulate and expressive voice of all is the one that presents them, provokes them, endures them, fools and is fooled by them and never stops commenting keenly on what is or may be going on. For the third great character in *Operation Shylock* is its narrator, Philip, who is driven between the pillar of Smilesburger's plot and the post of ordinary, daily, obdurately portentous, enigmatic, elusive Israeli reality. While not having come to Israel in the best of mental shape to endure the unremitting uncertainty that he is led through there, he still keeps those Swiss watch dialectical wits of his ticking away, precisely keeping the dark time of his life, the nightlong wrestle with the intimidating stranger (now Pipik, now himself) to whom the Hebrew words on the blackboard refer.

In journeying to the heart of the Israel–Diaspora matter, in breaking through its conventions and taboos, Philip's creator has gone further into his own genius, I think, than he ever has before. As Kafka wrote of himself, Roth can say of *Operation Shylock*: "I have...experienced states in which I completely dwelt in every idea, but also filled every idea, and in which I not only felt myself at my boundary, but at the boundary of the human in general."

Toward the end of the novel my son Ivan and I are portrayed meeting Louis B. Smilesburger and the author at Barney Greengrass, the Sturgeon King, on Manhattan's Upper West Side, the capital of the Diaspora. Roth has insisted that every word of *Operation Shylock* is true. So did this meeting really happen? Well, it has now and for a long time to come.

(1993)

Irving Howe's World of Ourselves

The first generation tries to retain, the second to forget, the third to remember. Jewish-American writing of the past thirty years is, for the most part, a literature of memory, a harking back to family, neighborhood, school, and other formative experience to recover the tracks of Jewish identity before they faded out in the shady streets of suburbia and the bright corridors of the professions. Why this interest, though? Why not "Stick to the present"? as my father would say. "The farther back you go, the more miserable it gets."

The main reason, I think, is that the third-generation Jew intermittently experiences himself as a case of cultural amnesia, the ancestral promptings and demurrers vaguely pulsing away. But the context of these intuitions of Jewish being—these moral slants and emotional tilts in the way he does his work, relates to her children, votes, justifies her life, chases his desires—remains elusive, full of blank spots, awkward sentiments, impatient questions. Why should it matter so much? asks the lapsed Jew, otherwise comfortable in his acculturation. So much influence from so little preserved content. This is one reason Philip Roth's fiction rings bells so sharply. The stories in *Goodbye, Columbus* turn upon the possessiveness of the Jewish ethos—a theme that develops into the aching comedy of *Portnoy's Complaint*, where Jewish conditioning and the Oedipal complex meet on the psychiatric couch to explain and explain the constrained desires of a model young lawyer with a lust for fashion models. But Roth's keen sense of the entailments of Portnoy's heritage is hardly the whole story of it, and so one reads Bellow and Malamud, Leonard Michaels and Grace Paley, Cynthia Ozick and I. B. Singer, et al., looking for fellow experience and perspective. Or one can study Judaism, even learn Hebrew, hoping to find the way back to the shaping significance that is hardly accounted for by the perfunctory bar mitzvah lessons and seders of one's childhood. Contemporary fiction, though, tends to be too, well, contemporary and idiosyncratic to supply much of the missing link, while Judaism, as one soon learns, is not in the business of providing self-revelation. Like all religions, it remains remote unless one meets it more than halfway. The fiction of Chaim Potok would seem to fill the bill, being plugged securely into the ethos of normative Judaism, but in the end a book like *The Chosen* remains parochial in its subject and tone, and reading it is like going to synagogue only once a year, a way of revisiting the gap between the religious Jew and the rest of us.

Jewishness, then, is like a language in which one knows only a few words and phrases and yet is strangely responsive to its intonations and rhythms, its lights and darks of feeling. Like Russian, as I found out on a recent visit. Or more to the point, like Yiddish—that mysterious language in which our parents kept their secrets from us. What remain are a few expressions; a coarseness to the ear which once had a stigma attached, like slurping soup; also a certain singsong rhythm that makes it seem a little dizzying; also a reverberant tonality whose middle register seems devoted to various shades of resignation. So one puts his bits of Yiddish and its intonations into his English, particularly with other Jews, to provide some fellow feeling, an acknowledgment of roots. Imitating Yiddish seems to confirm something basic in one's nature, a kind of free area of expressiveness as well as a contact with one's earlier self. The same is true of telling Jewish jokes in dialect.

And so, like Poe's purloined letter, the missing link to the past has been there all along, right before one's eyes or, rather, on his tongue. For much of the secret source of one's "Jewish" ways, as one recognizes and recognizes in reading Irving Howe's *World of Our Fathers*, turns out to be *Yiddishkeit*, the culture of the immigrant generation.

Howe has written a splendid book, a richly detailed and interpreted narrative of two generations of "bedraggled and inspired" Jewish immigrants on the Lower East Side and beyond, in its manifold political, economic, social, and cultural bearings. A work of history and of art, *World of Our Fathers* is brilliantly organized and paced by brisk, pithy chapters that make up large perspectives: the detonations of new hopes and renewed fear that drove the immigrants out of the Russian Pale after the assassination of Alexander II and the pogroms that followed; the wretchedness and culture shock of the first two decades in New York; the daily family and work life in the filthy, noisy, jammed streets off East Broadway; the dynamic rise of the Jewish labor movement; the emergence of the remarkable Yiddish theater and press, as well as modern poetry and fiction movements; and finally, the rapid, fated dispersion into middle-class America. All of which is exhaustively researched and documented, often in the words of the people themselves. At the heart of *World of Our Fathers* is a complex story of aspiration, fulfillment and incompletion. A work of sage meditation and ironic vision, it is lucidly and warmly written, and fleshed out with choice photographs which touch and bemuse. A richness everywhere.

If you are Jewish, you will find that Howe has written a necessary book, particularly if you need its blow on the head to deliver you from your amnesia and help you to understand yourself. Not that Howe's pages are ever particularly startling. Their effect is cumulative—the slow, dawning realization that this world is as familiar to your intuition as it is fresh to your eyes. You will discover, for example, that the Yiddish word for excommunication, *heren*, became the word for boycott, and a little crease of consciousness becomes activated and tells you why you've instinctively been pro-labor. Similarly, Howe's image of Jacob Adler, the matinee idol of the Yiddish theater, lying in state, as he instructed, in English morning coat, Windsor cravat, and talis. Or, at the other extreme of *Yiddishkeit*, a sketch by Z. Libin—a writer from the terrible first years, the era of the *farloyrene menschen*, the "lost souls"—about a worker who fears that because a wall blocking his window has been torn down he will have to pay more rent. My favorite trip into the dream life that joins the Jewish generations is provided by an unpublished memoir by David Goldenbloom, one of the self-educated garment workers who become the composite hero of Howe's narrative:

> [When] I was about seventeen I began to take an interest in books. Since I had also gone a little to the Russian school, I began to swallow—I mean, really swallow—Russian books. . . . Turgenev was my favorite, perhaps because there is such a sweetness to his voice. And then Tolstoy and Dostoevsky. I read, of course, Sholom Aleichem, who made the ugliest things in life seem beautiful, and Peretz, who, in his own way, taught me not to lose respect for myself.

To perceive the force of the attitudes and values that Yiddishkeit pumped through the generational conduits, one has to grasp the conditions that fomented and shaped them. It is a platitude, for example, that Jews are mercenary because our forefathers were desperately poor, or that Jewish mothers dote on and stuff and worry about their children because of the immigrants' experience of hunger and illness, self-sacrifice and hope. Yeah, yeah, yeah, one says, until he reads Howe's harrowing account of the poverty of the Lower East Side during the 1880s and '90s.

"Have you ever seen a hungry child cry?" asks the social worker Lillian Wald, explaining the dedication of her life. By 1885 the crying was everywhere. Wages in the garment industry—the main source of jobs—were cut in half. The population density of the Lower East Side was soon greater than in the worst sections of Bombay, the mortality rate was double that of the rest of the city. Project these figures into conditions and you get men working seventy hours a week in the unspeakable sweatshops and then taking piecework home in order to scrape by, of people sleeping five or six to a room with their boarders, of near epidemics of dysentery, typhoid fever, and of course tuberculosis, the "tailors' disease." For twenty years or so, it was as though the fabled wretchedness of the steerage passage never ended, that those vile, packed ships came up on land and turned into factory lofts and tenements.

What was most traumatic was the inner darkness. Totally uprooted and alien, driven by a tempo they had never known before, their austere, decorous spirits assaulted and derided by the brutal dog-eat-dog conditions of their existence, their religious institutions in disarray, the immigrants seemed to lose their main possession, the culture that had preserved so many generations of the Pale despite poverty and other oppressions. The collapse of its center, rabbinical authority, is brought home by the anecdote Howe tells of the attempt to establish a chief rabbi to restore order. Soon there were three—a Lithuanian and a Galician (traditional antagonists) and a newcomer from Moscow. When asked who had made him the chief rabbi, the Russian replied, "The sign painter."

"They were Jews without Jewish memories or traditions," reports one Yiddish writer. "With every day that passed," recalls another, "I became more and more overwhelmed by the degeneration of my fellow-countrymen." And in the words of the poet Moshe Lieb Halpern: "If a wolf stumbled in here / He'd lose his wits /He'd tear his own flesh apart." In a radical newspaper of the day, Howe tells us, "the word *finsternish*, darkness, recurs again and again. . . . their lives are overcome by *finsternish* and it is to escape from *finsternish* that men must learn to act." So they listened meekly to their flamboyant agitators, went on bitter and usually doomed strikes, saved their pennies for the Yiddish theater, but mainly lived on their last hope that they might yet see their sons and daughters move on to something better.

Finsternish didn't begin in the New York ghetto. It came in the immigrants' luggage and dreams, the darkness of being cooped up for centuries in their decaying villages and prayer houses and in their sustaining but hapless messianism. But in the Russian Pale it was already lifting, thanks in good part to the Bund, the nascent Jewish socialists from the cities. Here is David Goldenbloom again:

> …just a few years before I came [from Russia] people of my generation became very restless. We heard of the Bund, which had recently been started, and to us it meant not only socialism but the whole idea of stepping into the outside world. When a speaker

from the Bund came to our town, we saw him. . . . as a new kind
of Jew, someone with combativeness in his blood and a taste for
culture on his tongue. . . . He was our lifeline to the outside world,
and that was enough.

In America, it was the distinctively Jewish socialism developed
by the Bund that largely rebuilt the community and morale the immigrants had lost. Indeed socialism, mostly through the organizing
of the garment trades, provided a collective enterprise, not only as a
consequence of despair but also as a movement toward the vision of
a "normal life" at last, not merely as a response to privation but as a
recycled religious teaching. Jewish socialism derived, as Howe shows,
from Jewish messianism, in which the worldly and otherworldly were
aspects of the same destiny, a tradition that was quick to produce
political and social movements that had a strong utopian, universalist
cast and fervor.

The radicals of the early Lower East Side had been mostly Rus-
sian-style anarchists to whom the benighted workers were the shock
troops of revolution, good for strikes but hardly worth organizing.
The socialists from Warsaw and Vilna who came in droves after 1905
brought organization. They also brought the idea that the Jewish
trade unions should reorganize the Jewish community and bring it
into the twentieth century by replacing the religious framework with
more adaptive and effective social and cultural institutions. The Bund
leaders saw their opening in the great strike of the shirtwaist makers
in 1909, many of them, like their leader, teenage girls, and of the cloak
makers in 1910, in which, as the writer Abraham Liessen declared,
"the 70,000 zeroes became 70,000 fighters."

From these strikes rose the intense feeling that the Jews had once
again fought their way out of captivity and darkness; this élan, along
with the moral and psychic restlessness of believers who were rapidly discarding the religious worldview, was rapidly channeled into
the ILGWU and the Amalgamated Clothing Workers. The socialists
produced the major Yiddish newspaper and set up organizations such

as the Workmen's Circle, which provided health and life insurance, hospitals and sanitariums, schools that offered a secular Jewish education, as well as all manner of lectures, courses, and other cultural activities, mostly in Yiddish. From this example, all of Jewish unionism would take its cue: Thus the communists would challenge the socialists with their own children's camps and schools, cooperative housing projects, theater, dance, and choral groups, mandolin ensembles and literary panels, as well as an excellent newspaper. In short, in trying to revolutionize the world that ground them down, the immigrant Jews revolutionized themselves both to resist it and to help their children rise in it.

Reading Howe's pages on Jewish socialism and the labor movements—meticulously fair and even-tempered, though patently written by the editor of *Dissent*, one of the remaining few to whom socialism was a belief "to which they would pledge their lives"—the reader can see the powerful strains of Jewish idealism and skepticism working away like yeast in bread. Also, in Howe's descriptions of the intricate, shifting, but always bitter struggle between the socialists and the communists, of the slow giving way of radical aspirations to practical ambitions in the rank and file, one can find an evolving paradigm of the political behavior of Jews in America as well, perhaps, of the ideological tensions that mark one's own politics. This comes home in Howe's argument with the revisionist view that the Jewish socialist movement was mainly a mode of acculturation instead of a force dedicated to a new society, which was the way it mostly saw itself and the way it actually transformed the consciousness of masses of Jews.

The other powerful force that brought the immigrant community together and enabled it even to flourish was *Yiddishkeit*, also initially an East European movement of the late nineteenth century. Its marrow was the vernacular of the Jews, "a language crackling with cleverness and turmoil, ironic to its bones." Its substance was the Jewish way of life, through thick and thin, the "shared experience, which goes beyond opinion and ideology." Its function was to hold together a people who were undergoing one challenge after another, including, after 1881, dispersion and acculturation in a totally strange secular society. Its spirit was an ironic acceptance of its role of straddling two world-views—the religious and the secular—which were slowly moving apart and one of which was crumbling.

Even so, *Yiddishkeit* performed wonders while it lasted. It carried the fragmented, rivalrous East European Jews into the modern world. It provided an essential network of communications between the Pale and New York that reached into their respective theaters, union halls, newspaper offices, poetry movements, political cells, lifestyles, schools of fiction. It also negotiated the uneven and fateful transactions between tradition and modernity, between communal and individual expression, between its own survival and its people's acculturation. In its very premises that the Jews could remain Jews and yet regain their worldly bearings and lead a "normal life" in Russia and America lay the sources of its enormous energies and contradictions, its startling full life, and its inexorable self-destruction.

In his chapters on the *Daily Forward*, Howe describes how this leading newspaper functioned as a teacher of the tribe—a kindergarten that taught new manners and a university that explained the intellectuals to the masses (and vice versa); a counselor in all manner of family, work, and personal problems; an organ for high socialist essays and lurid crime stories, for Yiddish soap opera on one page and the fiction of I.B. Singer on the next. In sum, as Howe puts it, "a large enclosing mirror that reflected the whole of the world of Yiddish—its best, its worst, its most ingrown, its most outgoing, its soaring idealism, its crass materialism, everything." It was all held together by its editor, the remarkable Abraham Cahan, who wrote the one distinguished novel in English about the immigrant experience, *The Rise of David Levinsky*, whose theme is the melancholy wages of success. Cahan knew from the start that the more the *Forward* built a bridge to America, the more of its readers would cross it. At the same time, his newspaper held up the idea of the underlying unity of a culture that would strongly mark the work of American Jews, from the movies of Hollywood to the pages of *Commentary*.

Yiddish theater began as the one refuge in the years of darkness, serving up lofty sententiousness, flooded emotionality, and low pageantry: Moshe Lieb Halpern called it a cross between a synagogue and a brothel. In the fifty years that followed, it tried to inch its way toward modern realism and theatrical art, especially the Russian model. But its audience continued to clamor for the war-horses of historical spectacle or family *schmaltz*, preferably a touch of both, such as *Mirele Efros*, sometimes called "The Jewish Queen Lear," in which ungrateful, worldly sons eventually return to confirm their mother's wisdom. Such plays provided the audience with what they wanted: the brilliant genre acting of Adler, Thomashefsky, Maurice Schwartz, in the higher and lower registers (the best acting in New York, according to Stark Young), and a plot that confirmed the old wisdom that a persecuted minority requires strict family discipline—i.e., Mama knows best. Yet it was just this function that enabled Yiddish theater to flourish, creating something akin to Italian opera, in Howe's view, by the expressiveness and vigor of its uncomplicated theatricality. Perhaps in time, with the development of more sophisticated Yiddish audiences, the theater would have caught up with the aspirations and abilities of its Jacob Ben-Amis and H. Leivicks. But there was no time: "a wink of history and it was over."

There is also Howe's luminous chapter on Yiddish poetry—the soul of *Yiddishkeit* and the most highly developed of its literary arts, leading the charmed and bitter life, as poetry usually does, of public neglect. But then all of the Yiddish arts began to lose their public as America beckoned in English to the next generation. With the rapid development of a middle class in the 1920s, *Yiddishkeit* developed a kind of fugitive second life as an infiltrator of American culture. This insight provides a subtle undercurrent to Howe's treatment of the dispersion of the immigrant ethos, through the comedians from Eddie Cantor to Lenny Bruce, the artists such as Jacob Epstein and the Soyer brothers, and the American novelists from Henry to Philip Roth. Here Howe bears down on the point I began with—the legacy of Yiddish culture in the deeper levels of consciousness and moral will. For example, the abiding commitment to the aesthetic of Judaism itself: "beauty is a quality, not a form; a content, not an arrangement"—the moral and aesthetic belong to the same realm. Even in fiction one sees that the creation of a new Jewish-American prose has a trace of Yiddish flavor, and a carrying out of the strategy of the great Yiddish actors—"realism with a little extra," as Harold Clurman put it. At the same time, Howe observes the waning of the Yiddish influence under the same paradox that governed its rapid development and attenuation.

The sense of this rich and terrible brevity provides the tone of *World of Our Fathers*—the note of up-and-doing, striving, even frenzy, mingling with the note of frustration, sacrifice, attenuation. This tone, now brisk, now elegiac, also arises from Howe's feeling for the poignant dialectic of his story—that the "normal life" that these self-educated workers and their tribunes strove to create proved to be but a staging area for their children's escape from the family, community, and culture. Perhaps the last word fittingly belongs to David Goldenbloom, whom Howe, like the world he lived in, has rescued from near oblivion to tutor our obliviousness:

> What else can I tell you. My children went their own way. I am proud of them, but there are things we can't talk about. Still, I have no complaints. My circumstances were what they were. My family has been a whole world to me. I still take pleasure in Sholom Aleichem, and to me Bazarov and Raskolnikov are like friends of my youth. But to think of them is to be reminded that there was a door which, for me, never opened.

(1976)

204

The Strange Jews of A.B. Yehoshua

There has been an apparent disjunction in the writings of A.B. Yehoshua, Israel's pre-eminent novelist, between the Israelis in his fiction and the ideological position that he defends in his political essays. An eloquent spokesman for classical Zionism, as distinct from the military/religious revisionism that has been in the saddle for the past two decades, Yehoshua argues that a Jew can best lead a normal, coherent and challenging life in Israel, and that the Diaspora is essentially a neurotic solution to the identity conflict between the Jews as a people (like any other) and as the Chosen People (like no other). In America, the secular and the orthodox stay out of each other's hair by ignoring the identity problem, one that Israelis confront every day, thanks to the West Bank settlements, and in Jerusalem twice on Shabbat, thanks to the growing number and influence of the men in black suits and hats. The Diaspora Jews pay for their evasiveness, through a weakening of identity and the consequent mounting losses to assimilation. The Jews of Israel, Yehoshua argues, can make this problem an opportunity by instituting religious reforms that would "expose the commandments to the complexities of life"—that is, to those of a national life. This would be the first step in naturalizing Judaism, as it were, in its modern homeland, which would enable its citizens to preserve their heritage while becoming a people like any other.

Given this position, which Yehoshua develops with all his mind and heart, it is surprising, to say the least, to find that his novels and stories might almost as well be set in the Diaspora as in Israel. Far from representing Israelis struggling with the religious-secular split, his characters seem oblivious of it. And far from even indicating the greater stability and fulfillment that is to be gained in Israel, they are typically deluded, anxious, and perverse and remain so.

His first novel, *The Lover*, is built around an obsessive quest by a wealthy auto shop owner to find his wife's lover (who disappeared during the Yom Kippur War) and around his relationship with a young education-starved Arab employee whom he eventually sends back home, a village where the boy's love of classical Hebrew poetry will hardly thrive. *A Late Divorce* conducts the reader through several branches of a dysfunctional family and its victims. The unhappy marriage of Ruth and Yehudah Kaminka culminates in her stabbing him, which leads her to be committed and him to immigrate to America. They produced one son who cannot consummate his marriage, another son who is nastily driving his married lover around the bend, and a daughter who is completely dominated by her boorish husband. Containing overtones of *The Sound and the Fury*, the Kaminkas of Jerusalem and Haifa are most reminiscent of the Compsons of Jefferson, Mississippi, in their mixture of haplessness and cruelty. Yehoshua's last novel, *Five Seasons*, is a brilliantly observed but monotonously unyielding account of the blind failures of a middle-aged accountant to free himself from his state of arrested adolescent love for his dead wife.

In the stories collected in *The Continuing Silence of a Poet*, the psychological and moral weather in Israel doesn't improve. An old widower and lapsed poet is stuck with a late-born retarded son who struggles to emulate him. Two stumped graduate students fill in dead time, one by vindictively babysitting the son of her former heartthrob, the other by minding a forest that he allows to be burned down by an Arab whose tongue has been cut out. An old schoolteacher who has seen too many of his students sent away to die in battle is informed that his son, from whom he is alienated, has fallen; though this proves to be a mistake, his mournfulness continues. A convalescing engineer destroys the love letters sent to his daughter by a soldier, and then runs him over with a car. And so on. These stories are finely, intricately written, but they read like an assimilated American Jew's jaundiced view of the Israelis. What is Yehoshua's left hand doing that his right seemingly knows not of?

One of the interests of *Mr. Mani*, Yehoshua's new novel, by far his most ambitious, visionary and powerful one, is that it suggests the coordinating element between his Zionist ideology and his fertile imagination of slow, family disaster. It does so by bringing the Diaspora into this chronicle of a bizarrely fated family and by steeping it in modern Jewish history—the first time he has done either in his fiction. The narrative moves backward in time through five intense dialogues about the Mani family, four by outsiders, involving the climactic events in the life of the firstborn Mani of each generation who acts out a strange proclivity for self-destruction. Each is related by an overwrought witness and sometimes an accomplice, whether intentional or inadvertent, to the deed. The relationship of the teller to the listener has its own tensions and implications: a disillusioned S.S. misfit speaks to his Bismarck of a mother; an effete physician speaks to his Zionist father, etc. Since the responses of the listeners are omitted, what they're saying has to be intuited by the reader, a device by which Yehoshua creates a high degree of reader involvement and narrative voltage that steps up the current running through each of the accounts. Further, his use of recurrent details and actions (a black overcoat, forms of binding, identification with Arabs, among many others) creates a sense of destiny inexorably playing out in the lives of the Manis, much as a recurrent place, a telltale garment, fraternal trickery is used in *Genesis* to the same end. All of which becomes overpowering, luminous and mysterious in the final tale, the source of the sources, the climax of the climaxes.

The teller is Avraham Mani, a Salonika spice merchant and unordained rabbi, who has just returned from Jerusalem, where his son, Yosef, was killed soon after the young man's marriage. The time is 1848, the place an inn in Athens. His auditor is Flora Molkho, the aunt of Yosef's young widow; also in the room is Flora's venerable husband and Avraham's beloved mentor, the renowned Rabbi Shabbetai Haddaya, who has suffered a severe stroke that has left him paralyzed and speechless. In a voice that mingles Judaic learning, Levantine culture, mercantile worldliness, family passion—the voice, that is, of the Sephardic Diaspora (I'm told that the Hebrew original is linguistically amazing, and Hillel Halkin's translation is certainly remarkable)—the first Mr. Mani relates the strange events leading up to and away from his son's death that implicate Doña Flora and, with mounting hysteria and despair, Avraham himself.

Many years before, when Avraham was a lesser disciple of Rabbi Haddaya and himself a recent widower, the rabbi had proposed him as a husband to the beauteous Flora; she refused the ardent merchant-rabbi but accepted Rabbi Haddaya despite his advanced years. Some years later Avraham sent his son Yosef to study with the rabbi, and Doña Flora, an upright woman but a childless and often lonely one, doted on the handsome teenager, as did the rabbi, allowing him the run of the household, including their bed when the venerable authority was on one of his frequent trips. Doña Flora also arranged Yosef's marriage to her niece, Tamara, who much resembles her. As Avraham insinuates, with oscillating reverence and rage toward Doña Flora, this resemblance proved to be the undoing of the marriage, at least of his consummating it; pining for the distant Doña Flora, the unhinged young bridegroom could only give himself to his *idée fixe*: that the Arabs of Palestine are really Jews who have not yet awakened to their true identity, which it was his task to bring about through instruction and, if necessary, chastisement.

Though Avraham had intended only to visit the young couple in Jerusalem, he stayed on to try to save both Yosef's son's marriage by bringing it to fruition and his life by following him during his reckless forays into the Arab quarter. He relates to Doña Flora that he was successful only in the first task and could not prevent Yosef from running amok on the steps of the Dome of the Rock, where he was stabbed to death by the guards. Then, after she leaves the room, he confesses to the rapidly sinking rabbi that the marriage remained unconsummated, that he himself is the father of the infant Mani, and worse...

And I, my master and teacher, was outside the gate, I was watching from afar while listening to the distant bell of a lost flock, silently, wretchedly waiting for the worst of the night to wear itself out and the morning star to appear in the east, faint and longed-for, so that I might go to him, to the far pole of his terror and sorrow, whether as his slaughterer or whether as the slaughterer's inspector, and release him from his earthly bonds…

We are meant to know which of the two he is from having listened to the tale as well as to the teller. While confessing to the rabbi and asking for judgment as to whether he should kill himself ("'Twould take but a nod"), Avraham has been loosening the garments and diaper in which the paralyzed old man is swaddled. The motif of unbinding evokes the Akeda, the binding of Isaac. The name and act of the speaker and perpetrator, the four suicidal actions in the preceding sections and the details (such as the lost flock) in this passage, which foretell details of the family destiny to follow from the sins of the father: all of this completes the revelation that this Abraham has slain his firstborn son. At least, so I read it.

Political Zionist that he is, Yehoshua regards Judaism as playing a large part in the abnormality of the Jewish people. In one of his polemical essays he points out that it is God the father who gives birth to his chosen people and bestows their homeland through Abraham, a foreigner. Instead, then, of the normal development of a people who have become such by inhabiting their homeland, the Jews owe all to their father figure, which goes to prove his absolute singularity as well as theirs. Yehoshua goes on to argue that Yahweh's command to destroy the people of Canaan stems from Judaism's strongly felt need to fundamentally impair a more natural relation with the motherland: the reiterative warning not to "defile the land," the hostility of the prophets to the cult of the earth, the deferral of the return until the Messiah comes are further examples of the compulsion to assert the supremacy of the father not only over the children of Israel but also to proscribe a normal bond among them. And since the collective identity of the Jewish people is intensely masculine (ask any observant Jewish woman), the obsession with defiling the land, etc., bespeaks the mother of all complexes in the Judaic psyche. Yehoshua infers from this analysis a kind of primal rationale for the Jews remaining in Golah, or exile, for 2,000 years: keeping the son away from the mother and under the exclusive sway of the father.

All of this is a directional arrow pointing to the connection between Yehoshua's Zionism and his fiction: That is, disturbed family relations and their surrogates are emblematic of the condition of the Jewish people, whether in the Diaspora or Israel. Thus marital distress, generational conflict and child neglect tend to be staples of Yehoshua's fiction—the disordered home life at least partly standing for the still-to-be-achieved homeland. Read in this way, a realistic novel like *A Late Divorce* takes on strong parabolic overtones: The elderly Kaminka, a *yored* (Israeli émigré), returns from America to get a divorce from his wife because he has fathered a child. His wife suffers from a dual personality, and his two sons, one hysterical, the other cynical, are both sexually impaired. By the end of the novel there are double meanings everywhere.

In *Mr. Mani*, the disorder takes the form of the manias (in Hebrew, *manya*) incorporated into the family name. Unable to receive a judgment from his rabbi, who died during Avraham's confessions, he lived on for a number of tormented years, ending as a rabbi and cantor in Mesopotamia, as we learn from one of the biographical sketches that follow as well as precede each tale. This, of course, is the original home of his biblical namesake, the primal seedbearer. Avraham Mani's obsession with his son's seed is also meant to further the association that weighs on him and his descendants with resonating significance: that is, another Jerusalem family that is the bearer of the Jewish vertigo, as Harold Rosenberg called it, and in this case through the past hundred years.

Three of the four tales of self-destructiveness in *Mr. Mani* are set in the context of epochal events in modern Jewish history. Dr. Moses Mani, Avraham's surviving son, meets the occasion of his destiny at the Third Zionist Congress in the person of a beautiful young Polish woman, a redhead like his mother and great-aunt. An obstetrician and a dandy, he has a mania for women; for him the Zionist congress is merely a place to interest wealthy women in himself as well as in his clinic in Jerusalem, which he has made into a mirrored shrine to the eternal feminine. His devouring passion for one Linka Shapiro is strangely abetted by her enervated brother (just as Yosef's for Doña Flora was by her aged husband). Taking her back to Poland from Jerusalem leads to the consummation of Dr. Moses Mani's even deeper desire: "The only hope is the maggot," as Avraham puts it.

Yosef, Moses's son, is obsessed with the politics of the Ottoman Empire; his particular calling, like his uncle Yosef's, is to straighten out the Arabs of Palestine toward the end of World War I, when the British have arrived to drive out the Turks and change things utterly. His *idée fixe* is that the Arabs must be prepared for statehood because a competing state will now surely come to pass in this land. A crack interpreter for the British Army, Yosef spies for the Turks in order to have access to his uncomprehending Palestinian pupils, and then more or less arranges for himself to be captured and convicted of treason by the British (there is a quasi-legal British passport in the family—one of the many instruments of its destiny) so that he can give his most electrifying speech before he is to be hanged.

The bizarre machinations of this Levantine cafe prophet are related by his military prosecutor, Lieutenant Ivor Stephen Horowitz, who is about as culturally distant from him as Westminster Abbey is from the Wailing Wall, particularly since Horowitz is relating it to a newly arrived judge and war hero whom he takes for granted to be anti-Semitic. (However, since almost everything is connected in this cunning mosaic of irony inlaid with family and tribal déjà vu, Horowitz's mother is Sephardic, and two of the previous Manis were pets of the British consulate.) Along with being a superb rendition of Anglo-Jewish anxiety, Horowitz's tale is charged, as are the others, by the power of the Manis to make each of the witnesses who tell their tale into accomplices of their singular destiny, even revenants of their genetic nightmare of guilt and atonement, beginning with Avraham of his Arab-dazed son's.

Behind the deadly antics of these *folies à deux* that give the novel much of its pace and spin lies a thesis: namely, that the Manis, like the Jews of Yehoshua's polemical essays, are responsible for their own fate. In "The Constant Shadow of War," an essay on the Palestinian conflict, he writes:

> I sometimes ask myself whether the obduracy of this conflict perhaps derives from the deep roots of that ancient struggle between the Jews and the world. And can it be that secretly we Jews fear the termination of this conflict? For then we will finally find ourselves at the beginning of a harmonious, or at least essentially normal, relationship with the world. Do the Jews really want simply to be happy? wondered Hermann Cohen....By this question, no less and perhaps even more than by all his philosophy, he expressed a distinctly Jewish sensibility. For the Jew fears that something essential to his identity will be lost if he stands in a normal relationship with the world.

The acid test for this thesis, as for the novel, is the Holocaust, which finds Yosef Mani (who was spared from being hanged as a traitor) on the island of Crete, along with his son, daughter-in-law and grandson. Faced with the banality of Jewish collaboration but committed by his story itself to it, Yehoshua comes up with a narrative strategy almost as startling as the climactic one involving Avraham. The witness and accomplice is an S.S. medic, a devotee of Hellenism, who captures the Manis in the ruins of King Minos's palatial labyrinth, where they have the guide and trinkets concession. And labyrinthine become the relations between Private Egon Bruner and Yosef and Efrayim Mani, which include the binding and death of Yosef as a hostage and a renunciation by both Egon and Efrayim of their respective identities that have brought them to this juncture— though their respective guilt then insures that the will of the Manis, like that of the Führer, be done.

The only half of a dialogue that is less than riveting is, unfortunately, the first one, in which another lovely young redhead tells her mother of her encounter with the suicidal father of her lover. At this point, we are in contemporary Israel, and the self-destructive demon in the Mani blood has become a ghost of itself, a kind of *Schadenfreude* in the otherwise sober makeup of Judge Gavriel Mani, who even manages to resist the lure of dangerous Palestinian towns. Otherwise, the family's enigmatic paternalism toward the Palestinians is left to dangle without issue just at the point in history when something even more rich and illuminative than what has gone before could have been made of it.

But if the opening section is problematic, the rest of *Mr. Mani* is a marvel. Yehoshua has set himself the task of narrating one hundred years of suicide in a way that is both coherent and yet unexpected. Except for Garcia Márquez's *Chronicle of a Death Foretold*, I can't think of a recent novel whose technique is such a tour de force of re-created suspense and enfolding pattern. Such books set the novel back fifty or seventy-five years—to the era of Faulkner, Conrad and Forster, when innovations in narrative form and voice and the detection of destiny, the perennial subject of great fiction, went hand-in-hand. As such *Mr. Mani* is an original and daring re-envisioning of the Zionist view of Judaism, which uses the previously apparent disconnect betwen the political position of Yehoshua the staunch Zionist and the domestic fiction of the saturnine novelist, to dramatize a deep vision of the Jewish fate that is playing itself out today on the West Bank.

(1992)

Meyer Liben and His Generation

Meyer Liben was a quiet member of the clamorous community of New York writers and intellectuals that has come to be identified with the halcyon days of *Partisan Review* and that has now faded into history and legend. Like most of them, Liben was the son of Eastern European Jewish immigrants, had been raised in New York, and had gone to City College in the 1930s, one of the main ports of entry for the ideas of Marx, Lenin, and Trotsky, Freud and Jung, which like many of his fellow alumni, Liben was to take a hand in adapting, refining, and modifying as time went on. Though he was a close friend of Paul Goodman and Delmore Schwartz, as he was later to be of Harold Rosenberg and Dwight Macdonald, Liben did not take up at first their careers as freelance intellectuals but instead went into his family's tire business, and when, after a heart attack, he retired early and settled in Greenwich Village it was not to raise bohemian Cain or bourgeois hackles but rather a family. Though he had played on the basketball team at CCNY during the famous Nat Holman era, Mike, as he was known as by his friends, was the most unassuming of the writers I have known well. In his writing he eschewed the aggressive point-making style and somewhat preening erudition of the *Partisan Review* group, and instead developed a spare, unassuming, conversational prose of a man of middle sensibility, as the French say, with a lively, open mind—a kind of higher curiosity. Similarly, he tended to take the characters and themes of his stories from the Jewish middle class he remained part of—small-business men and modest professionals who carried within their practical, enterprising minds a poetry of fugitive desires.

The sense of the second-generation Jews—the so-called business generation—may be no more than a stack of tendentious and superficial images, minted from the coin of their post-war prosperity. Whether presented by his apologists or by his critics, the second-generation Jew is typically a hard-driving businessman and a sentimental ethnic, still a little anxious, perhaps, but basically at ease in the suburbs. Whether hailed as a hero of individual and communal enterprise or bitterly criticized as a materialist and a chauvinist, the second generation Jew has suffered a reduction of his experience: the struggle of the 1920s to get out of the ghetto and to get the ghetto out of oneself, the social and political intensities of the Depression years, the trauma of the Holocaust—all these have become, in one way or another, merely stages along the route to Great Neck. All the vulgarity belongs to the second generation, all the sensitivity to the third; all the complacency to the second, all the crises to the third. And, recently, all the struggle, spirit, and color to the first generation. Under the spell of false nostalgia and devious revenge, as well as of writers such as Singer and Malamud, my generation seems to be cultivating the idea that the only authentic Jews are the impoverished, bizarre, or long-dead ones.

All of which is a pretty misleading state of affairs. The rebels who like to write novels about the lower East Side with Hasidic overtones did not spring fully armed from the head of the Lubavitcher Rebbe, nor did the supercilious young intellectuals stumble all by themselves on their great tradition of Marx, Freud, Einstein, *et al.* Most of us— whether literary or advertising men, psychiatrists or tax specialists— follow the common fate, are living out the dreams of the business generation, just as its members lived out the dreams of the immigrant workers. The aspirations link up all the way back to the emancipation, as do the discontents—whether one calls them "*angst*" or "aggravation" or "*tsores.*"

Under these circumstances, the fiction of Meyer Liben is particularly valuable. In his modest way, Liben is a kind of Sholom Aleichem of the older, middle-class urban Jews, who expresses the ironies of their lives and attitudes by remaining faithful to the sources of his own values and to the continuity of experience linking the East Harlem of his childhood, City College, and Greenwich Village; linking the family life of the generations; linking the worker, the businessman, and the writer. Here is one of his typical characters, a distributor of encyclopedias who drives himself hard—"I get a certain pleasure (if not basic) out of buying cheap and selling dear…there's no standing still, you either go ahead or retreat"—but who deeply envies the man in the next office because he earns his living by dreaming up products, is reputed to have invented the yo-yo and the hula hoop.

> Whether he was indeed the creator of these remarkable toys I do not know, but certainly that was the way his mind ran—toward the creation of the absolutely simple, what answers a universal emotional need, the kind of thing that, once on the market, causes people to say: "Absolutely obvious. How come I didn't think of it?" without realizing how hard the perfection is to come by and how hard it is to wed the perfection to the obvious, the universal.

Most of the stories in *Justice Hunger* are told in the first person, and the narrator is usually the same type of man, whether he is the graduate student of history in the novella "Justice Hunger," who is trying to keep his head above water in the ideological riptide of the Thirties; the office worker in "A Note on Chivalry" who rescues an elegant girl from a socialist's jargon; or the tireless go-getter in "Ball of Fire" who rediscovers a sweet vein of lassitude in himself through reading *Oblomov*. Liben's imagination is essentially a reflective one: his heroes are generally designed to express his point of view, to speak with his voice, to stand in his shoes. They are sensible fellows, devoted to the work of the world, to their practical opportunities and responsibilities; but they carry in themselves a hunger for romance, whether of action or thought, that secretly opposes the patterns of their compunctions and repressions and wishes to dislodge them.

"Position is everything in life," says the narrator of "Justice Hunger," "that much at least I had learned in the poolrooms." His sense of position, however, is characteristically prey to deeper yearnings, like a pool player who is tempted by the fancy combination shots. In this case, the narrator is an earnest young liberal who is attracted to a girl who glows with the radical convictions of the Thirties, an ex-dancer, a divorcee, a Midwesterner with a Gentile background: in sum, the image of all his secret desires. He struggles to overcome his temperamental bias for political detachment and objectivity ("I thought of that fine word 'disinterest' and how it was slowly losing its meaning"), his aversion to the atmosphere of the Marxist enclaves, both grandiose and grim (a "loveless cynicism"), as well as his shyness and uncertainty ("I should have liked to come closer but did not know how"). The division within between passion and realism, pleasure and prudence, sensitizes his consciousness, makes him a tireless analyst and conversationalist—the verbal flow being his way of bridging the inner split and of connecting to the world, of fighting off "the sense of separation and loss that is forever crowding us." But he remains a man who cannot line himself up for long with his opportunities, for his hunger is basic to his nature, seemingly a state of permanent dissatisfaction that determines his divided view of experience, organizes his sacrifices and compensations, curtails his aggression, and leaves him standing on the sideline.

In story after story, Liben describes this situation with unusual subtlety and poignancy. The speaker in "The Locking Gas-Cap" has been engaged for six years to a girl who is hung up on the image of her father, an adventurous civil engineer who died when she was very young, as well as on the possessive strategies of her mother. The couple own a car together, a sort of surrogate home, over which they delight and worry, "the primary cathexes," as he puts it in his mock jargon, "having attached themselves to the secondary phenomena." One day she reports that the gas-cap has been stolen for the fourth time. He judiciously suggests a ride in the car to calm her down; she embraces him ardently ("I must say she seemed unusually aroused by the theft of these accessories from our car"). With a show of masculine competence (or is it his worrisome prudence?) he suggests a locking gas-cap, takes her to a garage, goes through the usual small humiliation of such places (though he has been a salesman of automotive parts, knows the owner, and hopes to show off a bit—

always competing, as he feels, with the girl's dead father). But with the new cap in place, her passion suddenly turns sour; she worries about the device (suppose she loses the key), then about her mother's latest depression. Always perceptive, always obliging, he dissipates the tension by suggesting they take her mother to the movies with them that night. It is, as he puts it, "a perfectly stable unhappy situation," the two of them cooperating expertly to maintain a common front against the risks of deliverance, getting in just enough desire to keep their inhibitions lubricated, their regressions in working order.

But that sounds more pat than it is; like the symbol of the gas-cap, the story is both immediately clear and rich in implications. Like much of Liben's fiction, it employs in the service of the variations of individual character, the nuances of the living moment. The woman is overly attached to her parents, but she is still a complex and desirable woman. The narrator's subservience in the name of "understanding" her keeps him standing on a dime, emotionally speaking, but does not rob him of wit, affection, awareness. Liben's heroes may lose out, but they are always more than the conventional portraits of the *nebbish,* and there is always more at stake than their weakness, their failure. Most of them are, peculiarly enough, bachelors, though tied to their mothers in the standard Jewish way. But the mother of the narrator in "The Office Next Door" is not the standard devouring monster, nor are his feelings toward her caricatured in the current fashion. He explains his attraction to the inventor's secretary as follows:

> She looked to be the age of my mother at the time that I was twelve or thirteen. It was then, for reasons I never clearly under-stood (though I now assume it must have been related to some crisis in the family life), that my mother turned toward me with love, affection, and, yes, need of an extraordinarily intensity. I think she realized that this feeling was too powerful for my own good, too powerful for her own good, but she seemed unable to control herself. I was impressed, flattered, as well as confused by this tor-rent of affection. Never since has a woman loved me the way my mother loved me for that unforgettable year....She went with me to unlikely places, up to Yankee Stadium, for example, to look at

those games, about which she could not have been more ignorant, from both a technical and historical view. There she sat at my side, gazing at this complex choreography, occasionally asking questions, less out of desire for knowledge than to make it appear that she was interested and so, she thought, adding to my pleasure.

In going out with girls, I have always felt uncomfortable in being with those of my own age or younger and have shied away from those older, though it was to these older girls that I was most strongly drawn.

Much of Liben's temperament is reflected in this passage, one that suggests the sources of the basic hunger that he writes about as well as the emotional tones and themes that grow out of it: a sense of exile and loss and frustrated deliverance well up naturally in his fiction. So does a tenderness toward the unfulfilled, a highly developed feeling for the fantasies of desire and guilt. So does an awareness of the shifting bases of a relationship and of the buried structures of feeling that can lie beneath a word or gesture.

As in Freud, the discontents of Liben's characters are also embedded in their social drives; in this case, those of a generation whose main business in life was to climb and remain on the precarious ladder into the middle class. The basic hunger works to keep them hustling after its goods and values, underwrites their prowess in business, stimulates their strong political interests ("we [were] all hungrily reaching out to one another, to create a sense of individual value, a sense of communion"), and supports their striving for culture. Liben's characters are, typically, involved in that great pursuit of what used to be called "refinement" (the courtship in "Justice Hunger" is mainly carried on at lectures, recitals, foreign movies; the hero of "Ball of Fire" sits up at night in a hotel room in St. Louis meditating on *Oblomov*; a secretary in "Solomon's Wisdom" uses the time when her boss is out of the office to write poetry).

What also rings true throughout *Justice Hunger* is a certain wry tone—both commonsensical and cultivated, a quiet blend of irony, curiosity, and conviction—which expresses the higher ethos of the second generation. It is a tone that is beginning to fade into history, though one still hears it, *mutatis mutandis*, in the poetry of Charles Reznikoff or the fiction of Daniel Fuchs. Perhaps it can best be characterized as a decorum of the spirit, a residue of Jewish spirituality.

Justice Hunger is an uneven collection of Liben's stories, a couple of which bear the marks of his apprenticeship, just as he allows the long title story to spread out rather thinly in places. Nonetheless it is a unique, gently lit, and lovely book, one that I especially commend to those members of my own generation of secular Jewish intellectuals who are looking for their actual roots.

(1967, 1986)

PART FIVE

The Literary Community

An earlier version of the following was given as a talk on the occasion of the 1996 Whiting Awards.

For the past two decades Gerald Freund has been one of the most important members of the literary community in America, as important in his way as John Updike to fiction or Robert Bly to poetry or Harold Bloom to criticism or Robert Silvers and Leon Wieseltier to literary intellect or Dan Halpern and Sam Hamill to literary publishing. This evening ten writers will receive $30,000 worth of free time, their most needed working condition, and the approval of their peers, the most enabling recognition writers can earn. These ten writers join the hundreds of poets, fiction writers, essayists, and dramatists whose careers Freund has aided in these two basic ways.

Hundreds is no hyperbole. The Whiting program alone now accounts for 120 of them; add to that the 100 or more literary recipients of the MacArthur Fellowships, which Freund ran and helped to keep alive during its early, traumatic years; add to that the 60 Lila Wallace Reader's Digest Writing Awards, which he created. Now there are also his Rona Jaffee Awards for the young gifted writers. And this doesn't take into account his years of funding writers through the program he directed at the Rockefeller Foundation and, in the past decade, through a network of smaller grants he assembled.

In sum, he has created a support structure that spans the abiding and often necessitous uncertainty of most literary careers. The Rona Jaffee Awards reach into the mass of aspiring writers churned out by the MFA programs, identifies several of the most gifted, and confirms their shaky sense of vocation. The Whiting Awards help the accomplished younger writer to know that he now has a career, that she has crossed the mountains and desert and reached the sea. The Wallace Awards help those who are in full career to navigate the treacherous middle of the voyage, often against the powerful tide of current trends and fashions and the high winds of change in publishing houses that have been blowing many fiction writers and poets hither and yon, and sometimes right back into the oblivion they thought they had put behind them. Finally, a number of the MacArthur recipients have been elderly and/or sorely neglected innovative writers who have been given the chance to complete careers that might other wise have exhausted their resources and morale.

I am not only paying tribute to a man, I am also pointing up his cause—the identification, nurture, and support of vital writing in America today. *Vital* in both senses, *alive* and *necessary*: writing that finds the enduring in the topical, reclaims the complexity of life from the sitcom and the crime series, from the news story and the talk show, from pop fiction and theater. Thus, along with the nurture, care, and relief of individual writers, Freund has helped to maintain the literary community itself, which has been staggering through deep struggles of identity and values in the past two decades because of the ever more intense commodification of publishing, the campus warfare between traditional writers and postmodernists, the impact of multiculturalism on literary norms and standards and book sales, the erosion of support for the small press movement and the independent writer. Such a small outpost of our culture and yet so fragmented and under siege.

I'm not going to deliver another jeremiad about the literary-industrial complex or revisit the vexing issues of literature as art versus literature as a major resource of gender, sexual, racial, regional and ethnic identity and expression. But there is another corrosive consequence of our market-driven and promotion-directed society to talk about, a consequence that the Whiting and the other prestigious awards help to check and alleviate. As we know, big-time publishing lives cheek-by-jowl with the magazine, TV and movie business; in many cases, its houses are subsidiaries of the infotainment conglomerates such as Fox and Time-Warner, and they are increasingly part of the mass media, the great leveler of cultural distinctions. Pursuing synergies and profits of scale, publishing has picked up the media's inordinate and contagious interest in topicality, celebrity, trendiness, and knowingness. In a word, the Buzz—the circuitry that connects book, author, publicity, gossip, and market and that, along with the bottom line, is the chief measure of a book's success. If you read the *New York Observer*, for example, you can see the publishing business turning into show business before your eyes.

The importance of the Buzz doesn't stop with the media. It goes out into the culture, even the literary culture. I taught in and visited a number of MFA programs where the Buzz reverberates in the intense questions I'm asked about marketing and promoting one's fiction; or the Buzz resides in the fiction itself which approaches a current trend or niche with wide-open arms. What these writers are responding to is not the old spur of eventual fame but the new one of well-planned celebrity. They're aware of the writers, painters, and musicians who have been able to place their pulse on the media's finger and turn it into Buzz, the soundtrack of fame in our time.

It is squarely against this phenomenon that the Whiting and the other literary awards stand and in so doing give hope and reassurance as well as money. Instead of mindless media interviews which make you wonder who you are and a tiny audience at a Barnes and Noble reading which make you wonder what you're doing there, awards like these provide recognition and confirmation and a small portion of genuine, clarified fame from the community that matters most to quality writers. That is what we are doing here this evening—keeping the faith that there is still such a community because for this hour or two, just as the Whiting judges have been doing in their meetings to select the winners, we are rallying the community's members and supporters as well as asserting its values.

As I've said elsewhere, the literary community is becoming like catacomb Christianity in a Roman empire whose household gods are wealth, power, status, and prurience. The community still lives on in a publishing house where the book culture leads a shadowy, compli-cated existence in the interstices of the marketing culture, and often in the same mind of a publisher and editor and even sales manager or publicity director. It lives on in the creative writing and human-istic interstices of the English departments, where novelists and poets and literary critics contend with the regnant dogma and growth in-dustry of sell-regarding literary theory. It exists in the interstices of high-tech word processing where small presses set up shop and keep the flow of new writing circulating. It lives on must importantly of all in the personal and enabling relationships between and among writers and between generations of writers. The literary community may be small, it may be bitterly divided, it may be losing newly won ground to the philistines. But except for the '60s and a while after, it's never had it easy in America, where it's not an institution as it is in France or Germany or the U.K. But it's still out there in America and hanging in, still resourceful, and still able to reinvigorate itself and its members—with a little help from its friends like Gerry Freund. As the poet and poetry editor T.S. Eliot put it, we're not trying to prevail but just to keep something alive.

As a New York literary editor and reviewer and occasional writ-ing teacher, I was in touch for most of the past forty years with the literary community and its resources and problems, but I understand better now what it is and how it works for a writer because in recent years I've been living the life of an isolated and increasingly obscure member of it. About five years ago I left my place in the limelight and the Buzz, such as my portion was, and went off to live in a little town near Hampton Bays, Long Island: the working man's Hampton, where culture begins at the little local library and ends at Blockbuster Video. Though I had anticipated and hoped for the solitude it con-ferred, I was surprised and dismayed to find out how soon the phone stopped ringing. The silence in my new study was matched by an even stranger silence in my head: not the silence of peace and con-templation, but the silence of inertness. I had taken my mind away from publishing and was crestfallen to find that, without its relationships and routines jogging my brain cells, not much was going on in there, except, now and then, a pounding cognitive dissonance.

As the wise say, be careful what you wish for. I had retired from publishing mainly to write a memoir, the story of my family and myself. Along with the time and solitude that early retirement confers, I felt I needed precisely the absence of the Buzz, which would be at best distracting and at worst destructive to my task. For I knew what the buzzers wanted, having so recently been one myself. I particularly knew what they wanted from an author like myself: they wanted to know all about what it was like to work at *Commentary* when Norman Podhoretz was changing his mind back in the '60s; or about editing *Book Week* by myself during the five month strike of the *World Journal Tribune*; or about the experiences of starting and maintaining *New American Review*, preferably with the lowdown on working with Philip Roth, Norman Mailer, and Susan Sontag *et al*; or about my relationships with the New York Jewish intellectuals and the counterculture renegades; or about my adventures in trade publishing with both the Helen Wolffs and the Richard Snyders. That's what I, the erstwhile buzzer, would want to acquire and not some oft-told story of two immigrant East European families and of growing up Jewish and American in the 1930s and '40s. So I mainly retired to East Quogue because I couldn't afford to have one side of my mind saying to the other, "Come on, Ted, who cares anymore about this personal and dated stuff?" Or, "Who is going to buy this book?"—the leading question of the career I had just left. I couldn't afford to have those worries—but try telling a writer what he can and cannot worry about.

The dissonance between what would likely get a nice contract and what I wanted to write and needed to learn how to write, if the later, career material wasn't to turn into the higher gossip, I've come to see as an inevitable part of the reeducation of someone who had stopped being a literary editor and moonlighter and who has begun to be a novice memoirist—that is, someone who is lonely and very unsure of himself. After a month or two, I couldn't stand it. To get the phone ringing again, to have another author for company, to keep my hand in, my name in print and most of all to feel again that I knew how to write, I went to work as a regular contributing editor to *The Nation*.

This went reasonably well for two years or so, that is until the day a new dissonant dialogue started up, this one between the busy professional literary journalist and the neglected amateur memoirist who was bitterly saying, "You didn't have to retire to write about the paperback publishing mentality that increasingly dominates hardcover publishing or to defend Irving Howe's legacy or to review John Cheever's journals. That's not what the chance you were giving yourself was about." Finally, the mediator between the two, my writing conscience, said, "The amateur is right. Give him his full chance."

I reminisce in this shameless way on this occasion, which belongs to you ten writers, because the experience has given me a much clearer and deeper awareness that there really is a literary community that has sustained you, that it's not just a hopeful fiction or a metaphor for gossip, status seeking, and networking for reading gigs. My conversion to imaginative writing didn't happen overnight or in a week or a month. It took more than a year before the voice of the Buzz stopped for good and the voices began to flow into my mind from the literary community, the living and the dead.

The novelist (and converted editor and publisher) E.L. Doctorow instructed me to "trust the writing process." That became a mantra— the simple, difficult Way. A number of writerly truths followed from it. One is that you find out what the pitfalls are in your approach by occupying them, that the memoir process, for example, isn't as interested in your family background as it is in your conflicts. Another is that you find your way by apparently losing it. You start the chapter with a clear idea of what you're going to tell and the process takes over and soon you're writing about something that has nothing to do with it or that you can hardly remember or even know if it really happened. Before long, you're lost. You have the feelings of being lost, of doubt and fear, which you learn to live with and even welcome. Philip Roth, another of my new allies and instructors told me,

"It's when I get lost that I feel I'm getting somewhere because some new stuff is getting freed up." When I sent him the lengthy autobiographical sketch I'd written for the Contemporary Authors series and thought was more or less my book in miniature, he said, "What you have to do now is take this and shatter it," which was dismaying, perplexing, but proved to be necessary advice if I was to penetrate the superficial, feel-good "line" we hand out about ourselves and get to the real story of my early life. I also began to mind the words of my main colleague on *American Review*, Richard Howard, who had said, "Only the risky is really interesting." Jerome Charyn helped me with his advice that you have to get a rhythm going in the work. Some words of Russell Banks reminded me in my cynical moments that cynicism is usually the sign of a writer who is losing it.

Another of the members of the community who took up residence in my head was Henry James who kept telling me, "We work in the dark—we do what we can—we give what we have. Our doubt is our passion and our passion is our task." He'd told me that before but now he was telling it to me for keeps. In the midst of the darkness and doubt that went on for the next four years, he and my other allies in the literary community, of whom I've mentioned only a few, sustained the passion that grew out of doubt as it diminished and enabled me to complete the task. Probably the most important message I got along the way was from Hayden Carruth who crustily told me after reading the first hundred pages to stop worrying, that I was getting somewhere, to keep going.

What I had to do, in effect, was to take off the comfortable shoes I'd been wearing for thirty years and start walking barefoot so that I could feel my ground, to throw away the crutch of writing about other writers' imaginations and make my slow, stumbling, often backward way with my own. I had to join the seven fiction writers we honor this evening because, as I found out, when I'd gotten the hang of what I was doing, the memoir worth writing is the envisioned and intuitive narrative under the memories that it retrieves, connects, and weights with meaning, shades with nuance and implication. To cope with my old habits of the literary pundit and the Village Explainer, as well as to keep on "shattering," I relied heavily on D.H. Lawrence's "Trust the tale, not the teller," or in current parlance, "It's a story, stupid." I also had to join the three poets we are honoring to the extent that I found out that the way to cull the important experiences from all the others that swarm around a family and a life is by going to the painful ones, even the shameful ones, and to the joyous and affirming ones. These can be no less repressed to the novice memoirist, no less in need of being teased out by listening to your language.

So to you ten much younger writers I can say now I know what you've been through. I understand what this award means. But I feel I should add Alfred Kazin's remark that "the trouble with being a writer is that you never know where you stand." For if Alfred Kazin doesn't know, who does? The media glare and buzz of a Whiting Award will soon vanish, and in a year so will the money and the time it's freed up. The recognition this evening from your peers, from your real community, will not tell you where you stand once you're back in the stillness of Portland, Oregon or Auburn, Alabama, or in the Buzz of New York and Los Angeles. But I hope that you'll let this award go on recognizing that you've been doing something important in your work, something right for your process, something good for others writers and readers as well as for your publisher, your editor, your agent, your copy editor and publicist who are grateful to you for confirming the significance of their work and renewing their connection to the literary community. Believe me, they need you.

(1997)

A Few Good Voices in My Head

Many years ago, probably around 1971, a young writer came to see me. He wanted to write an essay for *American Review* about the sudden decline of the counterculture, and we talked about that for a while. He seemed both jaunty and troubled, as many young people were in that fading era of fresh alternatives, but he didn't seem to have much of a grip on his subject. I suggested that instead of talking, he might do better to sit down and write and see what he really wanted to say. He said that that was the other thing he wanted to talk to me about. He had been having trouble writing lately and he thought that writing for *American Review* might get him going. "I don't know who to write for anymore," he said.

I asked him whom he had written for in the past. Well, he'd started out as an English major at Yale and written mostly for his professors. "I came on as a sort of young Northrop Frye." After college he landed a job at *Time* and became a staff writer, which was a welcome change from fancy literary jargon, and he did it happily for a couple of years. But then, "I got tired of the *Time* style, of having to come up with clever locutions like 'sluburb' and 'peace-monger.'" Also, as he said, "My politics were changing and some of my friends were writing for *The Village Voice* or *Rolling Stone*." So he began to moonlight for the then alternative press, and after a while he left *Time* and traveled around the country, writing reportage about the new street communities, communes, and so forth.

Why, then, didn't he write this piece for, say, *Rolling Stone*? He explained that writing for the youth culture had become like the flip side of writing for *Time*: you were just "enthusiastic and snotty about the opposite things." Also you had to deal with another standardized style—words like "downer," and "heavy," and "hassle," and spelling America with a *k*. That's why, he said, "I'd like to write for *AR*—you don't have any one style, any one point of view, and that grabs me. On the other hand, it's hard to know what you're looking for."

He was watching me carefully, as though I might inadvertently reveal the secret requirement. I said that *AR* published different kinds of pieces but mostly they were ones that seemed necessary for the writer to have written, which is why I suggested he try to find out what he really needed to say. He nodded but pressed on. "Okay, but look—you write yourself, right? Who do you write for?" I thought for a moment and said, "I guess I write for a few good voices in my head." At which point he suddenly smiled, relaxed, looked at me in a companionable way, and said, "A few good voices in your head—far out!"

Well, I've been thinking about that idea off and on ever since. I don't think it's as far out as the young writer found it. I think it's the way people start out writing—or painting, or composing, or doing scientific research: for one or two powerfully meaningful figures in their lives. And I think that those who continue as artists remain in touch with complementary and internalized versions of those early good voices. Needless to say, there are also bad voices in one's head—voices of doubt and despair and intimidation, particularly intimidation, which can also have a powerful effect early in one's career, and late as well. Harry Stack Sullivan calls these voices "supervisory presences" or "personifications of the self." They are evident in daily behavior; they prepare our faces for the faces that we meet, put us at ease or turn on the anxiety, tell us to be gentle or firm or tentative or to keep quiet, to let yourself go or to cut the crap. And so with writing. Sullivan describes his own writing supervisor as a "charming pill, bitterly paranoid, a very brilliant thinker and a wrongheaded imbecile, whose harassment in the name of an impossible clarity is all but entirely responsible for the fact that I almost never publish anything."

But to return to the benign voices. Literary scholarship, at least the more conventional kind, looks for another kind of supervisory presence, which it calls "influences." Thus scholars say that Hemingway was deeply influenced by Gertrude Stein and find the main import of this in Hemingway's sparse idiom, his use of repetition, his sentence rhythms, his impassive point of view, etc. But such studies of stylistic influence or imitation of content seem to me to focus upon the signs rather than the substance of the indebtedness, which has less to do with imitation than with validation. Perhaps what Hemingway got most from Gertrude Stein was confirmation—that his way of being a writer was all right, or rather that this way, one of several possibilities for him, was the right way because it brought out the precarious best in him. So I shall try to write about influence in a positive way, in the spirit of Gorky's statement about Tolstoy: "As long as this man is alive, I am not alone in the world."

Actually, Tolstoy's role in Gorky's sense of himself and his vocation, his encouraging, testing and confirming presence, probably came relatively late in Gorky's development, and was preceded by other good voices, good supervisory presences, beginning with his loving, story-telling grandmother, the one redemptive figure in that disaster area of poverty, brutality, and uprootedness that was Gorky's childhood. The reason a writer needs such presences is that they minister to the ongoing identity conflict, sometimes acute, sometimes dormant, but probably never resolved, that is characteristic of the literary vocation itself.

A writer's identity, according to Erik Erikson, often begins to be formed in late adolescence, and points to the individual's unique core, and its intimate relation to his own group's inner tradition. As Erikson puts it, "the young individual must learn to be most himself when he means most to others, the others being those who mean most to him." A writer's "identity," then, involves a mutual relation, between what earlier ages would have called one's spirit or soul and the persistent ability to share it with kindred spirits, particularly those from the tribe, as it were, he belongs to. Without this early and then ongoing transaction, the problem of my young visitor is likely to arise, for he was trying to tell me he no longer knew who he was as a writer, so dependent had his identity become on a succession of immediate, receptive, but transient audiences, so removed had he become, in trying to accommodate them, from his unique core.

The young writer is typically beset on both sides of the issue of "being most himself" and of "meaning most to others." On the one hand, he is likely to be just emerging from the adolescent turmoil in which his creative self has been under attack from his conforming, socialized self for being freakish, timid, unpopular. On the other hand, she is also beginning the process, likely as not, of challenging the values of her home and community, which are felt to be inimical to a literary career but which are also connected to the "inner tradition" that she sooner or later finds she abandons at her peril.

Hence the importance of the right literary role model. "As long as this man is alive, I am not alone in the world." Such a figure nurtures the young writer in the estranged and divided state that William James calls being "twice born," which is true of most writers I have worked with, including myself. Part authority figure, part ally, whether real or imagined, the right older writer confers upon the enterprise of writing a more powerful and refined version of *your* way of feeling, *your* sense of significance. His durable presence instills within you a hopefulness that you can somehow, someday, embody— not imitate but embody—the same felt values that this higher kindred spirit does. By being there, if only in your imagination, he prevents you from being an orphan as a writer—merely your parents' son, on the one hand, and your dubiously sensitive inner side, on the other. From this influence can come the beginnings of a style, because as you fall under the spell of the writer, you try to make the bond a little tighter and more intimate by being adopted, as it were, by his voice. But the durable influence, I believe, is from the kindred but refined attitude and values behind the voice, which center and inspire you by evoking the new but "persistent sameness of self." It's not so very different from finding a best friend or a good psychotherapist who brings out and confirms your better nature, who prompts your clearest, most personal, most truthful voice. It's also not so very different from prayer.

Not all influences, as I said, are centering and enabling ones. Erikson observes that the twice-born are particularly vulnerable to new ideologies that provide answers to those pressing questions that come with a new identity and also offer a way of repudiating the past life which nourished and frustrated the self. At the time, for example, that I was starting to think of myself as a writer, there was a prevailing literary ideology, known as the New Criticism. Its principal canon was that literature was best read hermetically and hermeneutically. The true meaning and emotion of a poem or story or a novel were to be found in the text itself, especially between the lines, where the deeper content was hidden away from common view in the form of ambiguity, irony, paradox. Literature was the Great Tradition of sacrosanct texts, and a literary vocation was like a priestly one, in which you first mastered these texts and the mode of interpretation before you were really entitled to practice the rites. There was even a recondite, mysterious language—"sacramental vision," "social anagogic," "the heresy of unintelligence," and so forth—which bespoke the hieratic aspiration. Bathed in Catholic or Anglo-Catholic or American-Protestant doctrines, the New Criticism trailed in its wake the anti-Semitism of Eliot and Pound. Nonetheless, I was caught up in it by the time I was a junior at Michigan, and was carried far away from my coarse, practical, middle-class Jewish background and its liberal sentiments.

Erikson observes that the twice-born person does not generally solve his identity problem when he adopts a new ideology; instead he may well be creating a kind of pseudo-self and a subsequent crisis at the point when he "half-realizes that he is fatally overcommitted to what he is not." This was to be the story of my next five years: a pretentious literary self with fetishistic notions of detachment and purity of style and covertly placed meanings. Mostly I wrote stories over and over again, modeled on the austere surfaces of Joyce's *Dubliners* or Flaubert's "Un Coeur Simple," beneath which lay a circuitry that was switched on only at the end by an epiphany that was supposed to cast a subtle retrospective light. Or something like that. A full account of this dead end is in an early essay, "Silence, Exile, and Cunning."

Fortunately, life did not leave my pseudo-self alone. While I was still at Michigan I wrote a review for the *Daily* of the stories of William Carlos Williams. Since he, too, was part of the modernist pantheon, I assumed that his stories were much more complex than they seemed and I gave them the exegetical treatment, as though Williams were Kafka, ambiguities and paradoxes everywhere, whereas his stories were really much more like those of his fellow physician Chekhov—all eyes and heart. The review was rejected as too "obscure." At first this didn't dismay me. What would a college newspaper editor know about symbolic meaning? Looking for vindication, I showed my review to my favorite English professor. He said that my writing style had certainly changed a lot since the last time he'd read it. He also said that reading my review made him feel as if he'd been hung by his suspenders.

His name was Herbert Barrows. He wasn't a New Critic either, but I took his response hard. He was the most civilized man I had yet met, a Boston bachelor who might have stepped out of the pages of a Henry James novel, one of those discreet tutelary figures like Ralph Touchett or Lambert Strether, who say little but understand everything. That Barrows had thought well of my writing had been one of my first and abiding incentives to become a writer. I'd also hung around him because he made me feel interesting to myself: there was a Jamesian encounter going on between us—between Cambridge, Massachusetts, and Elizabeth, New Jersey, as well as between a seasoned literary mind and a green one. I particularly loved his sense of humor, its wryness, freshness, accuracy—which was his way of relating to life while keeping his retiring distance. I once asked him, for example, if he'd been at Michigan when Auden was. No, he'd come there shortly after. "But you could pretty well follow his doings by the trail of sulfur he left." Barrows had no literary method to teach me, other than to read a writer until you'd gotten "the hang" of his work.

He seemed to have the hang of everyone from Henry Adams to Henry Miller. What he had to teach me was more primary than method: it was the primacy of literary taste, which he communicated with his whole being. For, living alone and being rather reclusive, he was sustained by the arts and treated their works accordingly, as nutritive and pleasurable or not. Hence his judgments were unaffected by fashions, conventions, and pretensions and came directly from his character. He said that a good style was like a simple, expensive black dress that you could then make expressive in your own way: a bad style was like a gaudy dress from Woolworth's that you couldn't do anything else with. Perhaps he told me that on the day I sat in his office with my William Carlos Williams review and realized I was becoming not a little screwed up: i.e., "fatally overcommitted to what I was not." He said that he was going to teach a course in something called "practical criticism" and suggested that it might be helpful to me.

It was a swell course or, better, a kind of literary workshop in which we learned how to trust and develop our personal response to a work. During the early sessions Barrows would read us a story or a poem (the poem twice) and ask us to jot down what struck us about it. The first few times I was left at the post in a kind of panic. I could barely make out the lines on one or two readings; how was I supposed to read between them? But this, of course, was the point of the exercise, which had to do not with ingenuity but with a kind of basic responsiveness known as paying attention, and with letting an impression grow inside you, and with articulating it. Clearly I had a lot to learn, beginning with the distinction between having an impression and making one. The pretender-critic in me, the "pseudo-self," didn't have impressions, for that was to be impressionistic, which was the last thing a New Critic could afford to be in his pursuit of order and complexity. But someone with my name had better begin to have some impressions, if I was to stop having to read aloud and hand in my desperate gibberish.

I had a lot of help from Barrows and from the group itself. There was one student who regularly came up with an amazingly sharp and interesting response. He seemed older than most of us, and he wore a hearing aid, which at first I thought might be really a miniature recording device by which he would play back to himself what the rest of us had heard only once and were stumbling to remember. But as I began to see, his secret advantage lay elsewhere. Instead of groping about to describe or judge the poem or story—this poem is about X, what I like about it is Y, and so forth—he would find an image, which as he deftly developed it characterized the work and stated its appeal in such a way that it came back from his mind as freshly and distinctively as it had entered. I remember his speaking about a Yeats poem as being like a patch of ocean where two mighty warships had just fought and gone down, leaving a single empty lifeboat circling on the surface.

So I began to see that practical criticism was not only trusting your first impression but also using your imagination to take the measure of a work rather than merely interpret it. As time went on and I got the hang, it was like being let off a leash; my mind could nose around in a work, responding to what interested it, and then frame my response in a straightforward or witty way. Criticism stopped being the ponderous, anxious task of lifting up the lines and sentences to see if you could find the structural grid underneath, or of injecting an image or a detail with added significance so that the work became like a chicken shot full of artificial hormones; instead criticism became more like characterization: i.e. letting your response and the writer's work meet each other halfway. Toward the end of Barrows's course, I wrote a review of e.e. cummings's collection *Xaipe*, which began:

> cummings is back again at his old stand, working this time out of a satchel with this cryptic Greek word pasted on its side. . . . Again one can watch adjectives dance into adverbs and participles put on weight and sit down as nouns, while the commas plummet and the clauses disappear and the parenthetical expressions get sawn in half. Whole mountains are again given the chance to dance and city pavements to grow flowers. The individual is sung back to significance and the social outcast to humanity.

I remember writing this for Barrows with a kind of "Look, Mom" élan. According to the English psychoanalyst D. W. Winnecott, who has a great deal to teach about these matters, that's how creativity begins: exploring, self-expressive play under the auspices of a mother who frees the child of anxiety; who is, in effect, one's first and determining audience. To Winnecott, psychotherapy is or should be a mode of play in this sense, and so are those other inventive activities that take place on the interface between one's inner and outer worlds. As the sort of "holding" mother-figure Winnecott speaks of, Barrow's enabled me to relax, to open up, to trust my judgment and imagination, and to stop pretending, which is really a form of compliance bred by anxiety. By his kindness and probity toward me as well as by his example, he helped me to see that I had to find some way to be literary and still be myself. But he could not lead me to my "inner tradition." A different figure was needed for that.

His name was Isaac Rosenfeld. I first met him through a story published in a *Partisan Review* anthology. This was in 1954, a few years after I had left college and was living in Greenwich Village, working occasionally as a waiter to support myself in my state of "alienation." Though I was where I was supposed to be, existentially speaking—that is, 180 degrees from the middle class—I was still writing stories so self-consciously posed they couldn't live. I was trying to be like the Joyce of *Dubliners* without his temperament, not to mention genius. Rosenfeld's story was called "The Hand That Fed Me" and tells of a young writer named Joseph Feigenbaum. It is set back in the early 1940s, when he has reached bottom. The WPA Writers' Project has folded, the war effort has passed him by, the last six women he has approached have turned him down. He receives a Christmas card from a Russian girl who flirted with him one day three years before, took him home for lunch, and then dropped him. Touched and wounded, hopeful and bitter, he writes one letter after another, none of which she answers. He becomes more desperate, even calls at her home, and is turned away by her brother. Finally, Feigenbaum comes to rest in his yearning and humiliation:

For after all, what is humiliation? It does not endure forever. And when it has led us underground to our last comfort, look, it has served its purpose and is gone. Who knows when newer heights may not appear? I believe some men are capable of rising out of their own lives. They stand on the same ground as their brothers, but they are, somehow, transcendental, while their brothers are underground. Their only secret is a tremendous willingness—they do not struggle with themselves!

Here was Dostoevsky's underground man—but with a Jewish-American voice that I could immediately relate to. And not just his voice. Here I was, running around New York in a fake tuxedo looking for work as a temporary waiter. I, whose motto was Stephen Dedalus's "*Non serviam!*" Like Feigenbaum I was pretty screwed up, and like him I could no more stop struggling with myself than I could fly. But I had found someone who understood me, who knew better than I where I was coming from and what I was looking for. As Feigenbaum says to his beautiful, heedless *shiksa*:

> Be gentle to the unfulfilled, be good to it. We are accustomed to sing the joys of the happy, the fulfilled men. Let us also sing the joys of the desolate, the empty men. Theirs is the necessity without fulfillment, but it is possible that even to them—who knows—some joy may come.

This heart-flooded story that somehow managed to soar at the end—at least in my lofty mind, busy with its own unwanted offerings and resignations—was the first thing that fastened me to Rosenfeld. A couple of years later, when I decided to try graduate school, I chose Chicago, partly because I'd heard he was teaching there. He died before I met him, but that made him even more of a shining presence to me. I'd slip away, now and then, from the scholarly grind in the library stacks to hunt up his pieces in *Partisan Review*, *The New Republic*, *Commentary* et al. He had much to teach me, not the least of which had to do with my false consciousness of "alienation." One of his essays dealt with Sartre and the underground and began with the thought that modern writers like to believe they stand at a necessary remove from society, resisting, if passively, its disorder, amorality, and so forth.

> This has put a high value on confessions, disclosures of the private life and its feelings, usually revulsions, which earlier ages have found neither interesting nor tolerable. The tone of very much modern writing is, accordingly, one of malaise. But we are so accustomed to it, we are seldom aware of it as such; and when we do take this malaise into direct account, we readily mistake it for what it is not—a report from the underground.

The burden of this passage—as relevant today as it was thirty years ago—is that writers have no more right to their disaffection than anyone else, particularly in view of the self-preening uses to which it is put. This was a good thing for me to hear; it was also exhilarating to see Rosenfeld arraign Sartre for taking the view from the café—its "contactlessness, the emptiness and superfluity of existence, the sexual miseries and perversions, violence and self destruction"—as the leading truths of existence. Sartre, after all, was the leading intellectual in the West at the time, and existentialism was everywhere in vogue. Yet here was Rosenfeld, in his calm, clear way, exercising his right as he would say elsewhere, to "take a good look" at the attitude with which Sartre approached experience and to weigh it on a firm, moral scale. This was not like the New Criticism at all. Rosenfeld's criticism was full of immediate encounter and judgment ("I should like to say what I must about Jean Malaquais's war diary with the humility owing to a man who has been through hell"), yet was lucid and even-tempered and stable. I knew in my Jewish bones, well before Matthew Arnold confirmed it, that literature was first and last a criticism of life, and now I had found a voice that embodied this viewpoint in a warm, masculine, somehow familiar way. It was less like discovering a writer than like finding a terrific older brother.

The first significant essay I wrote was done under his spell. The

TLS was planning a special supplement on the American imagination and asked Philip Roth to write an essay on the Jewish role in American letters. He said that he didn't know much about it, but he had this friend in Chicago who did. I didn't know much about the subject either, but I did know my way around a research library by then so I got a new bundle of three-by-five cards and camped out in the stacks. I read Rosenfeld's colleagues at *Partisan Review* and *Commentary* and *Midstream*, and as much as I could about the historical background of Jewish writing in America. I had six weeks, and in dutiful graduate student fashion, I gave myself five weeks to do the research and one week to write. And then toward the very end, just as I was beginning to do the writing, I broke a finger playing first base for a local tavern. It seemed like a judgment. I could barely type, which was the way I wrote, and the whole project, hasty and shaky at best, began to collapse.

I sat there thinking: Here's your big chance and it's all going down the drain. In despair, I picked up a posthumous essay of Rosenfeld's which had just come out in *The Chicago Review*. At one point, he talks about himself as being "uncertain, alone, and much of the time afraid" when he wrote, which was exactly how I felt, and about the importance of the attitude with which you approached your experience of the subject. About the only thing I was sure of about Jewish-American writing was my attitude, which was one of enthusiasm for the contribution that so many novelists, playwrights, poets, and critics were making to American letters. Until now, I'd avoided Jewish chauvinism like the plague, but there was no getting around my discovery, amplified by my research, that the contemporary writers who interested and inspired me were Jewish—whether overtly so like Singer or Howe or Malamud, or more indirectly so like Trilling or Arthur Miller or Bellow. What I could trust, then, was my own excitement that the Jewish sensibility, however broadly defined, had suddenly come into its own, what Leslie Fiedler had called a "breakthrough."

That word, "breakthrough," began to resonate in my mind. I sat down again, with my broken finger, and my heart in my mouth, and began to write a passionate essay in real trembling. I sent it off, thinking it would be rejected summarily as being the babblings of an enthusiast. But it wasn't: it was published and was even well received. In fact, it got me a job at *Commentary*. After a few months in New York I met William Phillips, who asked me to write a piece for *Partisan Review*. If the *TLS* was august at that time, *Partisan Review* was out of sight for a young critic of my background. *PR* was the Castle. So I'd arrived. Or so I thought.

The truth is that virtually every piece I've written since has meant starting out again. At a certain point, the enterprise invariably breaks down and I don't see how I can write this review or essay; in fact, I shouldn't write any more at all. Because I continue to lose confidence, including the confidence that may have accrued from seeing the last piece in print: the reasonably clear, coherent product of all that disarray. It's the ongoing identity crisis I mentioned earlier: this constant struggle, this manual and psychic labor we perform against our doubts and misgivings and sense of unworthiness, in which we do rely, at times quite desperately, on those good voices in our heads. I know I do because each time the crisis hits full force again—when I say I must abandon this, it's just too painful to go on, I'm too ignorant, too superficial, I don't have enough time, I can't write anyway—I'll open a book of literary pieces, *An Age of Enormity* by Isaac Rosenfeld, read a page or two, quiet down, gather myself, and say to myself: Look, that's what it's all about, he's just telling his truth as best he can, get on with it.

(1982)

Writing in the Cold

During the decade of editing *New American* (later *American*) *Review*, I was often struck by how many gifted young writers there were in America. They would arrive every month, three or four of them, accomplished or close to it, full of wit and panache or a steady power or a fine, quiet complexity. We tried to devote 25 percent of each issue to these new voices and seldom failed to meet the quota. Where are they all coming from? I'd ask myself, though more as an exclamation than a question. They came from everywhere: from Dixon, New Mexico and Seal Rock, Oregon, as well as Chicago and San Francisco, from English departments in community colleges as well as the big creative writing centers. They came amid the twelve hundred or so manuscripts we received each month. America in the late sixties and seventies appeared to be on a writing binge, and eugenics alone would seem to dictate that half of one percent of the writing population would be brilliant.

But what has happened to all that bright promise? When I look through the cumulative index of *NAR/AR*, I see that perhaps one fourth of our discoveries have gone on to have reasonably successful careers; about the same number still have marginal ones, part of the alternative literary community of the little magazines and small presses. And about half have disappeared, or at least their names are again as obscure to me as they were when they came from out of the blue. It's as though some sinister force were at work, a kind of literary population control mechanism that kills off the surplus talent we have been developing or causes it to wither slowly away.

Literary careers are difficult to speculate about. They are so individual, so subject to personal circumstances that are often hidden, even to the writer himself. Also, what is not hidden is likely to be held so secretly that even the editor who works closely with a writer knows little more about his or her sources of fertility and potency than anyone else does. And those writers who fail are even more inclined to draw a cover of silence or obfuscation over the reasons. Still, it's worth considering why some gifted writers have careers and others don't. It doesn't appear to be a matter of the talent itself—some of the most natural writers, the ones who seemed to shake their prose or poetry out of their sleeves, are among the disappeared. As far as I can tell, the decisive factor is what I call endurability: that is, the ability to deal effectively with uncertainty, rejection, and disappointment, from within as well as from without, and how effectively one incorporates them into the creative process itself, particularly in the prolonged first stage of a career. In what follows, I'll be writing about fiction writers, the group I know best. But I don't imagine that poets, playwrights, essayists, will find much that is different from their experience.

The gifted young writer will say: I already know about rejection and uncertainty. I know what to expect. Let's get on to surviving. I have to reply: You know about them much as a new immigrant to Alaska knows about cold and ice and isolation. Also, if you come from an enlightened family that has supported your desire to become a writer and if you have starred in college and then in a graduate writing program, you are like someone who is immigrating from Florida.

When I came out of college and went off to become a writer in the 1950s, I expected to remain unknown and unrewarded for ten years or so. So did my few associates in this precarious enterprise. Indeed our low expectations were a measure of our high seriousness. We were hardly going to give ourselves less time and difficulty than our heroes—Joyce, Flaubert, et al.—gave themselves. Also it was such a dubious career that none of our families understood, much less supported, us. Nor were there any universities—except for two,

Iowa and Stanford—that wanted us around once we'd gotten a B.A., except as prospective scholars. Not that we knew how to cope with the prolonged uncertainty, isolation, indifference, and likely poverty that faced us—who does until he has been through them?—but at least we expected their likelihood and even understood something of their necessity.

I don't find that our counterparts of the past two decades or more are nearly as aware of the struggle to come, or have even begun to be emotionally and mentally prepared for it. As the products of affluence and an undemanding literary education, most of them have very little experience with struggle. Also their expectations of a writer's life have been formed by the mass marketing and subsidization of culture and by the creative writing industry. Their career models are not, say, Henry Miller or William Faulkner but John Irving or Ann Beattie. Instead of the jazz musicians and painters of forty years ago somehow making do, the other arts provide them with the model lifestyles of rock stars and of the young princes of Soho. Instead of a Guggenheim or Yaddo residency far up the road, there is a whole array of public and private prizes, grants, colonies, writing fellowships, that seem just around the corner. And most of all, there is the prospect, no longer as immediate but still only a few significant publications away, of teaching, with its comfortable life and free time. As the late poet William Matthews remarked, "What our students seem to mainly want to do is to become us, though they have no idea of what we've gone through."

I don't think one can understand the literary situation today without taking into account the one genuine revolutionary development in American letters during the second half of the century: the rise of the creative writing programs. At virtually one stroke we have solved the age-old problem of how literary men and women are to support themselves. Most fiction writers today mainly support themselves by teaching writing. To do so, they place themselves in an insulated and relatively static environment whose main population every year grows a year younger and whose beliefs, attitudes, and privileges become the principal reflection of the society at large. The campus writer also risks disturbing the secret chemistry of his gift by trying to communicate it in class as well as defusing and depersonalizing it in coping with student writing. Then, too, the peculiar institution of tenure prompts the younger writer to publish too quickly and the older one too little. It's no wonder that steady academic employment has done strange things to a number of literary careers and has tended to devitalize the relation between literature, particularly fiction, and society.

The graduate writing program is also a mixed blessing to career-minded young writers by starting them out under extremely favorable, that is to say, unreal conditions. At a place like Johns Hopkins or Houston or Sarah Lawrence or the twenty or thirty others with prestigious programs, the chances are that several highly accomplished, even famous, writers will be reading a student's work. If he is genuinely talented, his work will be taken very seriously because his teachers need to feel that what they are doing for a living isn't entirely a waste of time and spirit. As well as a dazzling ally or even two, the promising writer will also have a responsive and usually supportive audience—the other writers in the program—and a small, intense milieu that envisions the good life as a literary career, particularly the model supplied by his teachers. And of course, he will have a structure of work habits provided by the workshops, degree requirements, and so forth.

I think graduate writing programs are mostly wasted on the young. But at their best, they're often good correctives to undergraduate ones in giving the gifted a more realistic sense of where they stand among their peers (there are now three or four others in a class of fifteen), in guiding them in the direction of publishable writing, and in providing a certain amount of validation to a young writer's still green and shaky sense of vocation. In general, these programs are a kind of greenhouse that enables certain talents to bloom, particularly those that produce straightforward, well-made stories, the kind that teach well in class, and, depending on the teacher, even certain eccentric ones, particularly those patterned on a prevailing fashion of postmodernism.

At the same time, the graduate writing program makes the next stage, that of being out there by oneself in the cold world, particularly chilling. Instead of a personal and enlightened response to her writing, the young writer now receives mostly rejection slips. Instead of standing out, she now finds herself among the anonymous masses. Instead of being in a literary community, she now has to rely on herself for stimulation, support, and discipline. Also she now has to fit writing into the interstices left by a full-time job or by parenting. In short, her character as a writer will now be tested—and not for a year or two but much more likely for five or ten.

That's how long it generally takes for the gifted young fiction writer to find his way, to come into her own. The two fiction writers whose work appears to be the most admired and influential in the graduate writing programs just now are Bobbie Ann Mason and Raymond Carver. Mason spent some seven years writing an unpublished novel, and then story after story, sending each one to Roger Angell at *The New Yorker*, getting it back, writing another, until finally the twentieth one was accepted. In his essay "Fires," Carver tells about the decade of struggle to write the stories that grew out of his heavily burdened life of "working at crap jobs" and raising two children, until an editor, Gordon Lish, began to beckon from the tower of *Esquire*. (It would be another seven years before Carver's first book appeared.) Three novelists whose "arrival" I witnessed—Lynne Sharon Schwartz, Joan Chase, and Douglas Unger—were by then in their thirties and had already written at least one unpublished novel. My most recent find, Alan Hewat, the author of *Lady's Time,* is in his early forties and has written two unpublished novels.

Why this long delay of recognition? Each of the above writers doesn't regard it now as a delay. All of them say the unpublished novel or novels shouldn't have been published. They were mainly part of a protracted effort to find a voice, a more or less individual and stable style which best uncovers and delivers the writer's material. This often requires a period of time for the self to mature and stabilize, particularly the part one writes from. The writer in his middle twenties is not that far removed from adolescence and its insecurities. Indeed the sensitivity he is trying to develop and discipline comes precisely from that side of himself that he likely tried to negate only a few years ago as freakish, unmanly, and unpopular. Hence the painful paradoxes of his new vocation: that his most vulnerable side is now his working one, the one that has to produce, the one that goes forth into the world and represents him; further, that from the side that had been the most uncertain, he must now find his particular clarity about how and why he and others live and his conviction about what is significant in their ways and days as well as in his own. If he is writing a novel, he must also develop a settled and sustainable moral point of view if its meaning is to cohere. And all this from a self that is likely to be rejected each time it looks for confirmation by sending out a manuscript.

The second difficulty is that the typical M.F.A. in creative writing has spent eighteen of his, say, twenty-five years in school. Thus he is likely to be still fairly limited in his grasp of how people live and feel and look at things other than in books and films, sources he still needs to sift out, and other than in his family and its particular culture, from which he is likely still rebelling in typical ways that lead to banal content. Throw in a few love affairs and friendships, a year or two of scattered work experience, perhaps a trip abroad, and his consciousness is still likely to be playing a very limited hand. (There appears to be a long-term psychosocial trend over the past fifty years or so in which each generation takes several years longer to mature: Many of the postwar generation of fiction writers, such as Mailer, Bellow, Styron, Baldwin, Bowles, Flannery O'Connor, Truman Capote, Updike, Roth, Reynolds Price, were highly developed by their mid to late twenties.) As often happens, a young writer's gift itself may fake him out of understanding his true situation by producing a few exceptional stories, part of a novel from the most deeply held experiences of his life. But except for these, he has only his share of the common life of his age, which he must learn to see and think about and depict in a complex and uncommon way. This takes much more time.

A young writer I know won a national award a few years ago for the best short story submitted by the various writing programs. It was one of a group of several remarkable stories that she published, almost all of them about members of her family, gray-collar people finely viewed in their contemporary perplexities from her observation post as the kid sister and the one who would leave. But almost nothing she wrote after that came near their standard; the new fiction was mostly about a difficult love affair that she was still too close to to write about with the same circumspection and touch as her family stories. After they were turned down, she was left low and dry; finally, she went to work reading for a film company and learning script development. Recently she sold an adaptation of one of her early stories, is writing another script, and is looking to take up fiction again. By the time she publishes her first collection, if she does, she'll be in her thirties too.

What she has been going through as a fiction writer is the crisis of rejection from both without and within, and more important from within. For writers are always sending themselves rejection letters, as the late George P. Elliot observed, to this sentence and that paragraph, to this initial characterization and that turn of the story, or, heartbreak time, to the story that has eluded months of tracking it, the hundred pages of a novel that has come to a dead stop.

The gifted young writer has to learn through adversity to separate rejection of one's work from self-rejection, and with respect to the latter, self-criticism (otherwise known as revision and what one might call re-envision) from self-distrust. For the inexperienced writer, a year or two of rejection or a major rejection—say, of a novel—can lead all too easily to self-distrust, and from there to a disabling distrust of the writing process itself. Anxious, depressed, defensive, the writer who is suffering this distrust, whether temporarily or chronically or terminally, gives up her most fundamental and enabling right: the right to write uncertainly, roughly, even badly. A garden in the early stage is not a pleasant or compelling place: it's a lot of arduous, messy, noisome work—digging up the hard ground, putting in the fertilizer, along with the seeds and seedlings. So with beginning a story or novel. The writer can't get her spadework done, can't lay in the bullshit from which something true can grow, can't set her imagination to seeding these dark and fecund places if she is worried about how comely her sentences are, how convincing her characters will be, how viable her plot. But the self-rejecting writer finds herself doing just that. Instead of going from task to task, she goes from creating to judging: from her mind to the typewriter to the wastebasket. In time, her mind forgoes the latter two stages and becomes a ruthless system of self-cancellation.

The longer this goes on, the more writing becomes not a process of planting and cultivating—or, perhaps more accurately, of mining and refining—but an issue of entitlement and prohibition. That is, what the writer sets down or merely thinks about must be so promising that her right to write is suddenly allowed again. But even if she hits upon an exciting first sentence or paragraph or even a whole opening development, just as surely as night follows day, the dull stuff returns, her uncertainty follows, and soon she is back in court again, testifying against herself. To stay in this state too long is to reach the dead end of narcissistic despair known as writer's block, in which one's vanity and guilt have so persecuted one's craft and imagination and so deprived them of their allies—heart, curiosity, will—that they have gone into exile and into the sanctuary of silence.

Unless he is a graphomaniac, the gifted writer is likely to be vulnerable to rejection from without and within, and how well he copes with them is likely to determine whether he has a genuine literary vocation or just a literary flair. To put the matter as directly as I can, rejection and uncertainty and disappointment are as much a part of a writer's life as snow and cold are of an Eskimo's: they are conditions one has to learn not only to live with but also to make use of.

The trouble with most talented first novels is that they lack a prolonged struggle with uncertainty. They typically keep as much as possible to the lived lines of the author's life, which provide the security of a certain factuality and probability but at the expense of depriving the imagination of its authority. Laden with unresolved conflicts, the voice is too insistent here, too vague there. Such a novel is also typically overstuffed and overwritten: the question of what belongs and what doesn't being too easily settled by leaving it in. The writer, particularly if he has some literary sophistication, may also try to quell uncertainty by allying himself with some current literary fashion. At the same time, the struggle with uncertainty may be here and there strongly engaged and won: The material rings true instead of derivatively, whether from experience or books; a power of understanding is abroad in the narrative, however intermittently. If there is enough earned truth and power, the manuscript is probably viable and its deadnesses are relatively detectable. The rest is mostly a matter of the writer's willingness to persist in his gift and its process and to put his ego aside.

This can take some very interesting and illuminating turns. Douglas Unger, whose first novel, *Leaving the Land* was received with considerable acclaim in 1984, began writing it in 1976. He had already had a previous novel optioned by a major publisher, had rewritten it three times to meet his editor's reservations, only to have it finally rejected. "He literally threw the manuscript at me and told me to get out of his office. Since I didn't know what to do next, I didn't have an agent or anything, I enrolled at the Iowa Writers Workshop."

I met him there the following year when I used the opening section of his next novel to teach a workshop. It began with a young woman named Marge walking through a dusty farm town in the Dakotas, on her way to be fitted for a wedding dress by her prospective mother-in-law and barely able to put one foot after the other. It is just after World War II, in which her two brothers have been killed, and she has chosen the best of a bad lot of local men to help her father and herself to keep the farm going. Unger's writing was remarkably sensitive to the coarse and delicate weave of a farm girl's childhood and adolescence and to the pathos of her love life, in which her spunk and grace are manhandled by a series of misfits left behind by the war. At the same time, he wrote graphically about crops and farm machinery and the special misery of raising turkeys, and he brought the reader close to the local farmers' struggle with Nowell-Safebuy, a turkey-processing plant and part of a giant food trust that drives down their prices and wants their land. Marge's long reverie suddenly ends when a convoy of trucks transporting factory equipment rolls into town. In the midst of it is an attractive man in a snappy roadster. Sensing that her luck may have finally changed, she follows the newcomer into the local café. All in all, it was a terrific beginning.

About eighteen months later, Unger sent me the final manuscript. It was some seven hundred pages long. About one fifth was taken up by a separate story of German prisoners of war operating the turkey plant; the final third jumped ahead thirty years, to tell of the return of Marge's son to Nowell, which is now a ghost town, and then backed and filled. Along with its disconnected narrative line, the writing had grown strangely mock-allegorical and surreal in places, as though Unger's imagination had been invaded by an alien force, perhaps the fiction of Thomas Pynchon. Most disappointing of all, he seemed to have turned away from a story with a great deal of prospective meaning—the eradication of farmers and agrarian values by agribusiness—to make instead the postmodernist point of the pointlessness of it all. I wrote him a long letter, trying to itemize what had gone wrong, and ended by saying that I still felt there was a genuine novel buried inside this swollen one and hoped he would have the courage to find it. When he read the letter, Unger became so enraged he threw down the manuscript and began to jump on it, shouting, "But I've spent so much time on it already."

He didn't write anything for a year and a half. By then he was living on an unworked farm, owned by his wife's family, outside Bellingham, Washington, and had become a commercial fisherman. Then one night he woke up with the people he had written about on his mind, pulled out the manuscript, and began to reread it. His main reaction was a deep chagrin at the distortions he had made in telling their story.

> I was running up against people every day who gave the lie to what I'd done to my characters. Then one day my wife's older sister turned up with one of her sons, to try to get the farm going

again. I witnessed an incredible scene in which her will to revive the farm ran into his admission that he wanted nothing to do with it. This opened my eyes to the truth that the original version had gone off in the wrong direction. It was really about Marge's efforts all along—through her marriage, her staying in that forsaken community—to hold on to their land with the same tenacity her father had shown and pass it on to her son. Much of this material was already there, lying around undeveloped and untidy. In order to feel easy again, I had to rework it.

It took another three years to do so. I asked Unger what had sustained him, particularly in view of the crushing disappointment after revising his first novel. He told me that after he left Iowa City, he had spent some time in San Francisco with Raymond Carver, to whom he was related by marriage.

Anyone who knows Ray knows that you have to believe that if you write well you'll eventually get published. Also the one thing he kept saying to me was 'A good book is an honest one.' I knew that his whole career had been an effort to write honestly, so those words really sunk in. And they were just the ones I needed to hear. At Iowa I was so desperate to get published, some of the others already were or getting close, and I thought it would help if I put in a lot of postmodernist effects. Also, Barth and Barthelme and Pynchon were all the rage then and it was easy to be influenced by them.

He ended up with three novellas: Marge's early life culminating in her affair and marriage to the man in the roadster, who is the lawyer for the Safebuy Corporation and the farmers' imperious adversary; the prisoners-of-war story; Marge and her son twenty-five years later, her marriage long over, the farm and most of the area abandoned when the Safebuy scheme of "vertical ownership" fails, her life divided between the dying community and the bright lights of Belle Fourche, forty miles away, and her final effort to pass on the deed to her son, who can't wait to get away. A brave, sad, increasingly bleak wind of feeling blew through the final novella, joining it tonally as well as narratively to the first. Were they the buried novel? The prose of all three maintained the straightforward realism of the original opening, but Unger's style had grown diamond hard, with glints of light whichever way it turned. So the three were eminently publishable as they were. Unger decided to go for the novel and set to work revising the first and last to join them more securely together.

What enabled him to persist through all his rewriting and also to let one hundred fifty pages of very good writing go by the board? "By now I'd lost any egotistical involvement in the work. The book was coming together. I was very objective now, almost impersonally watching a process occurring. The book wanted to come together and I was the last person to stand in its way."

There are several morals for the gifted young writer to draw from this account. Perhaps the main one is that Unger needed a period of adversity and silence, not only to recover from my "litany of its flaws," as he put it, but also to reorient himself as a writer and to undo the damage that the frustrated false writer, who wanted to be fashionable and publish as soon as possible, had done to the uncertain true one who had started the project. Once that had been done, the characters, like rejected family or abused friends, began to return.

There is a theory, put forward by D. W. Winnecott and V. R. Fairbairn, that creativity is a mode of play which we do not only for its enjoyment but also to explore the interface of self and world and to make restitution for the damage we do to others and ourselves by our narcissism. The youth tuning up the family car, the man weeding his garden, the woman rewriting a description five times to get it right, are all involved, psychically speaking, in the same activity. Even more overtly was Unger's rewriting an act of restitution ("In order to feel easy again, I had to rework it") for the falsifications he had made about others, and for the harm he had done to his own craft and spirit.

Earlier I wrote of the time that the gifted young writer needs to strengthen and trust the self he writes out of. To put it another way, the struggle with rejection, uncertainty, and disappointment can help him to develop his main defense against the narcissism that prompts him to become a writer in the first place. Writing to a friend, Pushkin tells of reading a canto of *Eugene Onegin* that he had just composed, jumping from his chair, and proudly shouting, "Hey you Pushkin! Hey you son of a bitch!" Anyone who has written knows that feeling, but also knows how easily it can turn over into self-hatred, when the writing or the blank page reflects back one's limitations, failure, deadness. The writer's defense is his power of self-objectivity, his interest in otherness, and his faith in the process itself, which enables him to write on into the teeth of his doubts and then to improve it. In the resolved struggle between the odd, sensitive side of the self that likes to imagine and the practical, socialized side that wants results, the gifted young writer is likely to find his true sense of vocation, the one for building, the other for finishing. Moreover, writing itself, if not misunderstood and abused, becomes a way of empowering the writing self. It converts diffuse anger and disappointment into deliberate and durable aggression, the writer's main source of energy. It converts sorrow and self-pity into empathy, the writer's main means of relating to otherness. Similarly, his wounded innocence turns into irony, his silliness into wit, his guilt into judgment, his oddness into originality, his perverseness into his stinger.

Because all this takes time, indeed much of a lifetime, to complete itself, the gifted young writer has to learn that his main task is to persist. This means he must be tough-minded about his fantasies of wealth, fame, and the love of beautiful women or men. However stimulating these motives may be for the social self, for the writing one who perforce needs to stay home and be alone they are trivial and misleading, for they are enacted mostly as fantasies that maintain the adolescent romance of a magically empowered ego that the writer must outgrow if he is to survive. And this is so even if the fantasies come true, and often enough, particularly if they come true. No writer rode these fantasies farther or more damagingly than Scott Fitzgerald did, but it was Fitzgerald who said that inside a novelist there has to be something of a peasant.

Rejection and uncertainty also teach the gifted writer to be firm, kind, and patient, a good parent to his gift if he is to persist in it. As he comes to realize, his gift is partly a skill that is better at some tasks than at others and partly a power that comes and goes. And even when it comes, it is often only partly functioning and its directives are only partly understood. This is why writing a first draft is like ice fishing and building an igloo, as well as like groping one's way around a pitch-dark room, or overhearing a faint conversation, or having prepared for a different exam, or telling a joke whose punch line you've forgotten. As someone said, one writes mainly to rewrite, for rewriting and revising are how one's mind comes to inhabit the material fully.

In its benign form, rewriting is a second, third, and nth chance to make something come right, to "fall graciously into place," in Lewis Hyde's phrase. But it is also the testing ground of the writer's conscience, on the one hand, and of his faith, on the other. One has to learn to respect the misgiving that says, This still doesn't ring true, still hasn't touched bottom, still hasn't delivered me. And this means to go back down into the mine again and poke around for the missing ore and find a place for it and let it work its will. Sometimes this may mean re-envisioning the entire work: that is, finding another central idea or image, a new star in the area of the former one to navigate by. Revision is mostly turning loose the editor in oneself, a caretaker who tinkers and straightens out and tidies up and has a steadier hand. At the same time, one must come to the truth of Valéry's remark that no work is ever finished, only at a certain point abandoned. One has to learn to recognize when that point has come from the feel of the work coming together once and for all and of the writing having to be what it is, more or less. For beyond that point, rewriting and revising can turn compulsive and malignant, devouring the vitality and integrity of what one has found to tell and say.

In sum, the gifted young writer needs to learn to trust the writing process itself and, beyond that, to love as well as hate it. For writing is not, of course, always stoop labor and second thoughts and struggling with one tendency toward negation and despair and accepting one's limits and limitations. There are the exhilarations of finding that the way ahead has opened overnight, that the character who has been so elusive has suddenly walked into the room and started talking, that the figure has been weaving itself into the carpet. But if the gifted young writer persists in believing that for him the latter conditions should be the normal ones, otherwise known as "inspiration" or "natural talent," he will likely decide after a few years that he fatally lacks one or both or that he has developed a writer's block, and may well turn to a more sensible and less threatened mode of expression, such as teaching or editing or writing for one or the other of the media.

There appear to be better and worse ways to get through this long period of self-apprenticeship and to get the most out of it. Of the first novelists and story writers I've been involved with virtually none of them were teaching writing, at least in a full-time way. Teaching offers the lure of relatively pleasant work and significant free time, but it comes with the snare of using and distorting much of the same energy that goes into writing and tends to fill the mind with the high examples of the models one teaches and the low ones of student work. Moreover, it tends to be insulating and distracting during the period when the young fiction writer should be as open as possible to a range of experience, for the sake of his character as well as his material. A job that makes use of another skill or talent and doesn't come home with one seems to work best over the long haul. It's also well, of course, to give as few hostages as possible to fortune.

What the gifted young writer most needs is time, lots of it. Bobbie Ann Mason says that when she is asked by writing students how to get published, she feels like saying, "Don't sweat it for twenty years or so. It takes experience at life before you really know what you're doing." She began writing fiction in 1971, after she got out of graduate school, and for the next five years or so wrote in a desultory way, finding it hard to get focused. In 1976 she finished a novel about a twelve-year-old girl growing up in western Kentucky, who was addicted to Nancy Drew novels. "It took another two years before I began to find my true subject, which was to write about my roots and the kinds of people I'd known, but from a contemporary perspective.

It mainly took a lot of living to get to that point. I'd come from such a sheltered and isolated background that I had to go through culture shock by living for years in the North to see the world of Mayfield, Kentucky, in a way I could write about as I was now—in a kind of exile. Also it took me until I was in my thirties to get enough detachment and objectivity to see that many of those people back home were going through culture shock too."

My own sense of things is that young fiction writers should disconnect the necessity to write fiction from what it is often confused with and by, the desire to publish it. This helps to keep one's mind where it belongs—on one's own work—and away from where it doesn't—on the market, which is next to useless, and on writers who are succeeding, which is discouraging. Comparisons with other writers should be inspiring; otherwise they're invidious. Bobbie Ann Mason says that "the writer I was most involved with was Nabokov. It was because he was a stylist and had a peculiar sensibility. In some ways, comparing myself to him is like comparing Willie Nelson to an opera singer, but I felt connected to him because he had the sensibility of an exile, was working with two opposing cultures, which made him peculiar, the same way I felt myself."

If there is no necessity to write fiction, then one should wait and in the meantime write other things. Keeping a journal with some depth to it is a good way to discover and strengthen one's natural style and the best way to talk to oneself about the real issues of one's experience. My other suggestion is to look for other opportunities to write and publish and thereby give one's talent some chance of gainful employment. Thirty years ago there was a great fear of "selling out," of "prostituting your talent," etc. It was as though your talent was like a beautiful pure virgin whom the philistine world was waiting eagerly to seduce and corrupt. Literary mores no longer place as much stock in the hieratic model of the writer, which is just as well. Unless one is good at self-sacrifice, is endowed with an iron will and a major-sized gift, it's likely to be a defeating thing to insist on producing Art or nothing.

If one of the primary projects of the gifted young writer is to begin to create a neutral zone between his social self and his literary one, so that the latter can live in peace for a while, it is also true that both need exercise and some degree of satisfaction and toughening. Many novelists-in-progress find it helpful to take their talent at least some of the time out of the rarefied and tenuous realm of literature and put it to work in the marketplace to try to earn some of its keep. Even hack writing has the benefit of putting serious writing into its proper perspective as a privilege rather than a burden. At a respectable professional level, writing for publication makes one into someone who writes rather than, in Robert Louis Stevenson's distinction, someone who wants to have written. Writing without publishing gets to be like loving someone from afar—delicious for fantasies but thin gruel for living. It produces in time what Milan Kundera, in other contexts, calls "the unbearable lightness of being." That is why, to my mind, a strongly written review, profile, piece of reportage in *The Village Voice* or *The Texas Monthly* or *Seattle Magazine* is worth three "Try us agains" from *The New Yorker*. The young writer needs whatever grounding in the vocation she can get. Once in print, her words detach themselves from the fluttering of the ego and become part of the actual world. Along with the reality of type, there is the energy that comes from publication: the "let's see what I can do next" feeling. Unger found that once he began revising his novel, his other cylinders kicked over and he was soon partly supporting himself by writing theater reviews for the local paper and developed a piece for the stage with his wife. The reality of getting paid is also good for one's work habits.

By the same token, the first years the writer is on his own are a good time to let his imagination off the leash and let it sniff and paw into other fields of writing. From journal writing it's only a small leap into the personal essay. It's also liberating to get away from term-paper type criticism and begin to try to write about other writers in the way that other writers do, as, say, Updike, Mailer and Sontag do. There is also the possibility of discovering that criticism or reportage or some other mode is for the time being more congenial than fiction. A young fiction writer I know had about come to the end of his rope when he had the wit to turn one of his stories into a one-act play and has been flying as a playwright ever since. Similarly, inside a functioning poet there is often a lapsed fiction writer. One of the most deforming aspects of American literary culture is the cult of the novel. Another is the decline of the concept of the versatile man of letters, which less specialized times and less academicized literary cultures than ours took for granted. And still do in Europe, where a Graham Greene, a Sartre, a Grass, a Kundera, write in three or four modes, depending upon the subject, the occasion, and the disposition of his well-balanced Muse. Even if he doesn't become a triple-threat writer, experimenting with other modes frees up energy and also helps to demystify the writer's vocation, which, like any other, is an ongoing practice rather than a higher state of being. This is particularly so for a prospective novelist; he must get over regarding his medium as a tinted mirror before doing so fakes him out completely. Auden puts it very well when he says that the novelist

> Must struggle out of his boyish gift and learn
> How to be plain and awkward, how to be
> One after whom none think it worth to turn.
> For to achieve his lightest wish, he must
>
> Become the whole of boredom, subject to
> Vulgar complaints like love, among the Just
> Be just, among the Filthy filthy too.

Hence he must learn to think of his medium as not a flattering mirror but a lens that he must grind and polish himself so that he can see more sharply and closely and powerfully.

Virtually all the fiction writers I've been speaking to about these matters fix the turning point in their writing lives in the period when the intrinsic interest of what they were doing began to take over and to generate a sense of necessity. This is not to say they first had to renounce the world and its painted stages. A little support and recognition from outside tends to go hand-in-hand with the recognition from within. This seems to be particularly true of women writers. As Lynne Sharon Schwartz explained, "Most women don't give themselves the freedom to pursue their dream. Being brought up a girl has meant just that." She began to write stories when she was seven and did so again during and after college but without taking the enterprise very seriously. "I'd get a letter from *The Paris Review* inviting me to submit other work and I'd think, That's nice, and then put it away in a drawer. Writing fiction was one of several dreams that probably wouldn't be realized." She married, had children, went back to graduate school, which somehow seemed permissible, perhaps because no one does much dream pursuing in graduate school.

> I found, though, that I didn't want to write a dissertation when I got to that point. I just couldn't face the library part of it. Going down into the stacks seemed so alien to my real sources. About that time, a childhood friend who also was married and had children told me she had resolved to give herself five years to become a dance critic. It was the way she did it, putting everything else to the side: it was her fierce tenacity that inspired me. I gave up graduate school and started to write fiction again.

"Wasn't it scary," I asked, "giving up something definite and practical for something so uncertain?" "Not really," she said. "Mainly, I felt that I was finally doing what I was intended to do."

Over the next few years she worked on a first novel, which went unpublished. "Just as well," she says, "but it got me an agent and some nice rejection letters, which was encouraging." In time she developed a small network of women fiction writers, published two stories in little magazines and then a satire on Watergate in *The New Republic*. "Doris Grumbach, who was then the literary editor, called me up to tell me and asked me who I was, where I'd been all this time. So I realized I might be someone after all."

Now, four books later, Lynne Schwartz looks back at these years and sees mainly herself at work.

I had to learn to write completely alone. There was no help, no other writer to emulate, no one's influence. It was too private for that. Once I got started I wanted the life of a writer so fiercely that nothing could stop me. I wanted the intensity, the sense of aliveness, that came from writing fiction. I'm still that way. My life is worth living when I've completed a good paragraph.

The development of this sense of necessity seems to be the rock-bottom basis for a career as a novelist. Whatever may feed it, whatever may impede it, finally come to be subsidiary to the simple imperative of being at work. At this point, writing fiction has become one's way, in the religious sense of the term. Not that there are any guarantees that it will continue to be for good or that it will make your inner life easier to bear. The life of published writers of quality fiction is most often the exchange of one level of rejection, uncertainty, and disappointment for another, and to go on means to rely upon the same imperiled and durable trust in the process and the self that enabled them to emerge from the cold.

(1985)

The Literary Campus
and the Person of Letters

In several essays I have discussed the widening gulf between trade publishing and the literary/intellectual culture. Increasingly ruled by corporate values and mass-marketing methods, the publishing business can be said to have moved most of its product and spirit to the shopping mall. Meanwhile, in response to the loss of its institutional home, the community of letters and ideas has been moving its product and spirit to the campus, where many of its books, magazines, and authors lead their dispersed but sheltered lives.

I see, for example, that John Hollander, one of our most sophisticated poets, is being published by Johns Hopkins University Press. I learn that the fiction and essays of Isaac Rosenfeld, one of the important New York writers of the 1940s and '50s, will be reissued by Wayne State Press, after being out of print for fifteen years. The whole oeuvre of Harold Rosenberg—the eminent art critic and seminal intellectual as well as one of the great American prose stylists of the century is being published by the University of Chicago Press, as are the essays of his chief peer and adversary, Clement Greenberg. Nor is it an accident that *Habits of the Heart*, the most broadly illuminating study of the inner life of American society since *The Lonely Crowd*, was first published by the University of California Press. Twenty years ago, a list of new titles that included the prose of W.S. Merwin; the poet Grace Schulman's book on Marianne Moore; a reissue of Zora Neale Thurston's landmark novel, *Their Eyes Were Watching God*; an experimental historical novel, *The Greek Generals Talk: Memoirs of the Trojan War*, by Philip Parotti; and the writings of Howard Gossage, the Ezra Pound of the advertising field, would likely have come from a house like Farrar Straus or New Directions. As it happens, this list is from the University of Illinois Press and could be from one of ten or fifteen other university presses.

Most of the foreign literature that reaches America today is in the keeping of the university presses. The recent revolution in American literary criticism, structuralism and its several branches, could hardly have come into being off campus. Similarly, the development of feminism, the most influential ideological movement of our time, has largely been undertaken by the women's studies programs and disseminated by the journals and books that come from the no longer academic press. (The influential Feminist Press, for example, is now sponsored by CUNY.) The universities and their fringe culture also publish most of our literary, theater, and film magazines and virtually all of the intellectual journals. Any issue of *The New York Review of Books*, both in its reviews and in its ads, provides ample evidence that the life of the mind in general and of the literary culture in particular would be severely curtailed without the publishing ventures that the universities maintain.

So, too, would the literary and intellectual professions themselves, which by and large have packed up and moved to the groves and precincts of academe, as the one institution left in the mass society and consumer economy that values and can afford them. Teaching provides a living for most of the serious literary artists and critics at work today as it does for our political and social thinkers. Moreover, the proliferation of graduate writing programs has meshed with the Ph.D. programs to form the principal training ground of the literary and intellectual vocations. A gifted young poet today can begin as an undergraduate at, say, Cornell; move on through the M.F.A. program at Syracuse; take up a teaching career at SUNY Binghamton, where he edits *Mss*, its excellent literary magazine; contribute regularly to *Salmagundi*, published at Skidmore; and publish poetry and criticism collections with the SUNY Press—a complete literary career without leaving upstate New York. Once the ivory tower of literature— perched so high above its time that it could view only the literature that began at a distance of fifty years and extended back through the centuries—the English and comparative literature departments, along with the writing programs, have become the refuge of novelists, poets, and critics in a culture that views literature as a rarely profitable, occasionally glamorous, and mostly dubious form of merchandise.

But as the history of the arts demonstrates, every gain involves some loss, and so with this development. The hospitality and security the academic community offers comes with its relative insularity and remoteness from the common life and its overt and underlying issues that are pressing for expression. (This is less true, of course, of the colleges and universities in urban areas, particularly the public ones.) Also the security of a teaching career, particularly after it is tenured, provides much more time to write than it does immediate need and incentive to do so. And as I shall suggest, teaching may well begin to take over an important part of the writer's primary drive to make his thoughts and feelings known.

Certainly teaching has already significantly altered the practice of the writing vocation in America. By offering itself as a livelihood, it has been responsible in good part for the declining numbers of the man of letters as of the freelance intellectual. Both of these professions are still prominent in Europe, where the chances for a writer to earn his bread and butter by teaching literature are slim, and by creative writing, all but zero.

It is also true, of course, that European newspaper, magazine, television, and film cultures provides an alternative mode of income that hardly exists any longer in America as a sufficient one, at least outside the pages of *The New Yorker*. A few other magazines pay well but not to contribute to letters. Edmund Wilson could both do his work and make his living at a magazine like *Vanity Fair*. It's unlikely, to say the least, that he would be able to do the former at today's *Vanity Fair*, which, one can fairly surmise, would cut his essay on Fitzgerald's last years to the juicy parts and title it "Scott on the Rocks." As for movie and TV money, many are called, few cash in. The rest is the occasional book review, think piece, travel article, which earns a night out but hardly room and board.

V. S. Pritchett speaks of himself as coming at "the tail end of a long and once esteemed tradition in English and American writing." As he says of himself and his dwindling brethren: "We have no captive audience. We do not teach." Instead his livelihood depends upon writing books and articles that the common reader wants to read. But this bread-and-butter writing has traditionally had a wider objective in view, which preserves the freelance literary person from becoming a hack: this is to keep the torch of letters lit and circulating, even in a time as windy and dim as our own. In Pritchett's words:

> We do not lay down the law, but we do make a stand for the reflective values of a humane culture. We care for the printed word in a world that nowadays is dominated by the camera and by scientific, technological, sociological doctrine. We still believe, with Dostoevsky, that "without art a man might well feel that his life was not worth living."

Words like these, so modestly phrased, so deeply felt, are like the colors of a regiment whose brave last members are still holding their position, though the others have been killed, wounded, taken prisoner, or are missing in action. Though we have many literary writers at work today in America, many more than at any time in history, we have few men or, to bring the term up to date, persons of letters. Were it not for Gore Vidal, John Updike, Elizabeth Hardwick, Susan Sontag, Hayden Carruth, Diane Johnson, Eric Bentley, Robert Bly, and a few others, one would be hard put to know what the phrase has meant.

According to Pritchett, the person of letters knows two things: that "literature is rooted in the daily society" and that "it springs out of literature itself." These two points will seem like platitudes to us. For the functioning person of letters they constitute a lived truth, for there is no lofty separation between their daily life and literature. The one is the other: they write in order to live, they live in order to write. Moreover, one cannot readily speak of literary matters to the common reader without approaching him or her from the direction of the common life. Here, to take an almost random example, is Pritchett talking to us about Nathanael West's *The Day of the Locust*:

> The artificial lights of the freak show are off in this book and we see human absurdity as something normal. This is a novel about Hollywood. West worked in the hum of the American dream generators and he chose those people who have done more for American culture than their coevals in Europe have done for theirs: the casualties, the wrecks, the failures, the seedy and the fakes. They are the people to whom the leisureless yea-sayers have said "No."

It is only a long stride of attention from the common life to the public sector of society. Pritchett has generally refrained from taking it; his leading American counterpart, Edmund Wilson, was prompt to do so when the times or his own outrage provoked him. As the tribune of public consciousness and conscience, the person of letters has a lineage that goes back as far as Voltaire and Milton; in this country, it was associated with the literary vocation from the start by the example of Emerson and Thoreau and was taken for granted by writers as otherwise dissimilar as, say, Howells and Twain.

During the 1960s there was a great deal of this direct public writing by persons of letters which both defined and influenced the character of the age: Paul Goodman's *Growing Up Absurd*, James Baldwin's *The Fire Next Time*, Norman Mailer's *The Armies of the Night*, Philip Roth's *Our Gang*, Susan Sontag's "Trip to Hanoi," Mary Ellmann's *Thinking About Women* and Kate Millett's *Sexual Politics*, Allen Ginsberg's *Planet News*, Robert Bly's *The Light Around the Body*. But this kind of public prose and poetry, political in its thrust but literary at its core, was found everywhere. Such writing today turns up now and then in a piecemeal way, barely rustling the stare of apathy that letters turns toward the public sector. A notable exception is Jonathan Schell's *The Fate of the Earth*, which eloquently and powerfully portrays the total horror, from the personal to the ecological to the ontological, of a nuclear war, and in so doing reminds us how desperately such writing is needed to cut through our stupor. Of the prominent novelists today, only Gore Vidal persists in writing strong public prose, and among the critics it is only the neo-conservative ones who play cultural politics with a passionate intensity. Indeed the most telling sign of the passivity of most of the community of letters is how little opposition there has been to the extraordinary politicization of literary judgment that has been conducted by the militant anti-Communist, high-bourgeois ideologues such as Hilton Kramer and Norman Podhoretz and those who write for their respective magazines, the *New Criterion* and *Commentary*.

Much of the non-combativeness of the so-called adversary culture can be attributed to the liberal/radical malaise of recent decades rather than to its affiliation with the academy. But that some of it is due to the privatism and insularity of the campus-based writer can be inferred from the decline of interest and controversy not only in the public sector of letters but in the literary one as well. As Pritchett reminds us, the person of letters keeps the other foot in literature. He or she makes readers conversant with the significant literature of the past as well as present, provides a bracing and aggressive standard of judgment, and keeps the literary tradition visible and perking by transmitting the energy of his or her own interests in it: in short, minding and defending the store at least part of the time.

This was a function that serious writers until the recent past took for granted, partly because they made some of their income from doing so and partly from the felt need to stake out and protect ground on which to cultivate interest in and taste for their own work. The tradition of modern poetry, for example, was virtually charted by the critical and ruminative prose of Rilke and Valéry, Pound and Eliot, Yeats and Auden, Tate and Ransom, Louise Bogan and Randall Jarrell, *et al*. All of them were active poets and position takers. The only comparable figure I can think of in our own time is Robert Bly. During the thirty-year history of his self-published magazine, Bly has tried to rechart the mainstream of American poetry to show how it runs through his own work and that of his kindred poets, has maintained a provocative and coherent line of judgment of his peers, and has significantly internationalized contemporary American poetry by publishing his own and other American translations from various languages. In sum, Bly is an inspiring example of what one person of letters can accomplish on his own—provided, as Bly himself would be quick to add, he doesn't teach.

From my vantage point as a literary editor in New York, which has its own insularity, I'm mainly conscious of a huge expansion of the writing population and a continuing decline of literary community and authority since I wrote about it twenty years ago in *The Red Hot Vacuum*. The general state of letters pretty much resembles that of the society at large in its dullness, diffuseness, crowdedness, perplexity, and privatism. In a remarkable long essay, "The Post-Modern Aura," Charles Newman places these conditions in a perspective that combines the inflation of literary productivity and value with the fragmentation of the modernist heritage. "In such a situation," Newman writes, "both the critical and aesthetic intelligence often relinquish their traditional claims, preferring to explore what they imagine to be the richness of their own limitations."

Well, yes and no. Postmodern criticism continues to play its elaborate games of removing the author's presence from his or her work to make it more habitable for the critic and the limitations of his "discourse." Also much of the higher discussion of contemporary fiction has been dominated by the metafictionists and their admirers. Meanwhile the Bellows and Updikes and Carvers, who have been writing most of the fiction of the age, go on trying to get at the truth in their outmoded way. The really interesting and relevant literary talk that I've come across in recent years has not been in texts but at readings and panels and in conversations. It's Robert Bly saying that the trouble with the young writers today is that they're afraid to attack the older ones because some of them have been their teachers; that writing programs cool out this necessary opposition. Or it's Lynne Sharon Schwartz talking about the difficulty women writers have had in writing subversively. Nor do I find that writers generally are more indifferent to or imperceptive of political and social conditions than they were in the past. And when I listen to their talk, I often wish they would develop this strong point of view, that sharply angled opinion, their clearheaded sense of the literary situation, and publish it in order to clear the air, stir the pot, get the juices flowing again. And the truth that comes to me is that they don't because they teach: that is, they don't write in the main for their keep, and the public and literary sides of their sense of vocation are expressed and probably pretty well exhausted by the process of passing on their concerns and standards and provocations to their students. And the rest of their spirit, energy, need to impose themselves and have their say, goes into their own fiction, poetry, plays, on which their careers depend.

I also sense that this is so from contending with my own feelings of anomie (i.e., "an anxious awareness that the prevailing values of society have little or no relevance to one's condition"). When the muddle of greed, hypocrisy, mediocrity, and hype of big-time publishing gets to me, I find myself wanting to teach again, to close the door on the muddle and get in touch with the spirit of literature and try to pass it on. So I teach a writing course or a seminar, and after a few weeks the atmosphere of sweetness and light descends, and I think that the literary community has taken refuge on the campuses rather as the early Christians took to the catacombs—to nurture faith, reinforce belief, tell one another the gospel, promulgate the word, and prepare the missionaries.

2.

Still, if the writing programs and English departments and university presses are to become the home away from home of the writer, they will need to strengthen communication and communion with the common reader and the common life. I hope that one or two of the more ambitious university presses that have been expanding into trade publishing will see their way to creating the kind of broadly interesting and lively magazines that the publishing houses once took to be their responsibility and opportunity, from *Harper's* and *Scribner's* up to the days of *Evergreen Review, Noble Savage* and *(New) American Review*. There are, of course, various literary reviews emanating from the university presses today, but they tend to be rather narrowly literary, the poems and stories sandwiched between thick slabs of academic-type literary criticism, and to be parochial rather than national in scope and tenor. The type of magazine I have in mind stations itself at the crossroads (which need not be bloody) where literature and politics meet; where the main action is a "lively dialogue between private imagination and public concern," in Geoffrey Wolff's apt formulation. As the example of *Granta* in England testifies, there is nothing like such a magazine to begin to pull a literary culture together by the breadth of its quality, interests, and timeliness and the readability of its prose. If a magazine like *Granta* gets going here, I think it will be because the right young editor, probably at a university press, insists on starting it and keeping it going by his vision, his will, and his gifts, not least of which is his ability to hustle money for the enterprise.

The other way that the university community can provide a better home for letters is to professionalize its writing programs. By that I don't mean bringing more editors and agents to campus to talk about how to get into the big time. What I mean is developing the training and values that would inculcate a commitment to the profession of letters: i.e., the equivalent of the general professional training a medical school or a law school or a Ph.D. program provides.

If the graduate writing program is at its best a sanctuary and a staging area, it tends often to have the torpor of a boondoggle and the cynicism of a scam; also, in the poet Greg Kuzma's words, "the ecstasy of being associated with a growth industry." Thirty years ago, when there were only a few graduate writing programs, their loosely structured curricula, revolving around the fiction and poetry workshops, made more sense than they do today because of the presence of the genuinely gifted. In John Berryman's class at Iowa in the early 1950s were W. D. Snodgrass, Philip Levine, Donald Justice, Robert

Dana, Donald Petersen, Henri Coulet, and Jane Cooper, all of whom went on to have significant careers. Today, with twenty-five or thirty prestigious programs and a hundred or more that are looking to become so, the talent and seriousness of the students and their ability to teach each other become spread very thin. As Kuzma puts it, the writer "no longer teaches the few who really are dedicated to the art but the average and the many. . . the contentedly mediocre." Even in a workshop in a top-ranked program today there will likely be among the fifteen students only a few who have the talent for a literary career, only one or two who have the character; so it is hard to avoid a congenial tolerance of the ordinary, that is to say unnecessary, poem: what Donald Hall calls "the MacPoem." So, too, with fiction writing.

The tacit deal that is cut with the students whose enrollment pays for the program and its faculty is that since we can't give most of you a career, we won't ask much of you. We will mostly let you "critique" one another's work and sit in a few seminars where you'll have to do some reading but that will still leave you with plenty of time to concentrate on your handful of stories or poems, perhaps teach an introductory writing course, and hang out with the other writers. As for the talented few, about the best we can do is to steer you in the direction of writing publishable work so that you can get a job teaching writing too. More or less divorced from the standards and demands of the English department, having lost, in Kuzma's words, "the old sweet antagonism between the academic and creative writer," the creative writing industry becomes in part a curious division of the consumer economy, academic branch, promoting not the culture of letters but the culture of narcissism. For a devastating account of how the industry works and the typical work it rewards, see Kuzma's essay in *Poetry* (Winter 1986).

Some programs are more strenuous, some teachers more stimulating, but the workshop institution is limited not only by its popularity but also by the immaturity of many of its students, often just out of college; by the brevity of the program, that is two years at most; and by the narrow and more or less calcified curriculum. Why not, then, develop a program that addresses these problems and also might begin to replace the missing persons of the literary community, the persons of letters?

First of all, the persons of letters program (PLP) would not admit writers—except in rare circumstances, such as having had extensive military service, managed a farm, raised a child, or experienced some other mode of precocious maturation—until they have spent two years or more out of college. Along with probably having developed another skill besides writing (Gary Snyder has said that the best preparation for becoming a poet is being a good carpenter or mechanic), the older student brings to a writing program a stronger hand of experience to play, a more settled character with which to develop a voice, and a mature attitude, which regards the program not as a pleasant option to take a crack at but as a privilege that has been earned.

Along with choosing writers on the basis of their gift and their experience, the PLP would require them to have a personal literary culture, which is not often the case today. They should know well a work by at least twenty writers, distributed through literary history and the several genres, and by a few foreign ones in their original language.

The PLP, then, would depart from the current practice of producing prematurely specialized poets, novelists, playwrights, and nonfiction writers, and instead provide a training that would be both more broadly based and more rigorous. My model is the European practice of the profession, in which it is taken for granted that the writer is able to address the public in several forms, as do Grass, Kundera, McEwen, Handke, et al. The first year's writing course would be devoted mainly to the fundamentals of the different genres: a student would choose one or more experiences that have a strong personal significance and write one or the other as an essay, a story, a novella, a poem, a one-act play, a film script, the emphasis being on the basic techniques and resources of each genre.

How would such a course be taught? By team teaching in a rotational way: a poet and a playwright, say, teaching the poetry and play-writing phases. The advantage to this arrangement is that it replaces the dialogue mainly of one, the coaxing of responses, that makes teaching writing often a dulling experience for everyone. Also it would be stimulating and challenging for the teachers to think in other genres than their own, and the principle of rotation would lessen the burden of their own banality and reduce burnout. Team teaching would bring the faculty together in a common effort to develop a pedagogy of teaching writing, which at present rarely progresses beyond the catch-as-catch-can group criticism of the workshop.

The PLP would also rejoin the writing program to the English department and extend it to the comparative literature one, so that each could benefit from the other's resources. Donald Hall has written about the value to the writer and student alike in turning the former loose in a literature course, where he or she can show the different character a literary work takes on in the hands of a writer who is looking for its source and circuitry of power rather than schematizing its meanings. By the same token, I've known literary scholars who would have been magical in a workshop. And again, both types of teachers would benefit from this interplay. The PLP should enrich and revitalize the teaching of writing as much as it does the learning.

So, too, with the foreign-language component. With the exception of the structuralists, American letters has been losing companionship with other languages and literatures and becoming more provincial with each decade. Hence one of the requirements of the PLP would be that each student translate at a professional level at least one work by a foreign writer and be conversant enough with his or her oeuvre and leading contemporaries to write a publishable introduction to the translated work. The idea would be to use the requirement to tutor the flow of the student's interests rather than to prescribe what they should be. Also, access and intercourse would he encouraged from the other side of the language barrier. The writing courses would be open to gifted writers from the other departments, as they would be to those in English Lit. Good curricula possibilities proliferate once the writer and the university begin to take each other seriously rather than regard each other in the mutually distrustful, resentful, and exploitative way that often obtains today: the undergraduate course in poetry writing having to add another section, while the one in the seventeenth-century lyric is canceled for lack of enrollment. Why not let a course like the latter be a requirement for the former and put some of the writing program poets into it to strengthen the discussion? The PLP would also bring literature and writing students together to learn from a professional how to write a publishable fiction, theater or film review. The writing student in, say, a Melville seminar would be enabled to write an essay for his term paper that weaves recent scholarship into a literary essay as a Kazin or Hardwick would do.

I'm sketching some organizing principles and values for an innovative comprehensive writing program rather than specifying a curriculum.* It departs from the current Ph.D. in creative writing, which some of the programs offer, because we need more persons of letters and not more English professors who write fiction or poetry. The PLP might offer training in travel writing and children's book writing to give its graduates a better chance to survive by their pens instead of having virtually no alternative but to teach or to do something unrelated to writing.

Just as it would flow easily between the different departments, it would maintain easy access to and from the society. Students would be free to leave for a year or two in the middle of the program to write on their own and to try to get by. Along with the core teachers, who would provide continuity, professional writers and editors would come for a semester or two to teach their craft. Though broad in scope and loose in structure, the PLP should be as busy and intensive as a medical school or a law school: writers with much to do, just as they're likely to be, if they're productive, for the next twenty years.

*A program along the lines I've suggested has been instituted at UNLV

276

Yes, much of what I'm proposing is impractical as matters stand. But a combined M.A and Ph.D. program in literature takes four or five years at least. Why not a PLP one that takes three? What students in their mid-twenties would be attracted to such a program? Only the few who are gifted, serious, and mature enough for it. What universities would initiate such a radically different program? Only the creative few. What writers and academics would work harmoniously together in such a program? Only those, in V. S. Pritchett's words, who "do not lay down the law but make a case for humane values."

(1986)

The Pits of Fiction

Inside the mind of most literary critics, editors, and English professors there is probably a lapsed novelist, playwright, or poet skulking around, wishing life had been otherwise. It figures: young people with a literary flair don't usually want to end up deconstructing "Billy Budd," or reviewing three first novels or revising and promoting a piece of merchandise about a Greek goatboy who becomes a shipping magnate. Most of us start out wanting to be literary in a much more self-expressive and famous way, but at some point, whether from frustration or necessity or a moment of truth, we give up the ghost of the free imagination in the glittering arena and settle for a more sensible career on the sidelines of literature.

After two decades of editing, reviewing, and teaching fiction, I thought I had pretty well laid this ghost when one morning I slipped away from a publishing sales conference in the Bahamas to scribble down an experience I'd had with a crafty Yiddish writer and garter-snapper, urged to do so by a pretty publicist I'd been telling it to the night before. With a funny story to embroider and a muse beckoning me on, I found that fresh words and images were bounding onto the page and taking the experience into places it hadn't been. Before I realized it, I was writing a short story. Being so verbally agile, Saul Bronsky turned into a poet, picking up some traits and history from another Yiddish writer I knew and some from out of the blue. I even wrote one of his love poems: it was so-so, but I said that it read much better in Yiddish. Riffing, lying, faking, stealing—all the things I couldn't do as a critic, at least not this outrageously. I sped along and in three hours I was done. No pain, no strain. Just like Chekhov, who wrote many of his shorter stories in a morning. The stories I had written in my twenties, after the charmed first ones, had been all pain and strain: various foremen and one apprentice brick layer. But now something had happened. The dutiful husband had turned into a crafty and shameless seducer. I sent the "The Amorist" out and lo, it was accepted by a prominent quarterly. But by then I was back in the New York publishing life, my muse was seeing someone else, and my writing time was again mortgaged to moonlighting. Once or twice I pulled out an old story and tried to rewrite it in my new style but it was like putting a Lubavitcher into leather. My old resignation returned.

A year or so later I was sitting at my desk one Saturday night. I was going through a divorce that felt like a third strike, my sons weren't staying with me that weekend, I didn't have a date. I was fooling around at the typewriter when a voice began speaking to me.

"I'm in therapy. I have to tell you that because that's how the story began. Not because, as you probably think, it figures: another Jewish sensitive who wears his grievances on his sleeve, one of the ailing and glib, like Portnoy or Woody Allen. I'm being a touch defensive. The trouble with therapy is the company you keep in other people's minds."

Who was this guy? It soon became clear he wasn't me: he was 20 years younger and much jauntier. Also he was better-looking and came from a classier background. He'd been an activist at Columbia in the 60s and now, a decade later, was trying to "liberate myself from my liberation." Also he was about to have an experience I'd only fantasized about:

> I was beginning my fourth year. After the Wednesday evening session there was now a stunning creature in the waiting room. She was still youngish—early 30s—very put together and had the special reserve of a woman who is used to being stared at. I figured she was a model or an actress and probably narcissistic, which was why she was there.

After a few more weekly glimpses and much rehearsed greetings he decides to say "Hi." She responds with a brief, polite smile. He decides she is a very nice person who wants to be left alone to prepare for her session. He tries to inveigle just a few facts from his therapist who tells him he's not a dating service, which leaves his imagination much room. He fashions her into a moral figure rather than an erotic one, and takes the fact that he doesn't try to hit on her or use her in his fantasies as a genuine sign of the great change he has been working toward. She becomes what his therapist calls "a healing illusion" and he calls "my muse of therapy." In time he begins to return to the waiting room after she has gone in for her session to sit in her chair and bask in her odor and aura. One evening he falls asleep; she finds him there and a relationship slowly and ambiguously begins.

It had started as an interesting idea for a story. But it didn't want to stop at that. It wanted to go on and on, from one session on the couch to the next, from the fugitive glances to the first date, to the complications of having the same therapist, to a choice that really puts his feet to the fire of change. Having written a published story my unblocked imagination had apparently decided to move on to the novel.

By the time I reached page 50 or so, the "I" had evolved into a 40 year-old union official named Hal. He was named for a friend who had died at about his age and whose pizzazz and sweetness he'd inherited. At first I decided he was an actor and even sketched out the play he was starring in at La Mama in which he ran an employment agency for impostors. But in time that began to trouble the critic and editor in me: the Supervisor. He was worried that Hal didn't know what he was talking about and it would show when the story had to get down to the nitty-gritty of a theater career. Also I was getting too satirical whenever off-off Broadway came in. I was mixing tones, losing consistency in the point of view. "Stick to realism," the Supervisor advised. "Stick to what you know about. This is supposed to be a serious book."

Since this was also supposed to be fiction, I gave Hal the road I'd not taken. I started him out in the same waiters' union I'd been in and gave him the job as an organizer I'd turned down to go back to graduate school. But worried about the credibility and interest of that, I then moved him on to District 65, where he was presently organizing a publishing house, not unlike the one I was working at, and editing the union newsletter, and writing book reviews for *The Nation*. Also since I was dealing with his deep inner life, his father, an Ivy League neo-conservative historian, and his mother, a collagist, became tarted-up versions of my domineering father and son-struck mother. Hal had also taken on a son who lived with him part-time, not unlike my youngest one, and an ex-wife who had his number— in this case a composite.

His lady-of-the-waiting room was named Doris, not only because it was Greek for "gift" but also the name of a young dancer I'd been smitten by at a summer job when I was in college and lost to an older waiter who knew all about Ezra Pound. But as the relationship developed she too became more "realistic," i.e. less an imagined updated version of the girl I'd known and more like the woman I'd begun courting. I'd also drawn upon a recent girlfriend to give Doris a child with cerebral palsy to raise by herself which Hal discovers as part of the opportunity for change, growth, and the other therapeutic virtues he has been seeking.

So ended Part I. I then decided to see if the book was as absorbing and commercial (a love story between two people in therapy: the audience in New York alone would be legion) and as surprisingly deft as I thought. I gave it to a few author friends who said that it was interesting, that they'd like to see the whole thing: what I usually said when I didn't have to commit myself. My agent said he disliked the first 75 pages but he's French and regards psychoanalysis as a German plot. One friend gave me a few editorial suggestions and a bemused smile, as if to say, "So that's who you are."

All in all hardly a discouraging response. But no one said that he knew all along I was a novelist or that she hadn't ever seen anyone write about therapy in such a fascinating way or even that it was likely to sell. When I started Part II I found that some of the air had gone out of the tire. Up until then, the next two or three pages had usually been there the next morning in my word processor but now they weren't. Nor were they there a week later or a week after that. I didn't feel panic-stricken as I usually do when something I'm writing abruptly quits on me. Instead I felt a weariness with the project; a lack of interest in what would happen to Hal and Doris. My sense of the narrative loosened and turned fickle. Perhaps I should make Hal a teacher at City College during its crisis in the late 1960s. Perhaps Doris's daughter should only be mildly retarded. Perhaps the story should be more about Hal's relationship with his father whom he discovers had named names during the McCarthy period, whose ideology and career rests on this betrayal. But that would be a different kind of novel. The one I was writing had some good passages, but the way ahead, which had been so intriguing, now yawned with boredom. What had gone wrong?

2.

The following are some of the thoughts I've had about the project in the years since I abandoned it. They speak to some of the pitfalls of writing fiction from the point of view of the pits.

Particularly novels by novices written in the first-person. André Gide remarked that the hardest word in the language to use well is the word "I". That's partly because it's so easy. Our natural mode of communication is the first person—we think in it, speak in it, perceive otherness through its lens. Except to the extent we're trained in and practice some discipline of detachment, our consciousness is grounded in a continuous personal narrative. Thus by beginning in its voice, not much altered from the freer one I use for personal letters, I had a style, a point of view, and, almost immediately, a certain momentum of perception, easily confused with inspiration.

The way to this pit is hidden in the phrase "not much altered from." Though I initially envisioned Hal as different from myself I failed to give him a voice that would have held him at arms length until he had a freestanding identity—or, as fiction writers like to say, had "taken off." What had been freed up was not my imagination but my prose, much as it had in writing the story. But the difference was that in the story most of my words were vamping a horny and shrewd Yiddish poet who gets through a readings by finding a pretty woman or two in the audience to pitch it to and the words of a woman who writes him a letter because of the rapport she felt at his reading. Both characters kept my imagination on its toes so that it could see, feel, and shape a situation that the Yiddish writer had told me about and thereby create a story from it.

I had often asked myself despairingly why can't I write essays that are like my letters, when the prose easily picks up a natural pace and tone and seems right on the money. Now that it was doing so, as often as not, I was too busy and elated grooving on it to ask myself much about the character and story I was supposed to be creating. Also to do that was to set up shop in the dark room of the imagination where words get developed into people and situations. Having only spent a morning there a few years back, I found that a prolonged stay was unnerving, more guessing and groping than fun and games. Also the new me, the Stylist, found the dark room mostly a distraction. He much preferred the library of memory where there was plenty of light and the material could be easily located and checked out (in both senses). This was particularly true of the psychological stuff: going into someone else's neurosis and treatment seemed after a few tries pitch black.

Which is to say that the first person voice not only undermined my imagination but also its working partner, my nerve. "What nerve!" may be an invective in commerce and manners but it's a motto for the fiction writer whose method, as the poet seducer Saul Bronsky taught me, is based on a brazen assertiveness. This is what enables him or her to riff and fake and borrow and lie. I knew that all interesting writing is risky but didn't realize until too late that I was ducking the fiction writer's particular risk, that is, making things up and flying by the seat of one's pants. Instead I substituted the autobiographer's risk by leading up to and away from certain crushing insights from my own therapy and illuminations from psychedelic trips in order to dramatize Hal's struggle with his dark gods of dependency and guilt. Actually there was something cozy rather than scary about using this material, for it was both mine and yet proffered as fiction.

For these reasons, the first person voice inexorably became the personal and the personal became literally the point of view: i.e., the closeness of Hal's voice to mine infiltrated the ways he thought and behaved until they became virtually identical with mine. What I wrote was interesting not because it was risky but because it was about me. I had found what people are always looking for—a fresh way of talking about themselves. This brought into play one of my most ingrained roles: the village explainer, which I'd developed as an editor, teacher and critic. Explaining Hal through myself and vice versa became the route of the writing process when it should have been that of imagining Hal for himself.

I had sensed this challenge for writing fiction when I initially made Hal an actor. When that became too daunting I made him a labor organizer. But once I'd told how he had gotten to District 65 and discussed the problems of white collar unionism, I had mostly ignored his work, for it didn't much engage him or me. What he really wanted was not to organize Scrivener Press but to unblock his talent so that he could write the novel the reader was now reading.

At the time I didn't think that steering clear of ten hours of most of his days would be a drawback. After all, there are very few major modern novels in which the author troubles to show his protagonist earning his living. We don't see Nick Carroway selling bonds or Jake Barnes chasing newspaper stories in Paris or Horace Benbow practicing law in Jefferson, Mississippi. There have been many novels in recent years whose protagonists teach literature or writing but very few in which we see them in class, except when they're lusting after the student who will get them into trouble. So it didn't seem to matter that Hal's occupation was more or less nominal.

Except that in his case it did matter. In not giving Hal work to do that involved him and that he was good at, I was making him, in effect, a full-time patient and mooner. This reduced the book's stake in his world and in the daily play of the problems and resources of a life going on—two of the main reasons for writing or reading a novel. Of course, a genius might get away with it, an idea that wasn't completely foreign to my state of mind. What I didn't allow myself to see was that part of, say, Kafka's genius was that when he wanted to write about himself as a patient and mooner he wrote letters to his Felice or Milena and when he wanted to write a novel he wrote about a land surveyor vainly trying to contact the authorities who had hired him or about a defendant trying to respond to charges that are never made clear to him.

In other words the resistances and dilemmas in Hal's life are mostly of his own making. The spectacle of a man planted firmly in his own way is essentially a comic one. What made Hal different from Alex Portnoy or Moses Herzog or Woody Allen's habitual schnook was not that he didn't wear his problems on his sleeve, which as an analysand he quickly and inevitably had to do, but that he wasn't amusing or, after a while, even ironic. If the story doesn't energize and show the resilient side of a protagonist, then the tone has to. Comic irony is particularly useful for the passive character because it is the energy and resilience of the depressed. Again, I'd sensed this early on in putting Hal into a play about imposters (which spills over into his therapy as another way of looking at himself), but its wackiness seemed to derail the serious burden of the story. It needn't have: I just didn't know how to control disparate tones since essay writing uses a consistent voice.

There was a good deal more self-delusion in thinking that I could go from writing one publishable story to a novel. This is partly a matter of technique, since I had only one firm string and one loose one to my new instrument. From my experience as an essayist I knew something about how to write about consciousness but very little about creating a world and a long-term narrative. The descriptions of place are tellingly meager and moody instead of evocative, and the story is virtually unpinned to its time, though one of Hal's problems is that he is a product of the sixties trying to restart his life in the 1980s.

The main problem, though, was not learning new strokes but

breaking old habits. Just as one doesn't change from a baseball swing to a golf swing just by hitting downward, so moving from discursive to narrative writing means altering certain fundamentals through lots of practice. Had I written more stories I would have known practically, as distinct from conceptually, that the circuitry of fiction is made from incidents not thoughts, and the longer the story the more diverse and unexpected and intercharged these incidents should be. The incidents I was using in the first half were mostly therapy sessions which take a long time to cough up their idea or insight, and tend to be overdetermined, to say the least, as a situation. So the presentation of Hal's character gave another pit to a first novel's typical self-consciousness and the pace of the accompanying love story was painfully slow: 25 pages before Hal speaks to Doris, 50 before they begin to have a relationship, 100 before it becomes complicated. In effect, far too many pages were devoted to establishing his character for the developments to come rather than letting the development do so. In this respect, too, I was arranging matters as an expository writer—schematically rather than narratively. Lots of teller, very little tale.

So, too, I needed more practice to break the fiction critic's and editor's habit of viewing characters in an analytic way in order to imagine them come into being, as I'd done at first. What I thought of as just fooling around was the process of getting lost in a story, which was my primary task. Once the Supervisor talked me out of writing under the spell of improvisation and subjected Hal and the others to reality checks, I had no recourse but to draw more and more directly on people I knew, beginning with myself. But by planting one foot in memory and its probabilities I slowly relinquished the authority of the imagination. Would Doris respond this way or that? Would his therapist say *that* at this stage of the process? Instead of telling myself to make them plausible, I would have done better to say, "keep making them vivid."

John Gardner characterized novel writing as tracking a "vivid, continuous dream." What I was tracking, until it quit on me, became more like a belabored fantasy. A fantasy is mostly a dramatized wish;

as such it tends to be thin, simplified, repetitious, rigidly controlled to keep out life's complexity and unexpectedness, its outer and inner conflicts. A dream is more like life itself: thick, complicated, unpredictable, unruly, full of conflict. It makes the familiar strange and the strange familiar and in doing so becomes uncannily persuasive while it's happening and leaves much room for interpretation.

Most of the time I was chugging along in my manuscript I told myself I was following Gardner's program and entering into the dreamlike state, the fluency of the writing more or less testifying to that. Also some of the material came from my unconscious which was suitably painful, fearful, and weird. But most of the time I contrived to make things familiar, comfortable and pleasant to the ego. The relationship with Doris was mostly a bracing fantasy of redeeming love and the one with the analyst a therapeutic fantasy in which I contrived to star by playing both roles.

Being lonely and rueful and confused at the time Hal's voice first came to me, I can see now why both strands of the narrative should have been so appealing. I can also see the main reason that it eventually quit on me, or rather, I on it. That is, why the project suddenly became so heavy, so boring. This occurred precisely at the point at which Hal learns that Doris's daughter is badly crippled and retarded and has to cope with that, not only within himself but even more critically in his relationship with his own son who wants nothing to do with the situation. Since Hal overly identifies with his son and has been dependent and guilty toward him since the marriage broke up, he has a lot of work cut out for him. The second half of the novel was to reveal whether he succeeds or not.

All of which touched painfully close to certain circumstances in my own recent past. I'd gone with a woman who had a severely impaired daughter, had tried to make it work with a son who was living part-time with me, but then had given up when the going got tough. Coming to a comparable situation in fiction forced me to take a fuller account than I had at the time of the harm I had done by my savior behavior. I would either have to imagine a different book to spare myself the guilt I felt, which would be a second cop-out, or else finally pay the dues for the erotic and moral fantasy I had concocted and the actual situation in which I'd failed. Hence the oppressiveness of the project at the end that I rationalized as boredom. Like the word "forlorn" in Keats' "Ode to a Nightingale," Doris and her daughter were calling me back to my "sole self."

For years I had been telling young writers to go into their pain and secrets, whether personal or social, that was where their strongest stories were likely to be. Writing my own fiction showed me how much easier that is said than done. Even so, writing a vivid, continuous dream might have accommodated the pain and shame; writing a self-infatuated, evasive fantasy could not. In the end I was trapped by the underlying motive that had sustained and deceived me.

Anyone who spends much time with writers knows that they tend to have a lot of vanity. For writers are people who literally call attention to themselves. In the great arena of contemporary consciousness, the vast majority—including many who are very intelligent, articulate, and otherwise ambitious—are content to sit quietly and listen to the few who leap to their feet, as it were, and exclaim, "Listen to me. I have something urgent to tell everyone about life."

However vain they may be, though, fiction writers need to lose themselves in the task for the work to go forward. They do so by connecting with otherness and thereby are taken out of their own egoscape, just as their readers are. Otherness is the charmed realm of what we are not, the world freed from being a mirror for the ego. The one character who became freestanding was the man who began as a highclass version of my father but then took on a reality of his own. There was little fantasy there to begin with; it was hard experience of lasting domination that was transmuted by the changes the story imposed on the character and on me. As the process of envisioning him continued, he became fixed in his own being and circumstances, the object of a fuller understanding than I had of my own father whom I continued to see in the narrow terms of his effect on my life rather than who he was when I wasn't around, which was most of his life. The father is the figure the novel probably should have been most about (that story could well have been told in the first person), and its theme the liberal vs. neoconservative culture war, which was there in embryo from the time I put Hal and his father together.

Once my friends gave me a lukewarm response to what I showed them the vanity underwriting the enterprise began to negate it. The coup de grâce was delivered by another friend whom I showed it to after I had begun to lose interest and confidence. She had known me for a long time and said that Hal reminded her a great deal of the person I had been thirty years ago in graduate school. I didn't like to hear that and dismissed her reading as inappropriate. But once I began to reread the manuscript in the stark light of her observation, I could see what she meant and more. Not only was Hal the recovering adolescent I had been in my late twenties but also I had written pretty much the first novel I would have written at the time, at least one that would have been fraught with the same preoccupations and faults. Perhaps everyone has an egotistical, facile, relatively inert first-person novel buried inside and it doesn't matter very much what else you've become when you turn it loose. As a novelist I was still the 25 year-old novice I'd been when I quit writing fiction, once again exploring the troubled, deviant, adolescent self, which is where the vocation usually begins.

Once I realized I'd been led astray by vanity and had fallen into the pits of fiction and couldn't get out, not at least with this book, I looked at the months I'd put into it and thought, "What a mistake, what a waste." But in a writer's life nothing is wasted as long as he or she continues to write. I'm now working on a memoir about my father and myself that is benefiting from the detachment the aborted novel taught me. As Josephine Herbst said to a young writer who was complaining about his mistakes, "If it wasn't for my mistakes, Bill, I'd still be sitting on the front porch in Sioux City, Iowa."

(1994)

Ted Solotaroff was an associate editor of *Commentary* and the editor of *Book Week*. The founding editor of *New American Review* (later *Amerian Review*), he later became a senior editor at Harper & Row and HarperCollins. He has also edited several collections, most recently *Alfred Kazin's America*. His previous literary writings have been collected in *The Red-Hot Vacuum* and *A Few Good Voices in my Head*. He is also the author of the memoirs *Truth Comes in Blows* and *First Loves* and is presently completing another. He lives in E. Quogue, Long Island.